DICKENS AND MELVILLE IN THEIR TIME

DICKENS AND MELVILLE IN THEIR TIME

PEARL CHESLER SOLOMON

COLUMBIA UNIVERSITY PRESS
New York

The Andrew W. Mellon Foundation, through a special grant, has assisted the Press in publishing this volume.

Library of Congress Cataloging in Publication Data

Solomon, Pearl Chesler.
  Dickens and Melville in their time.

  Based on the author's thesis, Columbia University.
  Bibliography: p. [225]–227
  1. Dickens, Charles, 1812–1870—Criticism and
interpretation. 2. Melville, Herman, 1819–1891—
Criticism and interpretation. 3. Heroes in
literature. 4. Great Britain—Civilization—
19th century. 5. United States—Civilization—
19th century. I. Title.
PR4588.S64   823'.8'09352   74-13307
ISBN 0-231-03889-5 823.09

10 9 8 7 6 5 4 3 2

TO MY PARENTS
MINNA AND MORRIS CANICK

ACKNOWLEDGMENTS

This book began as a doctoral dissertation under the direction of Professor Steven Marcus of Columbia University. Only his students can know how uniquely fortunate I was to have had the benefit of his intelligence, his wide learning, his example, his kind ear. It is a pleasure to acknowledge my very great gratitude to him.

I should also like to thank Professor Quentin Anderson who read and criticized this book at several stages in its development, and whose ideas about American culture have considerably influenced me. Professor John D. Rosenberg's careful and sensitive reading of the manuscript was of immense help. Professor David J. Rothman was kind enough to give me valuable criticism and advice upon historical matters.

For his years of good-humored patience with my labors I want at last to thank my son, Andrew Chesler. Finally, I thank my dear husband, Seymour Solomon, for his help in turning the manuscript from a student work into a book.

Columbia University   PEARL CHESLER SOLOMON
May 1974

CONTENTS

DICKENS AND MELVILLE IN THEIR TIME

"Whereas, great geniuses are parts of the times; they themselves are the times; and possess a correspondent coloring." HERMAN MELVILLE

INTRODUCTION

This book attempts to trace the shaping force of history upon literature; to see some of the ways in which "culture" determines the themes and forms of fiction; to see to what extent history and "culture" form the writer. These are broad, unwieldy issues. I have dealt with them primarily by focusing upon concepts of the hero since, in a hero's career, the life of a time is delineated. And since fictional heroes are very often patterned upon their authors' lives, in the consideration of such heroes many of these issues coalesce.

Certain works of Dickens and of Melville lent themselves to such a study. Roughly contemporary, living in countries which shared a common language, a common literary heritage and, up to a point, a common past, both Dickens and Melville used aspects of their own lives as material for their heroes' lives—yet each produced works of fiction radically dissimilar in theme and form, and heroes of radically dissimilar ideals and values. And not only are Dickens's and Melville's heroes different from each other; they stand—as did their authors—in entirely different relationship to their cultures.

What had already emerged as a central difference between England and America in the nineteenth century—indeed, between all of Europe and America—was the individual's relationship to society. The common man was moving to more and more prominence throughout the Western world: Dickens was as much a man of the people as Melville, and his heroes, no less than Melville's, were taken from the people. But traditional hierarchal roles had already changed far more drastically in America than in England, and part of the task Dickens set for himself was to help democratic man into a future which might still be guided and encompassed by traditional values. On the other hand, life in America had tended from the first to cut man off from his past, and the American democrat, for the most part, was feeling this as a national blessing. It was Melville who first wrote of this freedom from the past as a burden, even a terror, for the men upon whom it fell. Most characteristically American about Melville's fears for the future was that they were fears not for society or for social man, but for the individual man, the "soul-toddler" adrift in this new world.

Watch yon little toddler, how long it is learning to stand by itself! First it shrieks and implores, and will not try to stand at all, unless both father and mother uphold it; then a little more bold, it must, at least, feel one parental hand, else again the cry and the tremble; long time is it ere by degrees this child comes to stand without any support. But, by-and-by, grown up to man's estate, it shall leave the very mother that bore it, and the father that begot it, and cross the seas, perhaps, or settle in far Oregon lands. There now, do you see the soul. In its germ on all sides it is closely folded by the world, as the husk folds the tenderest fruit; then it is born from the world-husk, but still now outwardly clings to it;— still clamors for the support of its mother the world, and its father the Deity. But it shall yet learn to stand independent, though not without many a bitter wail, and many a miserable fall. [*Pierre*, Book XXII]

But Dickens saw the democratic hero still supported by his mother the world and his father the Deity. Perhaps it would be truer to say that he saw to it that his heroes still supported *them*. It is on this point that American and Englishman most sharply diverge.

Dickens found the moral basis of his own and his heroes'

lives first in their allegiance to their families, and then to those human beings whom destiny or accident had put in their paths. In this he was spokesman for his culture, which believed that a man's duty to his family and to the social order should be his paramount considerations. For the dissociated individual, no identity is possible in this world view. Yet Dickens sometimes felt that he had symbolically dissociated himself from his own past, most of all from his father. In a society still strongly committed to a patriarchal ideal, Dickens had so far superseded and surpassed his father that he seemed almost to have created himself. He never permitted his fictional heroes such supersedence, keeping their lives much closer to the cultural ideal than his was. And he mitigated his own "self-creation" chiefly by means of his career, socializing the immense success which, considered in relation to himself alone, at times caused him to feel great guilt. Through his work—novels, stories, periodical publications, philanthropies—he turned his powerful will into a force for good in the world.

In an environment which defined itself almost entirely in terms of money, work, and success, Melville was a member of the minority opposition, and he found the moral basis of his own and his heroes' lives in asserting the individual's right to dissent; in safeguarding the ego at the expense of society. Yet the opposition value for which Melville stood was very close to the dominant ideology of his culture, which was the right of every man to create himself. Most Americans felt that for the first time in history God had given men His sanction to make themselves, to "outfather their fathers." But Melville saw that Americans had *been* unfathered, and that they had *had* to make themselves in order to survive. So he created American heroes who were victims of the majority ideal. As mankind's first dissociated individuals, Americans were the first casualties of the future.

Dickens, feeling the hierarchy that for hundreds of years had held mankind together beginning to disintegrate under the pressure of separate individual wills, stood firm for the social order, even at the expense of bending or breaking the individual's will. But Melville's culture had already lost the "social order"—had lost most traditional hierarchies, had lost the historical past, had "lost" the family; and with these things, it had even lost the assurance of mankind's primacy in the universe. With the loss of the patriarchal father, Melville felt, America had lost its "paternal gods" as well. In all these things Melville was not America's spokesman—who else in America was saying such things?—but he had learned these things *in* America nevertheless.

Dickens's message to his own generation—that individualism must be contained, that to save society, the self must pay—was in one sense an attempt to safeguard the next generation, to make certain that the next generation, and the next, could flourish. But Melville, and America, had unleashed the individual will and committed themselves to its fulfillment. And what of the next generation?

Moby Dick, which is Melville's allegory of man confronting an unFathered cosmos, has two endings. Ahab, who demands recognition from his God or from Nature, and who will sacrifice his world—the *Pequod*—to achieve his goal, leads the world to its destruction. Humanity is annihilated, and the indifferent sea rolls on. But there is a second ending to the novel. In the epilogue we learn that Ishmael is rescued by the *Rachel* which, in seeking her own lost children, "only found another orphan." The old order is past. Those who are still seeking their Father will die. Only Ishmael, cast out by his father, inured to loneliness and loss, is saved—and saved by another loser, by the now childless captain of the *Rachel,* whose own beloved sons have been lost. The old order is past, but perhaps a new one will come; perhaps a new relationship can take the place of the old familial one, one which will begin, perhaps, with the recognition that all men are now orphans.

Dickens had taken over from his father, and from his culture, certain restrictions and ideals about the relationship of the individual to society and had internalized them as part of his own conscience, or super-ego. These restrictions and ideals were, for the most part, a holdover from an older world—for, as Freud said, the super-ego is the "vehicle of tradition and of all the age-long values which have been handed down in this way from generation to generation." Yet in his own career, Dickens had identified himself with the most progressive group in his society—the more individualistic, the more striving and aggressive younger men who were using the new technologies of science, finance, government, manufacture, to further themselves. Out of the tension created within him between the morality of an older world, and his will to seize whatever opportunity a new world held out, he molded a new ideal: to use his power in the service of society, especially in the service of the weak: "my creed in the exercise of my profession is, that Literature cannot be too faithful to the people . . . cannot too ardently advocate the cause of their advancement, happiness and prosperity."

The problem of Melville's attitude towards his society is more complex, since he was one of those men who are not spokesmen for their age, as Dickens was, but more or less conscious prophets of a new age. He could not be spokesman for his age because he could not fuse his identity with the dominant economic and technological culture of his time. For reasons which will be discussed later on, Melville did not wish to be a "success," nor was he free to be one. And success was understood in America as outfathering one's father, as making oneself. Yet Melville saw it as America's destiny to do just that: to cast off the patriarchal past, to renounce the "paternal gods," and to create itself. It was America's fate to see that the past was dead, and to lead the world in that perception.

The world has arrived at a period which renders it the part of Wisdom to pay homage to the prospective precedents of the Future in preference to those of the Past. The Past is dead, and has no resurrection. . . . We are the pioneers of the World; the advance-guard, sent on through the wilderness of untried things, to break a new path in the New World that is ours. In our youth is our strength; in our inexperience our Wisdom. (*White Jacket,* Ch. 36)

Mankind, Freud wrote, "never lives completely in the present. The ideologies of the super-ego perpetuate the past, the traditions of the race and the people, which yield but slowly to the influence of the present and to new developments . . ." But Melville would not only leave the ideologies of the past—in his novels he showed that the ideologies of the past have left us anyway. He would have his heroes leap over the present itself, leap straight into the future, which is a leap into the Absolute. And on the threshhold of the Absolute his heroes—Bartleby, Ahab, Pierre—die. But that is always the way of the Messiah. Seen only as rebels from the majority, such men have no identities. But seen as Messianic heroes, they are discoverers of "the way"—they are the "advance-guard" of the world.

CHAPTER ONE

TWO CLERKS:
BOB CRATCHIT
AND BARTLEBY

I TALES OF TWO CITIES

London. Christmas Eve. Around the middle of the nineteenth century. A merchant and his clerk part for the holidays. The clerk, Bob Cratchit, is lovingly awaited at home by a wife and many little Cratchits, chief among them Tiny Tim, a crippled child. The master, Ebeneezer Scrooge, goes to his solitary rooms. There he is visited by the ghost of his dead partner who warns him that three Spirits will visit him in the night. The first, the Ghost of Christmas Past, shows Scrooge his own past: the lonely child shut out from his father's love; the happy apprentice to a fatherly master; the grown man, hardened by avarice. The second Spirit, Christmas Present, takes Scrooge to the home of Bob Cratchit, where Christmas is celebrated in poverty and familial love; then to the home of Scrooge's nephew Fred where Christmas is celebrated in a mood of romance, feasting, and games. From under the Spirit's robes there now appear two wolfish, starving children. Scrooge is told that they are Ignorance and Want, the children of Man. Finally the Ghost of the Future shows Scrooge two deaths, that of the beloved child, Tiny Tim, and his own, solitary as his life. Terrified, he wakes, vowing that henceforth he will live "in the past, present, and future." He sends a goose to the Cratchits, dines with his nephew, raises Bob's salary, and becomes another father to Tiny Tim.—Charles Dickens, *A Christmas Carol.*

New York. Wall Street. Around the middle of the nineteenth century. A lawyer employs two clerks and an office boy. Finding himself with additional work, he hires a third clerk named Bartleby. Silent and diligent, Bartleby refuses to do any office work but copying; at last he refuses to copy as well. His only response to all commands is, "I would prefer not to." The lawyer, who narrates the story, soon discovers that Bartleby never leaves the office, that he has no other home. He tries to dismiss Bartleby, whom he now considers to be mad, but Bartleby prefers to remain, spending all his time staring silently out of the window at a blank wall. Unable to rid himself of the clerk's presence by kindness, threats, or bribery, the lawyer moves to another office. The new occupant of the old office forcibly ejects Bartleby, who begins to haunt the halls of the building. At last Bartleby is arrested for vagrancy. He is removed to a prison, called the Tombs. There Bartleby prefers not to dine or to speak, and one day is found by the lawyer, his former master, curled up on the imprisoned grass, his face turned to the wall, dead.—Herman Melville, "Bartleby, the Scrivener, a story of Wall Street."

Here are two stories, roughly contemporary, both written in English and coming out of the same literary tradition, concerning similar characters in a similar relationship and similar setting: master and workman in a great commercial city. It is a relationship which is fundamental to the nineteenth century, almost as important as that of father and son. Yet the stories themselves are utterly unlike one another. What is apparent even in outline is that the meaning of *A Christmas Carol* has been made available largely through the plot, while we are completely in the dark as to the meaning of "Bartleby." Many things happen in *A Christmas Carol,* all bearing a direct relation to the regeneration of Scrooge's heart, which is central to the story. In the beginning Scrooge has withdrawn from life. We are shown the manner of his living death; the past, and the steps of his withdrawal; the present, with the consequences—personal, social, and economic—of that withdrawal; and the future as it will be if the present course of his life does not change. Finally we return from the three dreams and see Scrooge after his long journey in the country of the regenerate heart. It is a story with a beginning, middle, and end, because Dickens saw men's lives as having beginnings, middles, and ends; and the plot is rounded off by a lesson because Dickens saw life itself as a kind of learning process. This becomes clearer as soon as we compare *A Christmas Carol* with "Bartleby."

"Bartleby" also begins with a man who has withdrawn from life, but instead of travelling forward into self-knowledge, he takes one small step backward, and dies. Aside from this nothing has happened; one dead wall has been exchanged for another. The American story does not have a beginning, middle, and end in the same sense that the English story has and this may be so because, to Melville, life neither shapes itself into beginnings, middles, and ends, nor derives meaning from that form. Instead of a life proceeding from beginning to end and rounded off by a lesson, the action in "Bartleby" moves in an even, undifferentiated flow which is interrupted by one gesture—a negation—and then back to brick walls. It is a form that does not readily reveal meaning—that seems, rather, to conceal it. *A Christmas Carol,* on the other hand, seems designed expressly to yield up meaning. Why? The answer lies partly in the fact that Dickens wants to teach, a fact apparent from the shape of the story—it gets somewhere—and also from all the encounters in it between human beings. In Dickens's view, all men are travellers through the vale of soul-making, and their duty is to help their fellow pilgrims on their ways, too: "Mankind is your business." The lesson is explicit in the events of the story, as it is implicit in its form. What of the encounters between human beings in "Bartleby"? Man does not help man in "Bartleby," or teach man; rather, he is mystified by man. The lawyer, the clerks, the bystanders, the prison warden, all think Bartleby mad. And this is reflected in the story's narrative form, which also mystifies: both meaning and form are ambiguous and unresolved.

In "Bartleby" a man withdraws from life and chooses to die—to stop working, speaking, eating—and for no apparent reason. At least, we cannot find reasons expressed in the events. In *A Christmas Carol* some event dramatizes every change in Scrooge's development: as a child he is abandoned at school and then welcomed back home; as a young man he is apprenticed to a good master; later on, he grows avaricious, and rejects his penniless lover; as an old man he withholds charity and love and rejects family. "Bartleby," however, is lacking in any events which could serve to objectify the hero's feelings: Bartleby prefers not to proofread, then to copy, then to speak, then to leave the office, then to eat. All other people in the story are either unnamed or called by nicknames, endowed not with characters but with quirks, locked into their own idiosyncrasies. Negation and loss and muted acts of aggression are the only human feelings portrayed. But in *A Christmas Carol,* other people's moods and characters and needs are given outward shape in the same way that Scrooge's are. Bob gives form to human kindliness, his family to dependence and love,

Scrooge's nephew and niece to fecundity and romance, Marley's ghost to remorse. Even Ignorance and Want are personified. They are present partly because Scrooge's are not the only feelings important in the story, partly because Scrooge's is not the only point of view in the story, as his are not the only values. Indeed, Scrooge's values, like his way of life, undergo a profound change during the course of the story. Scrooge's mind and heart are not of necessity, and by the very nature of the story's world, inaccessibly self-enclosed. "Bartleby" is completely enclosed in point of view, in part because it is a first person narrative, and in part because nothing happens to anyone but the hero himself; and it is enclosed by the absence of any values but the narrator's. There are no objects, no ideas, no values, that exist outside the narrator and Bartleby.

What we finally sense from the plot of *A Christmas Carol* is a multiplicity and richness in the possibilities of life; what we sense in "Bartleby" is life's meagerness. There is no ideal in "Bartleby" of family or society; no ideal of love, either filial or romantic; no marriages; no women; no parents, no children. There are no homes. There are hardly any names. There is no food but ginger-nuts and beer. There is no ceremony but arrest. There are many walls, endless offices and streets; and one patch of grass, which is really a grave. In *A Christmas Carol* life—the outside world—is seen both as an enrichment of self and as an escape from self; in "Bartleby" life is business—copying, or not copying. The images of the two graves, at which both stories dramatically culminate, epitomize the two worlds. Scrooge's grave is "walled in by houses, overrun by grass and weeds, the growth of vegetation's death, not life; choked up with too much burying, fat with repleted appetite." It is food and greenness gone to hell; walled round like hell, and neglected by all living things. It is an image, to Scrooge, of unspeakable agony. And here is Bartleby's grave: "The yard was entirely quiet.

It was not accessible to the common prisoners. The surrounding walls, of amazing thickness, kept off all sounds
behind them. The Egyptian character of the masonry
weighed upon me with its gloom. But a soft imprisoned turf
grew underfoot. The heart of the eternal pyramids, it
seemed, wherein, by some strange magic, through the
clefts, grass-seed, dropped by birds, had sprung." Miracu-
lous greenness in isolation—not even other corpses for company. It is an image, to the narrator, of unspeakable peace.
Scrooge's grave shows him that he is damned, past all hope
of redemption; but Bartleby is asleep "with kings and coun-
sellors."

Again: a story without a beginning, middle, and end; a
story that does not try to teach, and that depicts a life in
which men do not learn from one another; a story that does
not easily open out into meaning but seems to close over
meaning; a story in which almost no events occur; a story
that is self-enclosed around a single point of view. Further,
this story ends in a man's death that is not essentially different from his life, but is nevertheless seen as a kind of
achieved distinction, if not absolute triumph; and the distinction comes not at all from the richness of the life that
preceded it, but from the willful arbitrariness of its end.
Not the splendid presence but the unexplained exit distinguishes Bartleby. Contrast with this a story where structure
points up meaning, where life provides lessons and morals,
and where the writer's task is to teach, and the hero's duty is
to learn; a story rich in events; a story whose values are
based on long tradition and grounded in the Christian religion. Further, this story ends with a man's return to life to
set that life to rights before he can die a death that draws its
triumph and its meaning not from itself but from the quality of life that went before it, and the number of living people who mourn it.

The master-workman relationship is almost as important

in the nineteenth century as that of father and son. In *A Christmas Carol* the two relationships are in fact almost identical, and they must be felt by the master to be identical if the workman is to live. Bob is entirely dependent upon Scrooge, and Tiny Tim can be saved only if Scrooge becomes his father. In "Bartleby" the two relationships are not identical. The relationship of Bartleby to his master is unconsummated, almost non-existent, each one living enclosed in his own identity or will; the master not in any recognizable way paternal, nor the clerk filial. But we remember that in the world of the American story no familial ties exist at all. Perhaps, then, Bartleby and his master *do* exist as a father and son of a certain kind—a father and son who do not know one another, and who cannot communicate with each other; unable to teach, unable to learn; whose only gestures of mutual recognition are withdrawal, dismissal, and death.

II   The Hero as Master vs. the Hero as Working Man

The fundamental relationship in both stories is that of master and working man. In the American story, it is the only relationship; in the English story, master and clerk touch each other at a crucial point in their lives, but they touch others as well: Bob has a family, which is another center of his life; and Scrooge has a family, a past, a place in society. But it is clear in *A Christmas Carol* as well as in "Bartleby" that the work relationship is very important, that in fact it is symbolic of all other relationships; and that in order to be a good master Scrooge must become a good father. In "Bartleby," too, we sense that Bartleby wants something more of the lawyer than wages, that he wants somehow to transcend the bare commercial relationship. We are uncertain what Bartleby wants the lawyer to do or be partly because there are no other relationships in the story with which to compare this one—no good masters, no families, no fathers. Yet we assume that it is some kind of paternal recognition that Bartleby wants, since that is the bond that their mutual ages and positions suggest.

If in *A Christmas Carol* Scrooge is a kind of father, and in "Bartleby" the clerk is a kind of son, then Dickens's hero is the father while Melville's is the son. The overt relationship in both stories, however, is that of master and working man. Much of what Dickens and Melville have to say is said around that relationship and in terms of that bond. It may be of crucial importance to understand why, in the English story then, the hero is master as well as father, while in the American story the hero is a working man as well as a son.

A hero must be free: free to exercise full rights as a citizen; free in the pervasive although not necessarily stated opinion of his culture; free in his own eyes. Further, he must be free to make significant choices, choices which affect not only his own life, but his ability to sustain life. Bob Cratchit can choose to have Tiny Tim live, but his choice is not significant because Bob is economically dependent upon his master; he prefers that his son should live, but Tiny Tim will certainly die unless Scrooge can be prevailed upon to share Bob's preference. Bob cannot be a hero because his role in life and in the story is entirely passive. His passivity is that of the meek who will inherit the earth—but not until the earth has passed away and the kingdom of heaven has come.

Bartleby's passivity is of another kind; it is the passivity of suppressed power. The narrator says that Bartleby is passively resistant, although it would be more accurate to say that he is passively aggressive. What is important is that he is passive by choice, not necessity. Assumed within his preference to deny and die is the guarantee that he might have chosen to affirm and live. Bartleby is so free a man that he can choose to die—and this freedom and this choice imply a world of political, economic, and philosophic assumptions entirely different from those of Bob Cratchit's world. Bartleby's passivity is really the arrogance of the inheritor who already inhabits the kingdom of heaven-on-earth, and has found that it falls short of his dream, and so turns his back upon it. It is his freedom to turn his back that makes him eligible to be cast in the hero's role.

The reasons that led Dickens to take as his hero a merchant rather than a Prime Minister or a peer were biographical, not historical; but the assumptions that led him to make his hero a master and not a wage earner were not personal, but cultural. The assumptions that permitted Melville to make his hero a wage earner and not a master were cultural, not personal. He may also have had powerful personal reasons against taking his hero from the middle class, but the conditions that made a working man available to be cast in the role of hero in America were cultural, and not the result of Melville's iconoclasm. That is, most Englishmen, including Dickens, assumed that the wage earner was not free; most Americans, including Melville, assumed that he was; and in both cases these assumptions were so widespread that they did not need explicit statement.

The source of the difference between British and American attitudes towards the working man—like the source of very many of their differences—lay in the land itself: the small island of Britain, the vast American continent. By the middle of the seventeenth century—the moment of the founding of New England—England had already undergone its period of colonization and settlement and was beginning a long process of land redistribution which would end in the concentration of land in the hands of a small minority of Englishmen and which would leave, in the minds of the dispossessed majority, a dream-like memory of a golden age before the poor had been robbed of their "patrimony," before "This huge monopoly, this intolerable usurpation of the soil" had made the common man a "lodger" in his own house.[1] But seventeenth-century America was just entering upon its period of settlement and expansion. For 150 years the common man's dream of free land was to be realized on the American continent. American settlers were conscious of the fact that what was only dreamed of in Europe could here be achieved, and this consciousness—whatever else it did—was to give them an unprecedented faith both in themselves and in the power of their dreams.

In England most common men—artisans, wage earners, poor folk—were not only landless, they were without political rights as well. It was property, real or moneyed, which was represented in Parliament, while the ownership of property was the criterion for enfranchisement. Therefore the laboring man was not on the side of the governing, but on the side of the property which it was other men's responsibility to govern. British attitudes towards working men *as* men did not really begin to change until 1867, when the passage of the Second Reform Bill made it evident that the lower classes were coming into political power. When men rather than property were for the first time to be given representation in Parliament, those men were anxiously scrutinized for signs of intelligence and social responsibility. An article appearing in Dickens's *All the Year Round* in 1867 reflects the new hope, and the new fear, with which England viewed its "new masters." "Meanwhile, the working man remains a study—in some respects, too, a problem—in

---

[1] Quoted in Wesley C. Mitchell, *Types of Economic Theory, from Mercantilism to Institutionalism* (New York, 1967), I, 415, and Christopher Hill, *Puritanism and Revolution* (New York, 1964), p. 118.

great part a difficulty—in much a contradiction—but, on the whole, a national hope and a national pride." [2]

The meaning which Engels had given to the term "working class," based on his study of the English working class in 1844—that it had become "for the first time, an integral, permanent class of the population, whereas it had formerly often been merely a transition leading to the bourgeoisie [with the result] that now, he who was born to toil had no other prospect than that of remaining a toiler all his life"— was largely true of England in 1850.[3] But it was not true of America, where the working class had risen out of entirely different origins into entirely transformed expectations.

The Pilgrims, arriving in America with English preconceptions about hierarchy and rank, and with English ideas as to the rights and disabilities of the laboring poor, found that distinctions based upon land tenure were meaningless where land was readily accessible; that the laboring poor could not be kept either poor or landless when an empty continent lay over the hill; and that where men's abilities and labor were sorely needed, their inherited status sank to insignificance. Within the first generation of settlement, servants whose periods of indenture had expired were regularly granted twenty-five acres of unmanned land, and other settlements followed similar practices.[4] Everywhere in the Massachusetts Bay Colony this drama of the settlement of new land and the unsettlement of old ideas was reenacted. Land grants were given to groups of English emigrants who distributed acreage amongst themselves accord-

[2] Quoted in Asa Briggs, *The Making of Modern England* (New York, 1965), p. 522.

[3] Frederick Engels, *The Condition of the Working-Class in England in 1844* (London, 1892), p. 16.

[4] William Haller, Jr., *The Puritan Frontier: Town Planting in New England: Colonial Development 1630–1660* (New York, 1951), p. 20.

ing to inherited status and property in money and goods. The apportionment of land—usually into personal lots and commons—remained unchallenged until a generation of younger sons, pinched for land, questioned the justice of old inequities; and then these younger sons, together with whatever radical or dissatisfied members of the older towns there were, moved westward to form new towns which they established on more egalitarian, and less English, principles than their fathers.[5] And this was occurring at a time when the common man in Britain was being squeezed off the land almost entirely. That is, the drama of the common man in America was running directly counter to that of the English common man—and the matter of land was paralleled by the political situation as well.

Early in the nineteenth century, Alexis de Tocqueville, speculating on the phenomenon of American democracy, wrote that "the chief circumstance which has favored the establishment and maintenance of a democratic republic in the United States is the nature of the territory that the Americans inhabit . . . God himself gave them the means of remaining equal and free, by placing them upon a boundless continent." [6] The early colonial laws that enfranchised much of the white male population were created not out of a theoretic belief in egalitarian democracy, nor in the belief that government exists primarily to represent men rather than to safeguard property. Such beliefs became current only about 125 years later, in Great Britain as well as in America. By that time they reflected a widespread reality in America, and so they were adopted by American lawmakers without causing any upheaval in already existing conditions, as they would have done in Great Britain even then. As

[5] See Sumner Chilton Powell, *Puritan Village: The Formation of a New England Town* (Garden City, N.Y., 1965).

[6] Alexis de Tocqueville, *Democracy in America*, 2 vols. (New York, 1945), II, 301–02.

Pennsylvania's representative to the Constitutional Convention said, "The British government cannot be our model. . . . Our manners, our laws, the abolition of entails and of primogeniture, the whole genius of the people are opposed to it." [7]

The really pressing problem surrounding the American working man was underpopulation, not overpopulation, as in England. America needed men, and because of this, the common man's economic and political expectations had become limitless. And this open-endedness of promise was the crux of the difference between the English working man and the American.

The economic abundance of the new world transformed the working man's large assumptions about life, and his large ideals; and it threatened homely values, too, and traditional niceties. William Cobbett wrote enthusiastically of the common man's life in America in the early nineteenth century, when the poor in England were suffering from rising prices and the loss of liberties; but homesickness and a sense of loss occasionally break in:

The dwellings and gardens, and little outhouses of labourers, which form so striking a feature of beauty in England . . . are what I, for my part, most feel the want of seeing upon Long Island. . . . We here see the labourers content with a shell of boards, while all around him is as barren as the sea beach . . . This want of attention in such cases is hereditary from the first settlers. They found land so plentiful, that they treated small spots with contempt.[8]

A sense of dislocation and loss was often felt by native Americans too. Tocqueville, the most brilliantly intuitive of

---

[7] Samuel Eliot Morison, ed., *Sources and Documents Illustrating the American Revolution, 1764–1778,* 2nd ed. (New York, 1965), p. 247.

[8] William Cobbett, *A Year's Residence in the United States of America* (London, 1964), p. 23.

nineteenth-century writers on America, felt the characteristic restlessness amidst plenty, the paradoxical sense of
nameless loss beneath the material gains. The American's
"prevailing frame of mind," he wrote, "is at once ardent
and relaxed, violent and enervated. Death is often less
dreaded by them than perseverance in continuous efforts to
one end." "No sooner do you set foot upon American
ground than you are stunned by a kind of tumult; a con-
fused clamor is heard on every side, and a thousand simultaneous voices demand the satisfaction of their social wants.
It is impossible to spend more effort in the pursuit of happiness." [9]

The American pursuit of happiness thus very early took a
materialistic turn, and while it is true that the material re-
wards were great, opening broad avenues of splendor and
opportunity to the common man that were closed to him in
England, it is also true that certain doors were slammed
shut—doors of stability, tradition, duty, perhaps content-
ment.[10]

And so Bartleby, the inheritor of two hundred years of

[9] Tocqueville, *Democracy in America*, I, 145–46; II, 259.

[10] Physicians, interested in medical causes for what they considered new forms
of insanity in pre-Civil War America, were in basic agreement with Tocqueville. In
The Discovery of the Asylum David Rothman writes: "Medical superintendents' explorations of the origins of insanity took them into practically every aspect of
antebellum society, from economic organization to political and religious practices,
from family habits to patterns of thought and education. And little of what they
saw pleased them. The style of life in the new republic seemed willfully designed
to produce mental illness. Everywhere they looked, they found chaos and disorder, a lack of fixity and stability. The community's inherited traditions and procedures were dissolving, leaving incredible stresses and strains. The anatomical implications of this condition were clear: the brain received innumerable abuses, was
weakened, and inevitably succumbed to disease." "There is no mystery in this,"
explained Isaac Ray [a leading medical superintendent of the period]. "As with the
stomach, the liver, the lungs, so with the brain—the manner in which its exercise is
regulated, determines, to a very great extent, the state of its health." Since American society made unprecedented demands on it, one had to expect that insanity
would increase "at a rate unparalleled in any former period." (Boston, 1971), pp.
114–15.

liberty and power, with the richness of the American continent at his back and of the American opportunity at his
fingers' ends is, although a working man, free to be a hero.
He exercises his birthright of freedom by choosing to turn
his face to the wall and die. Yet Scrooge, the English hero,
inheritor of privilege and power, is filled with terror and
remorse when faced by the wall, and turns his back to it,
and is reborn.

<h3 style="text-align:center">III   MASTERS</h3>

The fundamental relationship in both "Bartleby" and *A
Christmas Carol* is that of master and clerk. What is a master
as master to Dickens and to Melville? To what extent is
Scrooge's behavior and that of the unnamed narrator of
"Bartleby" culturally determined, and how far does the cultural determination affect their fictional roles? How closely
do they share the values of their contemporaries; or to what
extent, and to what end, do they stand as implicit critics of
those values?

We see Scrooge in the character of a good master for only
a brief moment at the end of *A Christmas Carol*. On the day
after Christmas, a new man, he greets his clerk with these
words: "A merry Christmas, Bob! . . . A merrier Christmas, Bob, my good fellow, than I have given you for many
a year! I'll raise your salary, and endeavor to assist your
struggling family, and we will discuss your affairs this very
afternoon, over a Christmas bowl of smoking bishop, Bob!
Make up the fires, and buy another coalscuttle before you
dot another *i*, Bob Cratchit!" And Dickens adds that
Scrooge "was better than his word." We don't follow
Scrooge into this better state because we have already seen
what a perfect master is—Scrooge's former master, old Fezziwig. Scrooge has explained why it is of such importance to

be a good master: "He has the power to render us happy or unhappy, to make our service light or burdensome, a pleasure or a toil. Say that his power lies in words and looks, in things so slight and insignificant that it is impossible to count 'em up; what then? The happiness he gives is quite as great as if it cost a fortune." Now Scrooge will become like old Fezziwig—and what is that? Fat, old, and kindly; loving Christmas and games and dancing and food and servants and apprentices and wives and children. He has a voice that is "comfortable, oily, rich, fat, and jovial," and this is what he says: " 'Hilli-ho!' cried Old Fezziwig, skipping down from the high desk with wonderful agility. 'Clear away, my lads, and let's have lots of room here! Hilli-ho, Dick! Chirrup, Ebeneezer!' "

Old Fezziwig is a perfect master and he is an all but perfect fool. Why? What is a good master, and why is he depicted by Dickens as one step from an idiot? Scrooge has said that the good master has the power to make his workers happy or unhappy, to make their service light or burdensome, pleasure or toil. But what are we to make of the fact that the master who can do these things is a fool, so much so that we can hardly believe that he can run a business at all; while those two preeminent men of business, Scrooge and Marley, are neither good men nor good masters? Isn't Dickens obscuring the fact that he really believes that good business and good hearts do not add up to large profits; that the good master deals in "words and looks," not pounds and shillings, and that the two cannot be reconciled?

There is another pair of good masters in Dickens—the Cheeryble brothers in *Nicholas Nickleby*. They are first cousins to Old Fezziwig, but they are presented at greater length and may make clearer what Dickens meant by good men of business. We never see the Cheerybles actually conducting business, only dispensing acts of charity. They de-

scend from heaven on the needy Nicholas and carry him off
to the great good place that is their warehouse, situated in a
bucolic-commercial London square, a rural-urban paradise
where the distant noises of the city are transformed into
sounds like the hum of insects, and butterflies miraculously
fly amongst iron railings. In this commercial oasis is the
Cheeryble warehouse where, as far as the reader can ascer-
tain, no business is conducted, no advantage, commercial or
otherwise, is taken of one's fellow men, and no profits could
conceivably be made. The brothers themselves (they are
twins) look like a cross between Father Christmas and the
Blessed Infant, their eyes "clear, twinkling, honest, merry
happy"; their faces "jolly" and "old" with a "comical expression of mingled slyness, simplicity, kindheartedness, and
good-humour"; their appearance quaint and odd, old and
old-fashioned, fat and clumsy and infantile. And Nicholas
himself, after ten minutes in their company, "sob[s] like a
little child."

In part, the question of why Dickens made his good masters fools is inseparable from his fictional technique; from
his habit of dividing the attributes of a single person or role
amongst several persons. By fragmenting his merchants
into their various aspects—in *Nicholas Nickleby* into the
grasping Ralph Nickleby and the charitable Cheerybles; in
A Christmas Carol into the miserly Scrooge, the regenerate
Marley, and the cherubic Fezziwig—Dickens is able to
present both good and bad masters, but he can also avoid
having to face his own ambivalence about the master, and
his uncertainty about the possibility of any man being at
once kindly and commercial. Yet Dickens insisted that the
Cheerybles were "drawn from life," at the same time that he
was evidently aware that they were drawn unconvincingly.
The sceptical world, he says in his Preface to *Nicholas Nickleby,* "will seldom admit a very strongly-marked character,
either good or bad, in a fictitious narrative . . . For this

reason, they [the Cheerybles] have been very slightly and imperfectly sketched." It is a curious and unsatisfactory explanation, and indicates that Dickens felt that something was amiss in his portrayal of the good-man-as-businessman (the Cheerybles) as opposed to the good man of business (Ralph Nickleby). There is no reason why a great novelist should be a great or even a consistent economist, but in this instance more than Dickens's own inconsistency is involved. His ambivalence is an expression and reflection of a larger cultural ambivalence. There was a side of the Victorian mind which was not certain that money-making *is* compatible with virtue. Its prophets were Carlyle and Mill and Ruskin and Arnold; but in the life-style of the Victorian merchants themselves there was an implicit *self*-criticism.

Social historians are agreed that although Great Britain was whole-heartedly launched on an unprecedented drive to make money in the nineteenth century, England never became a business society.[11] That is, the business of making money was not accepted by most people as an end in itself. For the successful merchant to achieve his own ideal of the gentleman, he had to repudiate much in himself that had made it possible for him to have become rich in the first place. To turn gentleman, he not only had to turn his eyes from his place of business, he also had to glorify those of his traits that were least like business traits and most like those of a gentleman. In this contemporary portrait of the ideal British merchant the greatest praise goes to those qualities of the man that are least narrowly merchant-like and most broadly humanistic:

There certainly is no character on the face of the earth more estimable than that of the British merchant. His enlarged intercourse with the world leads to an enlarged and liberal spirit of dealing with mankind; his necessary avocations exercise his mind

[11] See Asa Briggs, *Victorian People* (New York, 1955), pp. 10–11; Briggs, *The Making of Modern England*, pp. 410–11.

in a wholesome activity; his daily experience of the value of character and of a good name, stimulates him to preserve them, and trains him and fixes him in habits of truth and of fair dealing. Liberality is his motto, charity his virtue, generosity his practise.[12]

"Liberality is his motto, charity his virtue, generosity his practise"—this is pure Fezziwig. But Dickens is too intelligent and too honest to see such a merchant as entirely sane; while the actual Victorian merchant, as divided as Dickens, often solved his dilemma by creating an ideal Victorian gentleman out of the part of himself that was his son. He did this, significantly, by altogether removing the son from any possibility of contamination by the source of his wealth—that is, his own business.

The other side of this ambivalence was the British merchant's pride in having incorporated into himself *as merchant* some of the values of the gentleman—in being honest and gentlemanly in his commercial dealings. "This is the age that, more than any other, built up in the eyes of the world this concept of the honest trader, the English merchant whose word is as good as his bond, on whose quality and price the nations who are his willing customers can implicitly rely. . . . The Victorian philosophy of enterprise rested upon a conviction, in no wise a hypocritical one, that honesty *was* the best policy." [13]

Honesty was not the only virtue praised in the successful businessman. Writers like Samuel Smiles saw the commercial world as a school for character building, and that not merely on a personal, but on a national scale.

---

[12] Freeman Hunt, *Worth and Wealth: A Collection of Maxims, Morals, and Miscellanies for Merchants and Men of Business* (New York, 1856), pp. 106–07. Hunt was the editor of a number of magazines and periodicals for businessmen, as well as author of several books. He was the most prolific of nineteenth-century American writers on business. *Worth and Wealth* is a compilation of articles taken from his own magazines and periodicals.

[13] H. G. Nicholas, "The New Morality," in *Ideas and Beliefs of the Victorians*, ed. Harman Grisewood (London, 1949), pp. 32–33.

British biography is studded over . . . with illustrious examples of the power of self-help, of patient purpose, resolute working, and steadfast integrity, issuing in the formation of truly noble and manly character . . . illustrating the efficacy of self-respect and self-reliance in enabling men of even the humblest rank to work out for themselves an honorable competency and a solid reputation. . . . It is strong individualism which makes and keeps the Englishman really free, and brings out fully the action of the social body. The energies of the strong form so many living centres of action round which other individual energies group and cluster themselves; thus the life of all is quickened, and, on great occasions, a powerful energetic action of the nation is secured.[14]

Such tributes to the British merchant's lack of single-mindedness in money-making are reflective of the whole commercial enterprise as it was pursued in England. According to the economist H. J. Habakkuk, British commercial acceleration had always been hindered by a value system not entirely harmonious with business. In the nineteenth century the British manufacturer's determination to enter the gentry caused a "haemorrhage of capital and ability from industry and trade into landownership and politics." [15] The English businessman's ambivalence toward his own calling ultimately affected his performance in that calling, and British economic progress, rapid though it was, was not as rapid as it might have been. It was in America that values and conditions created an atmosphere entirely favorable to business growth, making of the United States a "true" business society.

The conflict between good business and good men did not exist only in the world of Dickens's novels. Literature in this instance expresses quite faithfully, with only a slightly displaced emphasis, a cultural phenomenon. In fact, litera-

---

[14] Samuel Smiles, *Self Help: With Illustrations of Character and Conduct* (New York, 1860), p. 17.

[15] H. J. Habakkuk, *American and British Technology in the Nineteenth Century: The Search for Labour-Saving Inventions* (Cambridge, 1967), p. 54.

ture does more than corroborate in this case. It reveals what reportage such as Smiles's obscures: that the ideal is less easily achieved, and less clearly understood by the culture, than the culture is itself aware. But there are also instances in Dickens's novels where the kind of business morality which Smiles extolls and economists describe is expressed with absolute fidelity: in *Great Expectations,* for example, in the business house of Clarriker and Co., of which Pip is a partner and which he describes thus: "I must not leave it to be supposed that we were ever a great House, or that we made mints of money. We were not in a grand way of business; but we had a good name, and worked for our profits, and did very well." Here and throughout Dickens's work is an ideal morality that goes further and deeper than commercial honesty or a gentlemanly code. It is related to Scrooge's notion of the good which the good master can bring to his dependents, and is inseparable from Dickens's whole concept of the master as father, and of social bonds generally.

In the United States, where there was little to compete with business success as a source of social prestige, the "accepted ideal" was that a man "should rise as far in terms of wealth as his abilities could carry him." Class standing in England had for hundreds of years been based upon birth, family, education, manners, accent, possession of land, title; and there the "ideal of the 'all-round man,' the man of well-developed competence in many fields . . . was still strong." [16] But in America, the indigenous class structure was based almost entirely upon wealth.

. . . there is one element in the national character, one principle of action animating the entire mass of our people, which is greater than any other; nay, I will be bold enough to assert, more powerful than all others united. Whether it be called avarice, or

[16] Habakkuk, pp. 191, 192.

the love of money, or the desire of gain, or the lust of wealth, or whether it be softened to the ear under more guarded terms, prudence, natural affection, diligence in business, or the conscientious improvement of time and talent—it is still *money-making* which constitutes the great business of the majority of our people; it is the use of money which controls and regulates everything.[17]

The religion of the dollar can be seen simply as hypocrisy, which for the most part it is; but there is an element of expediency underlying it. If in England duty to society seemed to call upon the individual to limit greed, in America duty seemed to call upon men to unleash greed. The Bible taught that land was given to man that he might make it fruitful, and in the United States the promised harvest became its own excuse for the rapacity of the harvester. Only by swelling their ambition and so increasing their effort could Americans make up for their limited numbers. All the time that they were idle opportunity shouted. And always underlying the American's faith in progress as expressed in profits was his belief in Nature as the visible proof of God's covenant with him. The richness of the continent was proof of God's faith in America. "God has promised us a renowned existence, if we will but deserve it. He speaks this promise in the sublimity of Nature." [18]

Not only was American society whole-heartedly given over to business, but the business community was eager to embrace as business any activity that brought in money—to encroach on what would have been considered non-commercial values in England and to see them, too, in terms of cash: "here in our country every man is a trader. The Physician trades his benevolent care; the lawyer trades his ingenious tongue; the clergyman trades his prayers." [19]

[17] Address by Judge James Hall to the "Young Men's Mercantile Association of Cincinnati," 1846. Quoted in Hunt, *Worth and Wealth*, p. 224.

[18] Quoted in Perry Miller, *Errand into the Wilderness* (New York, 1964), p. 210.

[19] Quoted in Hunt, *Worth and Wealth*, p. 367. Compare this passage from the Communist Manifesto: "The bourgeoisie has stripped of its halo every occupation

The English professional classes drew a sharp line between themselves and the merchant class. In an article by Harriet Martineau which appeared in Dickens's *Once a Week*, they are scolded for their snobbishness toward the respectable merchant: [20] "There is something as ridiculous as it is melancholy in the contempt which the vulgar of the professional classes parade for commercial occupations." What Martineau herself despises in the merchant is his servility or "cowardice": "It is not to be denied that the aristocratic illusions of the professional classes are kept up by the characteristic faults of the commercial order, as, for instance, the political cowardice which is the conspicuous vice of the manufacturers and merchants of many countries of this day . . ." But the British merchant's servility was an expression in part of his wistful longing for the gentility that comes from inherited wealth; in part a prejudice in favor of the class above his, the class into which "he and his wife yearned to be admitted"; in part an internalization of that cultural contempt of which Martineau speaks.

In *Unto This Last* John Ruskin gives another explanation of British attitudes toward the merchant. Like Martineau and Smiles, Ruskin emphasizes the importance of the merchant class to England; like Dickens, he uncovers the cultural ambivalance in which commerce was enveloped, and cuts through to its moral root. Ruskin asks why members of all the "so-called liberal professions" stand higher, in the "public estimate of honour," than the merchant.

The essential reason . . . will be found to lie in the fact that the merchant is presumed to act always selfishly. His work may be very necessary to the community; but the motive of it is under-

---

hitherto honoured and looked up to with reverent awe. It has converted the physician, the lawyer, the priest, the poet, the man of science, into its paid wage-labourers." Karl Marx and Frederick Engels, "Manifesto of the Communist Party," 1848, in *Selected Works* (Moscow, 1951), I, 35.

[20] Harriet Martineau, "Representative Men," *Once a Week*, 5 (1861), 203.

stood to be wholly personal. The merchant's first object in all his dealing must be (the public believe) to get as much for himself, and leave as little to his neighbour (or customer) as possible. Enforcing this upon him, by political statute, as the necessary principle of his action; recommending it to him on all occasions, and themselves reciprocally adopting it, proclaiming vociferously, for law of the universe, that a buyer's function is to cheapen, and a seller's to cheat,—the public, nevertheless, involuntarily condemn the man of commerce for his compliance with their own statements, and stamp him forever as belonging to an inferior grade of human personality.[21]

Like Dickens, Ruskin measures the merchant against a more deeply serious moral scale than mere gentility or commercial honesty. Dickens wants a business enterprise to be run as if it were a family and the merchant were the father; Ruskin as if it were the Lord's vineyard and the merchant were the Father. Both find it impossible to abide the merchant without changing the nature of the profit-making enterprise altogether: Ruskin transforms profits into divine sharing, Dickens into familial sharing. Ruskin's model is an early Christian commune or monastery; Dickens's model is a pre-industrial work group. Ruskin has a characteristically restricted social ideal—a brotherhood of adult males. Dickens's ideal, characteristically, is both more broadly human— the family includes all human possibilities, male and female, old and young—and less far removed from possibility. The work arrangement as he wanted it had been the normal one in pre-industrial England, and was still extant during Dickens's childhood. Dickens's desire to have Scrooge embrace as family his clerk and his clerk's children, although retrogressive, is neither fanciful nor sentimental. What Dickens is criticizing in the modern world is precisely what Melville criticizes—and the criticism of each has, at this

[21] John Ruskin, *Unto This Last*, in *The Genius of John Ruskin*, ed. John D. Rosenberg (Boston, 1963), p. 240.

level, nothing to do with economics or even with morality, but with a profound psychological truth. The industrial work relationship robs the worker of all emotional satisfaction based upon love.[22]

Ambivalence breeds ambivalence; certainty breeds opposition. The unquestioning faith of most Americans in business bred a radical revulsion from it in those who did not share that faith. The narrator of "Bartleby" is a product of Melville's revulsion. He is a man who is totally absorbed by business values. He reveals this as he explains himself, stripping away his humanity in the process of describing himself as the perfect man of business.

"All who know me," he boasts at the beginning of his narrative, "consider me an eminently *safe* man." During the course of the story the word "safe" is played with, punned upon, and opened out into unexpected meanings. It is used to mean "safe" in the sense of guarded, cautious, secret, prudent, peaceful; and it also means "safe" in the sense of a safe, and vault, and tomb. Almost all of the various meanings of "safe" are used to mask their opposites. The narrator is "safe" in the sense that he is self-enclosed, shut off by his own ego from all human sympathy, and he is like a safe in the sense of being like a tomb, death locked within, on guard against the culprit life. Almost all synonyms for safe are used in this double sense. Peacefulness becomes identical with chilling indifference, and Bartleby's passivity turns out to be the weapon of his aggressive will. As a noun, "safe" is the dominant concrete image in the story. Wall Street itself is a safe, or vault, or tomb, as are the lawyer's chambers, bounded on all sides by walls. Finally, Bartleby's safe-tomb in the Tombs is a green turf between high walls.

[22] For a full discussion of the pre-industrial work group see Peter Laslett, *The World We Have Lost* (New York, 1965).

To be entirely safe, then, is to be entirely dead; and to be a "safe man" is to be a very dangerous man as far as life is concerned. And we remember that "safe" is the self-conferred epithet of this good man of business.

The lesson that Scrooge has had to learn is that mankind is his business. As a man he must assume responsibility for the lives that cross his; as a master he must count his profits not only in pounds and pence, but in words and looks, in happiness conferred and life secured. But the narrator of "Bartleby" has learned no lessons. He has used his encounter with the strange clerk to reinforce his own original perception about life: that the greatest virtue lies in safety—safety, again, being the exclusion of life. Nor has Bartleby attempted to teach anything. He has somewhat evasively demanded that the narrator respond in some adequate way to his own assertion of life. This the narrator, somewhat evasively, has refused to do, and he has couched his refusal entirely in terms of business, although both he and Bartleby realize that this, too, is an evasion.

The narrator's description of his other clerks has made it clear that business suffers whenever life threatens to break out, and he has therefore systematically robbed them of life. First, they have no names but nicknames, which are "expressive of their respective persons or characters." They are expressive, in fact, of their idiosyncrasies; had they no idiosyncrasies they would be perfect business machines and, like the lawyer himself, would need no names at all. Each of the clerks is good for business during only half the day, that half during which he is half dead. Turkey is useful in the morning: in the afternoon his face is like a "grate full of Christmas coals"; it is "red and radiant" and he himself is "too energetic" with a "strange, inflamed, flurried, flighty recklessness of activity about him." That is, he has come to life, and his life interferes with his usefulness to business. The second clerk, Nippers, is good for business only in the afternoon; in the morning, when he is a victim of "indigestion," he would "impatiently rise from his seat, and stooping over his table, spread his arms wide apart, seize the whole desk, and move it, and jerk it, with a grim, grinding motion on the floor." A good deal of repressed sexual energy is implied by his behavior, sexuality, like all natural functions, being threatening to business. Bartleby, who has reduced natural functions to a minimum—he hardly eats or sleeps or speaks or moves—seems at first to be the perfect clerk: "motionless . . . pallidly neat, pitiably respectable." He copies day and night, "gorging" himself on legal documents—the only food in the story which does not interfere with work. But he bridles at reading proof, which the lawyer himself describes as a "very dull, wearisome, and lethargic affair." "I can readily imagine that, to some sanguine temperaments, it would be altogether intolerable. For example, I cannot credit that the mettlesome poet, Byron, would have contentedly sat down with Bartleby to examine a law document." Nor will Bartleby. It is at this point that the conflict of wills begins, and Bartleby's passivity first asserts itself as aggression. For a moment it occurs to the lawyer to consider Bartleby's reason for refusing to read proof—"But my business hurried me."

The world of business has absorbed religion, too, into itself; and the condemnation of business extends to a condemnation of Christianity. When the lawyer's "old Adam" rises up against his insubordinate clerk, he preaches patience to himself by recollecting the Bible while in his counting-house—

simply by recalling the divine injunction: "A new commandment give I unto you, that ye love one another." Yes, this it was that *saved* me. Aside from higher considerations, charity often operates as a vastly wise and *prudent* principle—a great *safe*guard to its possessor. Men have committed murder for jealousy's sake, and anger's sake, and hatred's sake, and selfishness' sake, and spiritual pride's sake; but no man, that ever I heard of, ever committed a diabolical murder for sweet charity's sake. Mere self-interest, then, if no better motive can be enlisted, should especially with high-tempered men, prompt all beings to charity and philanthropy. [My italics.]

The divine injunction "saved"—or safed—him into a recollection of self-interest. Melville's satire seems heavy-handed until it is compared with contemporary business handbooks, and then, like so much in Dickens, it pales to reportage beside the real thing:

If a merchant wishes a clerk to be faithful, and attentive to his interest, he should take some care of the welfare of those in his employ. Any act of kindness, by which gratitude will be awakened, will go further towards making a good clerk, than a thousand severe, and sometimes irksome business precepts. A display of passion toward those who, by the nature of their situation, can make no defense, is not only galling to a sensitive mind, but it often leads to future evils, which no opposite influence can counteract.[23]

The narrator comforts himself with philosophy as well as with religion. He has been pondering over Bartleby's strange irrationality:

Gradually I slid into the persuasion that these troubles of mine, touching the scrivener, had been all predestinated from eternity, and Bartleby was billeted upon me for some mysterious purpose of an all-wise Providence, which it was not for a mere mortal like me to fathom. Yes, Bartleby, stay there behind your screen, thought I; I shall persecute you no more; you are harmless and noiseless as any of these old chairs; in short, I never feel so private as when I know you are here. At last I see it, I feel it; I penetrate to the predestinated purpose of my life. I am content. Others may have loftier parts to enact; but my mission in this world, Bartleby, is to furnish you with office-room for such period as you may see fit to remain.

Once again, Melville has been paraphrasing journalism.

Here is H. A. Boardman, a prolific authority on business

---

[23] Hunt, *Worth and Wealth,* p. 107.

ethics and author of *The Bible in the Counting-House,* advising the philosophic businessman in what light to look upon commercial reverses: "The very errors and reverses of commerce conduce to a moral end. . . . A careful observation of the causes which have produced the downfall of others, may prompt to a cautious and moderate policy, the disappointments to which even the most sagacious are liable, and are adapted to impress the mind with a becoming sense of God's universal Providence and our absolute dependence upon Him in every undertaking." [24]

The passage from "Bartleby" exposes the real human failure inherent in the canting religiosity of this one, which turns the downfall of others into neat self-help maxims. To turn mankind's agonies into caution and policy is really to turn men into objects, and this is just what Melville's narrator is always doing. His great talent is the dehumanization of all human beings who cross his path. If Bartleby has been "billetted upon" him by "an all-wise Providence" for some mysterious purpose relative to the narrator alone, then Bartleby is not himself a full human being; "harmless and noiseless as any . . . old chair," he may then be treated as a chair and, like a chair, he may be safely provided with office space. Melville's apprehension of the clerk in the commercial world, like Marx's apprehension of the worker in the industrial world, is of his reduction into an object or "instrument" for his master's use.

In "Bartleby," business is shown to be antipathetic to all human sympathy, and to life itself, and there is no ideal of business that *is* compatible with life. The only possibility opposed to imprisonment and death is the life of business; the only release from, or alternative to business, is death. In this respect, as in all its aspects, "Bartleby" deals in a very circumscribed world. The contrast between business and life seems so inadequate that we suspect that business is a meta-

[24] H. A. Boardman, *The Bible in the Counting-House* (Philadelphia, 1856), pp. 79–80.

phor for life itself, and Wall Street for the world. If all life is bound in by walls, then the business of Wall Street is as good a symbol as any other for human activity as it is conducted behind the wall—in nineteenth-century America, in fact, it is the perfect symbol. And the human failure of the narrator is not entirely, or even primarily, a criticism of him *as master*. The "good master," in the Dickensian sense, is not as important in America as he is in England. Bartleby is not dependent upon the narrator for his life, as Bob Cratchit is upon Scrooge; and the narrator is entirely aware of this. Bartleby does not want a raise in salary, or even kind words and looks, but something else; and the lawyer knows it. "I might give alms to his body; but his body did not pain him; it was his soul that suffered, and his soul I could not reach." It is the soul which he *must* reach, and his failure to do so is not a failure of the business society, but of the human society.

IV CLERKS

There were 20,000 insurance, Stock Exchange, mercantile, and law clerks in London in 1831.

In this body of clerical activity, poured daily into the City, drained from it at night, we have the central distinctive type of the Early Victorian period. The classes above it, Royal, noble, or propertied, legislators, merchants, members of the learned professions, had existed before, but for the first time they became dependent on the, so to say, negative virtues of a body of men who made nothing with their hands, except figures in books of account, and whose great quality was not manual skill, but probity as regards other people's affairs entrusted to them.

G. M. Young calls these men "the private servants of their masters." [25] The great age of the English *public* servant, the product of the competitive Civil Service examination, was

[25] G. M. Young, ed., *Early Victorian England,* I (London, 1934), 179, 180, 179.

yet to come. Those men, brought up to believe government service to be the highest vocation of a gentleman, were growing to manhood during this period. They were members of the middle class—that "virtuous rank," James Mill called it [26]— educated at the Universities, brought up in a tradition of public service, belief in work, and self-restraint.[27] But how were *these* men, the "private servants," members of the aspiring lower ranks, brought up to exercise the probity and self-denial necessary to their task? Many were educated in the Charity Schools, founded by Dissenters at the end of the seventeenth century, and still flourishing, under the direction of the Anglican Church, in the nineteenth. These schools were designed to teach discipline rather than knowledge, and their supporters always emphasized the fact that in them the poor were not to be educated into discontent with their lot in life.[28] "In the expanding world of commerce there was an ever-increasing demand for clerks, and these schools provided them. The attitude of the men and women who ran them was essentially Puritan. They believed, like their grandparents before them, in godliness, industry, and thrift." [29] It is a school that

[26] Quoted in Mitchell, *Types of Economic Theory*, I, 484.

[27] In 1854 plans were made for reforming entry into the Civil Service. By 1870 the scheme was in full operation and England introduced the competitive examination for Civil Service employment. England was "establishing standards to which all men might repair . . . Not only were they going to admit any man equally into the Civil Service but also, inside the Service, they were going to insist on scrupulous probity, anonymity, political neutrality, and public loyalty." H. G. Nicholas, "The New Morality," pp. 132–33. These virtues sound very much like those which the charity school sought to inculcate in the lower classes, and indeed the nineteenth century is a period remarkable for the widespread belief, through so many levels of society, in a similar morality. See Briggs, *Victorian People*, p. 3: "Belief in a common moral code, based on duty and self restraint" was shared in by all classes. "Institutions like the school, the voluntary organization, the trade union, and, above all, the family, emphasized the maintenance of those values which held society together."

[28] See Richard D. Altick, *The English Common Reader* (Chicago, 1957), pp. 37 and 143.

[29] J. H. Plumb, *England in the Eighteenth Century (1714–1815)* (Baltimore, Maryland, 1950), p. 31. See also E. P. Thompson, *The Making of the English Working Class* (New York, 1964), p. 401.

Bob Cratchit might well have been brought up in, and surely he must be its finest product—devout, hard-working, humble, always hoping for help from his betters but resigned to receiving none. Whatever happens, he and his family are "happy, grateful, pleased with one another, and contented with the time." [30]

Dickens was also aware of the other face of "godliness, industry, and thrift"—hypocrisy, diseased ambition, dishonesty, and corruption—which he paints unforgettably in *David Copperfield*. Uriah Heep (another law clerk) describes his charity school education to David:

"Father and me was both brought up at a foundation school for boys; and mother, she was likewise brought up at a public, sort of charitable, establishment. They taught us a deal of umbleness—not much else that I know of, from morning to night. We was to be umble to this person, and umble to that; and to pull off our caps here, and to make bows there; and always to know our place, and abase ourselves before our betters. And we had such a lot of betters! Father got the monitor-medal by being umble. So did I. . . . 'Be umble,' Uriah, says father to me, 'and you'll get on. It was what was always being dinned into you and me at school; it's what goes down best. Be umble,' says father, 'and you'll do!' And really it ain't done bad!"

It was the first time it had ever occurred to me that this detestable cant of false humility might have originated out of the Heep family. I had seen the harvest, but had never thought of the seed. . . . I fully comprehended now, for the first time, what a base, unrelenting, and revengeful spirit must have been engendered by this early, and this long, suppression. (*David Copperfield*, Ch. 39) [31]

---

[30] Bob's name alone indicates that he is the perfect clerk or scrivener. Cratchit is an obvious pun upon "Scratch it"; and Bob is slang for shilling, in which coin he gratefully counts his miserable salary. ("Bob had but fifteen 'bob' a week himself; he pocketed on Saturdays but fifteen copies of his Christian name.")

[31] This kind of education for the lower classes was not widely questioned until the Reform Bill of 1867 made the upper classes fear their ignorance, now that they were to become "the future masters of England." Henceforth a national system of education was felt to be essential. See Briggs, *The Making of Modern England*, p. 521.

It is tempting to us, who value self-expression at almost any cost and distrust repression for almost any reason, to say that Heep is more true to life than Bob Cratchit and that Bob is too good to be true. And yet, of the 20,000 clerks in whose probity their masters trusted, it is undoubtedly true that for the system to have worked—and we know that it did work—Bob must be closer to the truth than Uriah, on the level of behavior at least. Bob has internalized his lessons, and they have become a part of his own nature: Uriah, perhaps because he is more intelligent, perhaps because he was ground harder, has kept the lessons outside of himself, and only internalized the wounds. But it would be difficult to say which of the two men has suffered the greater mutilation from "this early and this long suppression"—although it is quite clear which of the two Dickens himself would select.

Dickens presses the type of the repressed clerk yet further in *Martin Chuzzlewit,* in the character of the old clerk, Chuffey. Chuffey's personality has been so entirely obliterated by his master's that he has become "an embodiment of nothing. Nothing else." He is Dickens's apprehension of the working man who is cut off from himself by work that is altogether alien, as Marx described him in 1844, the same year that *Martin Chuzzlewit* was published: "This is the relationship of the worker to his own activity as something alien and not belonging to him, activity as suffering (passivity), strength as powerlessness, creation as emasculation, the personal life (for what is life but activity?) as an activity which is directed against himself, independent of him and not belonging to him. This is *self-alienation.*" [32]

Chuffey is cut off from himself by his work; but to Dickens, this "self-alienation" is to some extent compensated for by Chuffey's utter absorption into old Anthony Chuzzlewit's

[32] Karl Marx, "Alienated Labor," in *Marx's Concept of Man,* ed. Erich Fromm (New York, 1961), pp. 99–100.

personality, just as Bob Cratchit's repression is justified, or at least mitigated, once his filial relationship is acknowledged by the regenerate Scrooge. In Dickens's mind, the really terrifying and unforgivable work relationship would have been what E. P. Thompson, following Marx, calls the "classic exploitive relationship" of nineteenth-century England:

The classic exploitive relationship of the Industrial Revolution is depersonalized, in the sense that no lingering obligations of mutuality—of paternalism or deference, or of the interest of "the Trade"—are admitted. . . . Managerial or supervisory functions demand the repression of all attributes except those which further the expropriation of the maximum surplus value from labour. . . . The worker has become an "instrument," or an entry among other items of cost.[33]

This is alienation piled on alienation—from the self as well as from the master. Neither Chuffey nor Bob Cratchit are "instruments" or "items of cost." Nor are they alienated in the same way that Bartleby is—self-dependent and self-enclosed to the point of absolute autonomy. Melville's equivocal feelings towards his hero—pity at his loneliness, admiration for his crazy assertion of self—would have been unequivocal pity and horror in Dickens. And Dickens's belief in the mitigation of the worker's self-alienation through the "obligations of mutuality" between master and worker would have been no mitigation at all to the fiercely democratic Melville.

In America, where even domestic help objected to the name of servant, it would have been impossible to call a clerk the "personal servant" of his master.[34] The democratic

[33] Thompson, *The Making of the English Working Class*, p. 203.

[34] Bayrd Still, in *Mirror Gotham: New York as Seen by Contemporaries from Dutch Days to the Present* (New York, 1956), quotes two European travellers on the question of servants and subordination in America. The first is a Mrs. Felton, a wealthy Englishwoman writing in the mid-1830's about the servant problem in New York City

assumption was that no man would remain long in a subordinate position, and writers of business advice urged the young only not to try to rise too fast:

The great characteristic of the young men of the present day is an over ambitious desire to become . . . masters of their profession, whatsoever they may be. . . . The haste of the young man to be master, instead of clerk, has thus led him on inevitably to his own ruin, and when he should be enjoying the ease and comfort attendant upon a salary prudently and safely managed, and the prospect of entering into business with those he has so faithfully served, he has by his undue haste, wasted his capital, tarnished his reputation, failed in business, and is seeking once more the employment of a clerk.[35]

The four clerks in "Bartleby" form a spectrum of *in*subordination. It is significant that Turkey and Nippers, who are at least half subordinate—they behave as they ought for half the day—are both English. Turkey, "a short, pursy Englishman of about . . . sixty," is, in the mornings, "the civilest, nay the blandest and most reverential of men." Nippers is a young Englishman of about twenty-five, with a "gentlemanly sort of deportment"; but he has already been bitten by the American bug, ambition. "Nippers knew not what he wanted. Or, if he wanted anything, it was to be rid of a scrivener's table altogether." He is one of those young clerks who is eager to rise to be master, and he surreptitiously receives clients of his own while still clerking it for

---

which, she said, was driving many New Yorkers to live in boarding houses: "Irish immigrants provided the chief source of domestic workers, together with the colored element in the population; but employers complained that the Irish put on airs almost immediately upon their arrival, and that servants generally took the equalitarian philosophy of the time so seriously as to insist upon being called, not servants, but 'helps,' 'helpers,' or 'hands'" (p. 91). And in 1825, Karl Bernhard, Duke of Saxe-Weimar-Eisenach reported similarly: "The servants are generally negroes and mulattos; most of the white servants are Irish; the Americans have a great abhorrence of servitude. Liveries are not to be seen; the male servants wear frock coats. All the families complain of bad servants and their impudence, because the latter consider themselves on an equality with their employers. Of this insolence of servants I saw daily examples" (p. 111).

[35] Hunt, *Worth and Wealth*, pp. 315–17.

the narrator. Ginger Nut, the office boy, is a native American boy on-the-make, the popular smart-aleck, without an ounce of reverence, and proud of his own insolence. Bartleby is the story's other native American. Melville apparently found it impossible to think of any American in a truly dependent position. The independence of the American working man was a point that would not have needed emphasis in Melville's day, when men were so urgently needed at all kinds of jobs that, for example, the *New York Times* was urging the employment of women in clerical positions in order to free men for more "active" jobs.[36] Yet Melville does emphasize it; he is particularly insistent that Bartleby is in every way a free and independent man. The story makes it clear that Bartleby would be provided with another job if he left this one; even that he needs no job at all since his savings, tied in a handkerchief, are enough for him to live upon.

In fact, Bartleby is dependent upon no one but himself. He is the quintessential American—independent of past and of future; independent of family, of friends, of human intercourse; independent of home or hotel or belongings; of money, of food, of life. It is this very independence which first inspires fear in the narrator; and Bartleby's extreme assertion of equality increasingly assumes a paradoxical air of aristocratic exclusivity. He has a "certain unconscious air of pallid . . . haughtiness . . . or . . . austere reserve" which intimidates the narrator. He has sprung from nowhere and will reveal no progenitors. He may, in fact, be a prince in disguise. Or he may be entirely self-created. It is certain only that his expectations of life are in no way circumscribed by his occupation. What was a position of permanent subordination for Bob is the ground of Bartleby's limitless freedom. Not Bartleby, but Bartleby's master, is enslaved by his position, forever bound over to safety.

[36] Quoted in Hunt, *Worth and Wealth,* pp. 499–500.

CHAPTER TWO

THE HERO BETWEEN TWO WORLDS

As an American working man, then, Bartleby is free—as free a man as Scrooge, the English master. Each is free to be a hero, set free by certain political, social, and ideological circumstances of their cultures to select their own paths. Although they are offered essentially the same choices, the paths they choose are radically different: one into the heart of the human family, one severing all bonds.

As heroes, they go the way of their cultures; as representative men, they select representative courses. It is Scrooge's "Englishness" that makes him embrace mankind as his business, while Bartleby's self-embrace is as representative an "expression of the American mind" as the Declaration of Independence.[1]

Bartleby and Scrooge are offered the same choices, connection with other human beings, or isolation from them; yet each story assigns an entirely different value and meaning to isolation and community. In *A Christmas Carol*, com-

---

[1] The phrase is Thomas Jefferson's, taken from a letter he wrote in 1825 in which he explained what his object had been in writing the Declaration of Independence. The entire sentence reads: "Neither aiming at originality of principles or sentiments, nor yet copied from any particular and previous writing, it was intended to be an expression of the American mind." Quoted in Carl Becker, *The Declaration of Independence: A Study in the History of Political Ideas* (New York, 1942), p. 25.

munity is what *must* be desired, and the burden of proof is put upon Scrooge to justify his selfish life in the face of the increasing evidence from past, present, and future, that he is wrong. In "Bartleby" the burden of proof is put upon the narrator to persuade Bartleby that his life would be better spent at work in the community of the office. At its bleakest, Scrooge's life is circumscribed within the commercial circle, where man is locked into relationship only with cash. Scrooge's death bed, like the living death of his office life, is surrounded by voices haggling over money; even the ghost of his dead business partner is accompanied by a lurid jangling of cash boxes. There is a progression of isolation even among the dead: Marley's ghost, caught up in the noise of the other damned spirits, is not so fearsome an apparition as Scrooge's solitary grave—the horrid culmination of his nightmare—and even it is described in terms of a teeming, diseased, inhuman liveliness. True riches, in *A Christmas Carol,* are represented by relationships with human beings and carry with them not only joy, but responsibility. It is both good and necessary to join the family of man, for others as well as for the self. Finally, a man's responsibility to other men is not open to question: it is the "given." The lesson, the truth, that is revealed to Scrooge is that mankind is his business—not his joy or comfort merely, but his obligation and his trust.

At the bleak end of Bartleby's existence, too, life is reduced to the cash nexus—or rather, to the business "relationship." At the rich end is solitude, and death. In "Bartleby" the business relationship is representative of all human relationships, relations which are based not upon mutual joy or mutual duty, but upon competitiveness and self-aggrandizement. Isolation in *A Christmas Carol* is almost identical with sociability in "Bartleby": both are loveless and self-centered. And opposed to such sociability is splendid isolation and triumphant death.

The values assigned to isolation and community seem to have been reversed by the American story. In *A Christmas Carol,* isolation is evil and community is good, and good and evil carry their full moral connotations. But in "Bartleby" it is isolation that is the "good," sociability the "evil." Good and evil have lost their absolute moral connotations and are good or evil only in relation to each other. Good is whatever is desirable, perhaps simply bearable; evil is whatever is undesirable, ultimately, to Bartleby, unbearable. That is, in "Bartleby" good and evil have psychological rather than ethical significance, which is another way of saying that they have been displaced from the social to the personal or private sphere. The individual is the measure of all things in the American story, not the community. The measure of Scrooge's life is almost entirely social; the measure of Bartleby's life is almost entirely personal.

Bartleby's option, which I have called the representative American option, is the self-embrace of the inescapably isolate or "personal" man. Scrooge's option, which I have called the representative English option, is the social embrace of the inescapably social man. Why are these the central tendencies of their cultures?

The change from the pre-industrial world to the modern world, which began in the seventeenth century, can be characterized in terms of change itself—in the pre-industrial world the order of things was believed to be fixed and eternal, in the post-industrial world change is looked upon as perpetual. Or it can be characterized in terms of the change from a patriarchal order of society—a society in which the model of an authoritarian Father was repeated in all areas of life, political, economic, and social—to a society which saw its origins and its model in a social contract agreed upon between men of equal and inalienable rights. Or it can be seen as a change from a society whose basic unit was the family to one whose basic unit is the dissociated individual. These ideas, born in Europe and carried over to America by Englishmen, took root and spread across America far more rapidly than they did in England or anywhere else in Europe. In the eager embrace of change for its own sake; in the loosening and letting go of the patriarchal way of life; in the deification of the individual man, America went to more radical lengths than England, and was carried far more rapidly into the modern world.

In England what chiefly retarded the rampant progress of change was the presence of the past—both its physical presence, its houses and monuments and cultivated fields, and its symbolic presence, its usages and ceremonies and customs. The post-industrial world was felt by Englishmen as well as by Americans to be more and more a place of accelerated change. So it was. But respect for tradition was in part a recognition of the Englishman's identity *as* Englishman; so that even when change was necessary it was often seen as the evolution of some older form into a newer, rather than as an entirely new departure based upon a present contingency. The English constitution was largely a matter of precedents and traditions; the law, too, was based upon traditional interpretations of freedom and restraint. In the late eighteenth century Blackstone "saw the mere survival of an institution through many centuries as evidence of the cumulative approval of many generations. Any institution, therefore, seemed deeply rooted in the popular will." [2] And any institution, as long as it was old, could be seen as enshrining *value*. In 1795 Edmund Burke wrote with proud irony about "the British government, loaded with all its incumbrances, clogged with its peers and its beef, its parsons and its puddings, its commons and its beer, and

[2] Quoted in Daniel J. Boorstin, *The Lost World of Thomas Jefferson* (Boston, 1960), p. 209.

its dull slavish liberty of going about just as one pleases." [3] "We want great alteration," Cobbett wrote, repeating the well-worn refrain, "but we want *nothing* new." [4]

Although progress from the mid-seventeenth century to the mid-nineteenth was in part a movement away from authoritarianism—from the authoritarianism of King, Lords, and Church—much of the symbology and tradition surrounding them remained, as well as what A. P. Thornton calls "the habit of authority," or what Gladstone called "a sneaking kindness for a lord." [5] But the strongest and longest survival of authoritarianism in England was that of the father of the family. According to G. M. Young, most nineteenth-century Englishmen still saw English society as a whole as a community of families. The "traditional culture and morality of England were based on the patriarchal village family of all degrees": "the father worked, the mother saw to the house, the food and the clothes; from the parents the children learnt the crafts and industries necessary for their livelihood, and on Sundays they went together, great and small, to worship in the village church. To this picture English sentiment clung." [6]

This ideal was so strong, Young says, that throughout the nineteenth century it inspired English poetry, controlled English art, and obstructed the formation of a "true philosophy of urban life." It was this ideal which controlled Dickens's imagination in *A Christmas Carol*. Considered from the point of view of its date of publication (1843), Dickens's attempt to turn the firm of Scrooge and Marley into the family of Scrooge and Cratchit was anachronistic; even more

[3] Quoted in A. P. Thornton, *The Habit of Authority: Paternalism in British History* (London, 1965), p. 170.

[4] Thornton, p. 172.

[5] Thornton, p. 172; Gladstone quoted in G. M. Young, *Victorian England: Portrait of an Age* (New York, 1964), p. 84.

[6] Young, *Victorian England*, p. 21.

anachronistic, then, was his attempt to turn London itself into a vast extended family on Christmas morning. But Dickens seldom exaggerates. London had in fact not yet been much touched by the industrial revolution, nor had the lives of its working people changed significantly in the past hundred years.[7] Poor clerks and other working folk still lived in the City; indeed, it would have been impossible, with almost no public transportation and none cheap enough for them to afford, for working men to live farther from their places of work than their feet could take them until well into the 1860's.[8] So Bob Cratchit lived close to his office, as Scrooge did, and as Fred and all his friends did too. The fragmentation of life which is caused by separation of one's place of work from one's home had not yet oc-curred in London and in that respect it was still possible to feel the city as a series of villages and all of its hierarchies as patriarchal. Dickens was of course aware that the city could be a place of terrible loneliness as well, especially for the poor. But his solution for their loneliness was to take them back into a family. In that sense Dickens, like most other Victorians, had no "true philosophy of urban life."

Above all, Dickens must see Scrooge as part of a family because the dissociated individual had no heroic stature in British eyes; had, strangely, less stature in 1843 than he had had twenty-five years earlier when, for example, *Manfred* was published. But the post-Romantic age did not eulogize the loner. Engineers and manufacturers were the individ-

[7] "The ordinary Londoner had only been touched lightly and, so to speak, patchily by those mechanical, scientific, and industrial changes which were making a new England. Before the railways came he had hardly been touched at all. Even after, he often escaped contact, living and working very much as his father and grandfather had worked and lived." J. H. Clapham, "Work and Wages," in *Early Victorian England* (London, 1934), 1, 25. The first railway was begun in London in 1836.

[8] The first workingman's fare was introduced in London by the Metropolitan Railway Co. in 1864. Asa Briggs, *Victorian Cities* (New York, 1970), p. 15. The Underground opened in 1863. Clapham, "Work and Wages," p. 21.

ualists most admired by the Victorians; that is, individualism was best tolerated in economic life. Laissez-faire economics was the doctrine that the businessman left to himself would do best for himself and for the nation; but by 1847, with the passage of the Factory Act, Parliament had decided that unrestricted freedom even in the conduct of business was not always best for the nation. And although the businessman was respected in Victorian England he was not respected so much there as he was in the United States, nor did he respect himself as much as his American counterpart did. Throughout the nineteenth century, the English merchant's and manufacturer's ideal remained the gentleman— and a gentleman, almost by definition, was a man untainted by trade. So when the rich tradesman had accumulated enough money he left his business and bought land, and on the land he abandoned laissez-faire for noblesse oblige— abandoned individualism for the social responsibilities of the country squire. And it was the picture of this patriarchal village way of life that provided English art with its themes throughout the nineteenth century. It was patriarchal English village life on all its levels which provided English literature with its heroes as well.

It is precisely on the issue of the heroic ideal that England and America diverged, almost from the moment of America's founding. If it is true that the source of the English ideal remained the patriarchal village family, that is because the cluster of images surrounding such a family— the uninterrupted flow of the generations, the traditional and hierarchical familial roles, the fields and gardens and churches and homes—had remained a reality of English life. In the children of those families of those villages Englishmen could still see themselves. In the cradles of the Shandys and the Bennetts, the Copperfields and the Pirrips, the Tullivers and the D'Urbervilles and the Pontifexes, the patriarchal village families of all degrees, the English writer could still find himself. But the American hero, almost from the beginning, had been born not into a family but into isolation; had sprung, like Gatsby, from his own Platonic conception of himself. Natty Bumppo had no family, nor had Ishmael, nor had Huck Finn; and Hester Prynne could not found a patriarchal family in the New World—could not even find a father for her child.

Even before the *Arbella* had landed in the New World John Winthrop, Governor of the Bay Colony, seemed aware that his people had left behind them the intricate web of necessity which in England had bound all men together. In his exhortation to his followers that they not forsake the Puritan ideal of community, he warned that the colony must "rejoyce together, mourne together, labour, and suffer together, allwayes haueing before our eyes our Commission and Community in the worke, our Community as members of the same body." [9] Whether or not Winthrop was a conscious prophet, wilderness did in fact destroy community. The Puritan ideal that "Society in all sorts of human affaires is better than Solitariness" was an English ideal—an ideal based upon the fact that in England a growing population was forced into a proximity which it could not even imagine away.[10] In America proximity was not a necessity, and a new ideal arose—the ideal of man alone, whom Melville named the *Isolato*.

What was unprecedented in America was that here there was a geographic habitation and a name for men living outside of society and beyond the reach of government. The habitation was always shifting westward, and this changefulness was part of its romance and of the romantic appeal

[9] John Winthrop, "A Modell of Christian Charity," in *An American Primer*, ed. Daniel J. Boorstin (Chicago, 1968), p. 40.

[10] John Cotton, quoted in Perry Miller, *Errand into the Wilderness* (New York, 1964), p. 143.

of the men who followed it—frontiersmen, trappers, trail blazers, mountain men. A new ideal had been born in the American West out of the continuously repeated experience of emigration to new lands. In one sense, the heroic is only the commonplace pushed to an uncommon extreme; and the most extreme American experience, that of the men of whatever frontier of whatever decade of the continent's first 250 years of settlement, was imaginable to every American in a way that it was not imaginable to Europeans—imaginable as part of every American's experience or possibility. And eventually this experience became self-perpetuating in America regardless of space or time, of frontier conditions, or of wilderness. The strangeness of unsettled land was unlike traditional atmospheres just because it had been formed out of the impossibility of living in traditional, historied ways. The endlessly repeated experience of finding traditional responses inadequate or meaningless for American conditions created, in Americans, a contempt for tradition that came to be transmitted as part of their cultural heritage. And an environment which required constant experimentation with new responses and techniques of life served to so modernize the American scene that every American immigrant, settling in the wilderness of nature or in the wilderness of modernity, found the amount of his usable past to be very small.

At its most extreme, emigration destroyed the practical value of the past. What one had learned in the European past was not necessarily fit for use in the American present. This threw a weight of authority onto the young which was unprecedented in Europe and which tended to divest old people, and what was old in general, of importance. If there is as much to be learned from the environment itself as from traditional knowledge, then the moment assumes more authority than the preceding centuries. There was no fund of past knowledge that could teach settlers of virgin land how to live their present lives, and old and young, parents and children, were equally at a loss. In fact, the young were at an advantage in the sense that they had nothing to forget.

American family life, education, politics, all reflected the immanence of the future in the present instead of, as in England, the immanence of the past. "There is a figure of rhetoric adopted by the Americans, and much used in description," wrote an English traveller in 1817; "it simply consists of the use of the present indicative, instead of the future subjunctive; it is called anticipation. By its aid, what *may be* is contemplated as though it were in actual existence." [11] American education and vocational training were based upon the anticipated needs of an uncertain future. The ideal American youth was described as "a sturdy Yankee who in turn tries all the professions, who teams it, farms it, peddles, keeps a school, preaches, edits a newspaper, goes to Congress, buys a township, and so forth." [12] This training for versatility laid the groundwork for the ideal of American liberal education, a non-specific training of the mind which easily turned itself into an ideal of education for self-expression, self-fulfillment, and self-enrichment, rather than for specific social ends. By the eighteenth century it was already clear that the continuity of the generations, as it was known in England, was to be continuously broken. For this reason American schools must train youth to be ready, in Benjamin Franklin's words, "for learning any business, calling, or profession." [13] By the nineteenth century, Americans believed that they were changing too

[11] Daniel J. Boorstin, *The Americans: The National Experience* (New York, 1967), p. 296.

[12] Hunt, *Worth and Wealth* (New York, 1856), p. 82. Hunt is actually quoting, with slight changes, Ralph Waldo Emerson's essay "Self-Reliance."

[13] Quoted in Bernard Bailyn, *Education in the Forming of American Society* (New York, 1960), p. 35. My discussion of American education is largely based upon Bailyn.

rapidly for any but the young to comprehend. An 1853 article describing "The Great West"—the area of most rapid change—exclaiming over the astounding thrust of the republic, burst out: "The change [that railroads are bringing about] is coming upon us so rapidly, that only the young can fully comprehend it. Like a splendid dream will it appear to people of mature age." [14]

In vocational training, emphasis was put upon versatility rather than specific skills, and in business and manufacture as well, versatility and change were of enormous importance. Everything in American life seemed to reinforce the need for adaptability and changefulness. Labor scarcity, for example, made it desirable for American manufacturers to search for labor-saving devices, and at the same time, made it advantageous for the worker to help in this search by inventing such devices himself. In England, on the other hand, there was a reluctance on both sides to bring about technological changes—from the manufacturer because what machinery he had was built more durably and would therefore outlast American machinery, which was always built cheaply because of the shortage of capital—and from the worker, because every new machine threatened job security.[15] The search for new ways to do things became a deeply engrained business practice in America. An observer in the 1820's wrote: "Everything new is quickly introduced here, and all the latest inventions. There is no clinging to old ways, the moment an American hears the word 'invention' he pricks up his ears." [16] Widespread economic health seemed to have bred a native optimism that many foreign observers noticed, and optimism itself—the willingness to take risks—intensified and increased economic health.

[14] "The Great West," *DeBow's Review*, 15 (1853), 50–53.
[15] See H. J. Habakkuk, *American and British Technology in the Nineteenth Century* (Cambridge, 1967), pp. 50–51, 142–43.
[16] Quoted in Habakkuk, p. 49.

At the same time that business was aided by American optimism and love of change, the rich businessman was tolerated by the basically egalitarian society, especially of the pre-Civil War years, because it was expected that wealth too would change hands quickly; that riches and bankruptcy followed each other fairly commonly within single lifetimes. Robert Rantoul, Jr., a Jacksonian politician and theorist, believed that inequalities both social and economic were tolerable in a free society entirely because of the rapidity of changeover; because of the social mobility prevalent in America "within and between generations"; and because the acquisition of great wealth by the small capitalist class was "held in check by the same grand principle of turnabout: a half century changes almost the entire class roster." [17] Instead of being seen as a threat to the social order, change itself became one of the guarantees of social stability as Americans understood the word, by guaranteeing the continuation of an egalitarian or republican social order.

The rhetoric of change, which in England was absorbed into the rhetoric of traditionalism, took on more and more significance in all aspects of American life. To have roots in one place was as detrimental to vocation as having only one skill or trade. And it was finally not the pursuit of vocation alone that caused the typical American restlessness. A qualitative change seems to have taken place. One changed jobs or location first to earn a living; then to earn a better living; and finally one changed to change. Restlessness and the need for excitement is one explanation for what emerges more and more strongly as an American characteristic; but the lure of wealth in the eighteenth and nineteenth centuries, like the lure of land in the seventeenth, seemed to provide the seeker with its own moral justification, even compulsion, for seeking it.

[17] Marvin Meyers, *The Jacksonian Persuasion: Politics and Belief* (Stanford, 1960), p. 213.

It is in American political theory that the rhetoric of change is furthest from the British belief in the authority of custom. The vitality of the present is the vitality of fact; history, on the other hand, is made up of what Paine called "the errors of tradition." The metaphor of the generation gap dates back to the very inception of the American Republic. "We may consider each generation as a distinct nation," Jefferson wrote, "with a right, by the will of its majority, to bind themselves, but none to bind the succeeding generation, more than the inhabitants of another country." [18] Constitutionalism as the English practised it—the gradual absorption of change into the existing body of the law—was inimical to this ideal of the constant march of generation.

No society can make a perpetual constitution [Jefferson wrote], or even a perpetual law. The earth belongs always to the living generation: they may manage it, then, and what proceeds from it, as they please, during their usufruct. They are masters, too, of their own persons, and consequently may govern them as they please. But persons and property make the sum of the objects of government. The constitution and the laws of their predecessors are extinguished then, in their natural course, with those whose will gave them being. . . . If it be enforced longer, it is an act of force, not of right. [19]

Jefferson's belief in the discontinuity of the generations is both fantastic—the great architect of the Republic never seriously envisioned implementing such ideas—and revealing, too, of his deep mistrust of perpetuity. Nothing could be further than this from the English common law principle that "custom acquired legal validity by being handed down from time immemorial—'a time whereof the memory of man runneth not to the contrary.' " [20] Like Jefferson, Walter Bagehot used the word generation in relation to the continuity of government, *not* as a divisive concept, however:

[18] Meyers, *The Jacksonian Persuasion*, p. 205.   [19] Meyers, pp. 210–11.
[20] Meyers, p. 209.

"Generally one generation in politics succeeds another almost silently; at every moment men of all ages between thirty and seventy have considerable influence; each year removes many old men, makes all others older, brings in many new. The transition is so gradual that we hardly perceive it." [21] Bagehot's use of the concept of generation, in its insistence upon gradualism and stability, seems a genuine expression of English history. Jefferson's use of it, in its cheerfully aggressive divisiveness, seems an expression not so much of American history as of one side of "the American mind."

The American lawmaker, like the American businessman, felt that discarding the past left him freer to deal with the contingent present and uncertain future. The "stilts and crutches of precedents" seemed of no use in dealing with the American future. At the same time, Jefferson's apprehension that all laws are relevant only for the generation that made them reveals his underlying mistrust of government altogether, as does his well-known dictum that the best government governs least. It is also revealing, however, of Jefferson's perception of what the conditions of American life were. In a country like America, "Kindly separated by nature, and a wide ocean, from the exterminating havoc of one quarter of the globe," "possessing a chosen country, with room enough for our descendents to the thousandth and thousandth generation," it seems logical that Jefferson should have believed that the least possible amount of government was sufficient; that all America needed was a government whose characteristics would be almost entirely negative, consisting in the absence of restraint and the protection of the individual ("a wise and frugal government, which shall restrain men from injuring one another, shall leave them otherwise free to regulate their own pur-

[21] Walter Bagehot, *The English Constitution* (Garden City, N.Y., 1962), p. 11.

suits of industry and improvement, and shall not take from the mouth of labor the bread it has earned").[22] This negative ideal of government persisted in America long after Jefferson's day, following the frontier, where the debate over "law" and "government" stayed alive as long as government did not move as quickly as men did; as long as law was the result of spontaneous communal activity and not of written codes. But it persisted in the East too, which had been a frontier only a few generations since. Thoreau, like all American writers deeply responsive to the West, could imagine a time when government would govern "not at all." Freedom, education, westward expansion, are not the product of government, Thoreau wrote, but had come about in spite of government, out of the "character inherent in the American people."

Government of some kind was necessary to the welfare of the individual members of each frontier community, but the way in which such governments were formed robbed them of the sanction of traditional value and prestige, and at the same time released their members from any compelling ideological commitment to sustain them. These were communities, going back as far as the Plymouth Compact, which depended upon the agreement of all members to submit to the "common will." Many settlers of the early colonies, "finding themselves without legal rights on vacant lands," signed compacts in which they agreed to submit to the common will.[23] A typical covenant of this sort was drawn up by the settlers of Exeter, New Hampshire, in 1639.

Wee, his [Charles I] loyal subjects brethren of the church of Exeter, situate and lying upon the river of Piscataquacke, with other

---

[22] Thomas Jefferson, "First Inaugural Address," reprinted in *An American Primer*, p. 233.

[23] Frederick Jackson Turner, "Western State-Making in the Revolutionary Era," *American Historical Review*, 1 (1895–96), 72.

inhabitants there considering ourselves the holy will of god and our owne necessity, that wee should not live without wholesome laws and government amongst us, of wch wee are altogether destitute doe in the name of Christ and in the sight of god, combine ourselves together to erect and set up amongst us such government as shall be to our best descerning aggreeable to the will of god, professing ourselves subject to our sovereign Lord King Charles, according to the liberties of our English colony of the Massachusetts.[24]

Almost 150 years later, settlers of Tennessee and Kentucky, in regions beyond the jurisdiction of federal laws or political institutions—the then "western lands"—found themselves in the same position as the Puritans of Exeter. They too drew up town laws based upon and sanctioned by the common will. In the 1840's and '50's, groups of pioneers forming wagon trains to travel West regularly adopted the well-established custom of the trail of making themselves into political bodies.

This method of forming laws, based upon expediency and without sanctions from a national government, from tradition, or from God, predisposed its makers to form certain assumptions about law and government, the most pertinent one here being that what man has made, and made within living memory, no matter how judicious and expedient, man can imagine unmade. The difference between such an American community and, say, an English village, is that the sanction of continuity and the sanctity of custom are missing. It takes a far more radically imaginative leap to undo what has existed since beyond the memory of man than to undo what you yourself created yesterday; and the possibility of dissolution both robs institutions of prestige and exonerates individuals who abandon them from blame.

Another aspect of the westward movement served to rein-

[24] Quoted in Turner, p. 72.

force the Jeffersonian dichotomy between community and government. In the nineteenth century, most western lands were held by the federal government. Western immigrants, settling haphazardly on these lands, were therefore "squatters"—technically, illegal occupants of federal land. But American squatters were only ambiguously lawbreakers; more accurately, they were preemptors, people who had gotten to the land before anyone else, sometimes before government had had time even to survey the land in question. Eventually, the law accommodated itself to these preemptors, reinforcing the settlers' feeling that "natural" law was stronger than "bureaucratic" law. To protect themselves from counterclaimants to the lands they themselves occupied, these earliest settlers often organized into "claim clubs" in order to protect their claims. The claim clubs took the place of courts of law, which had not yet reached the frontier. Strictly speaking, their activities were outside the law; yet they represented all the law and order there was. Where the law of claim clubs clashed with the federal law, the settlers' allegiance was generally with their own, self-made procedures. This method of law-making, and the attitudes toward government which it inspired, had developed to suit the needs of the "land rush"; it was repeated by the miners who went West during the "Gold Rush" where again the federal government came to be regarded if not as an enemy, at least as an outsider.[25]

Such government, although democratic in origin and intention, often led to the subversion of the judiciary. The Vigilance Committees of the Far West were the result of the absence of an established judiciary controlled by a central government. Created by frontiersmen and pioneers to deal with criminals, vigilante customs were based upon immedi-

[25] See Boorstin, *The Americans*, pp. 72–81, for the history of the Claim Clubs.

ate needs and conditions. In very new communities, or "on the trail," there were no jails; even where jails existed, it was expensive to keep men locked up.

One of the earliest and most popular of the western writers, Charles Webber, describes and explains the activities and origins of the vigilantes (whom he calls rangers) in his novel *Old Hicks, the Guide*. Some horse thieves have been at work, and the novel's hero, a mountain man,

called a council of our oldest and best men . . . it was determined to give these interlopers warning to make themselves scarce in two days. They defied us, and refused to go. I called together the Rangers and we went down to their settlement to see that our orders were enforced.

They fired on us; a desperate fight occurred, in which four of them were shot, and the other two taken prisoners and hung in ten minutes to a live oak in their own yard. . . . such a course was inevitable. We had no judicial organization; what else could we do? Be run over rough-shod, and have our property destroyed and stolen, and our honest working-men picked off from "the bush"? It could not be expected. What judiciary could we appeal to? They would have sworn each other through the meshes of the law in the best organised courts, if we had had them in existence among us!

We knew they did the mischief; we had circumstantial proof enough to satisfy us of that; we knew, too, that their neighbourhood would be in every respect fatal to the interests of our colony; and we took the law in our own hands, as we had a right to do. The remedy was a terrible one, but the disease was eradicated. Such is the stern necessitarian logic of the frontier.[26]

Webber's appeal to expediency—"what else could we do?"—seems reasonable. The "stern necessitarian logic of the frontier" imposed its own laws upon the helpless frontiersmen. But Webber's reference to the "meshes of the law in the best organised courts" is revealing of the mistrust, even contempt, in which the Westerners held the workings of es-

[26] Charles W. Webber, *Old Hicks, the Guide* (London, 1856), pp. 17–18.

tablished government and written laws. True justice, "natural law," came from the people and was dictated to the people by their most recent experience: the experience of the frontier, or of the trail, or of the moment. Therefore, only the moment could be trusted—and oneself. The vigilantes were men not of the states but of the territories—and when the territories had been absorbed into the United States, there was no longer any room for them. But the vigilante, the man of rough and ready "justice," remained and remains an American hero.

The absence of federal control along the western frontier led not only to a subversion of the judiciary, to "squatter's rights" or semi-legal possession of land, but to illegal land seizure as well. In the case of Indian treaties, the law was broken without fear of punishment, partly because it had come to seem inevitable that Americans should take over the continent, partly because successful occupation of land gives to the occupier a sanction irrespective of mere lawfulness. Whatever the reason, nothing succeeded like the success of the westward movement, and even those Americans who opposed the methods by which the United States seized much of the South and West from the Indians, and Texas and California from Mexico, probably would have been unwilling to see those lands returned.[27] Indeed, many Americans wanted to acquire Mexico itself as part of the United States. An editorial from the New York *Morning News* of 1845, entitled "The Popular Movement," exemplifies the common contradictory attitudes of Americans towards the settlement of the West.

From the time that the Pilgrim Fathers landed on these shores to the present moment, the older settlements have been constantly throwing off a hardy, restless and lawless pioneer population, which has kept in advance, subduing the wilderness and prepar-

[27] See Frederick Merk, *Manifest Destiny and Mission in American History* (New York, 1963), pp. 89–106.

ing the way for more orderly settlers who tread rapidly upon their footsteps. It is but a short time since Western Massachusetts, Connecticut and Rhode Island, although now proverbially the land of "steady habits" and good morals, presented a population no ways superior to that of Texas at the present day. As their numbers increased, law and order obtained control, and those unable to bear constraint sought new homes. Those latter have rolled forward in advance of civilization, like the surf of an advancing wave, indicative of its resistless approach. This is the natural, unchangeable effect of our position upon this continent, and it must continue until the waves of the Pacific have hemmed in and restrained the onward movement.

To say that the settlement of a fertile and unappropriated soil by right of individual purchase is the aggression of a government is absurd. Equally ridiculous is it to suppose that when a band of hardy settlers have reclaimed the wilderness, multiplied in numbers, built up a community and organized a government, that they have not the right to claim the confederation of that society of States from the bosom of which they emanated. An inalienable right of man is to institute for themselves that form of government which suits them best, and to change it when they please. On this continent communities grow up mostly by immigration from the United States. Such communities therefore inevitably establish the same form of government which they left behind and *demand* of them that they *come* into the Union. Mexico is a government professedly of the people. If that people choose to change its form they have the right to do so. They have already done so with the approbation of the world. If therefore Mexico, in whole or in part, becomes so settled by the Anglo-Saxon race that they have a majority and decide to alter the system to that of the United States model, and ask for admittance into the Union, the same inalienable right will exist and who will deny it? [28]

This editorial illustrates the ways in which such a "popular" movement is an American innovation, and it does so largely through its characterization of the pioneer. The phrases "subduing the wilderness," establishing "law and order," forwarding the "advance of civilization," although

[28] Quoted in Merk, pp. 22–23.

American enough, could have been written by any of the numerous English travellers who were sending home accounts of the New World throughout the nineteenth century. The "inalienable right of man" to change his form of government was, by 1845, an American axiom, as old as the Revolution. But the writer's obviously admiring characterization of the American pioneer—"hardy, restless and lawless"—is frontier American. It was this man, felt to be necessary to the growth of America and therefore not subject to ordinary moral laws who became the native American hero, and who had no forebears in European Romanticism. His hardiness is his courage; his restlessness is that energetic enterprise which had always kept Americans from being satisfied with any mere portion of the continent; and his lawlessness is his native American self-reliance which obeys not the outworn precepts of history, but the spontaneous dictates of his own heart.

During the early years of American settlement, the ideal remained that of man in community. But first men placed land acquisition in new communities above the old communities; and then land over settlement altogether; and finally the lone hunter and solitary trapper came into existence. By the eighteenth century, the accepted ideal became equally the self-reliant American whose philosophies were self-evident and whose laws would henceforth be self-imposed. A tension between the ideals of solitariness and community was acknowledged openly and would never again go underground; the weight of popular romantic appeal, if not of popular approval, would shift more and more to the "loner" as the solitary hunter, trapper, trail blazer, and mountain man were needed for Western settlement.

Toward the end of the eighteenth century, Hector St. John de Crèvecœur, a Frenchman farming in New York State, described what he called two stages of frontier development. The first stage, which consisted of clearing the wilderness, is accomplished by the "most vicious of our people," men who, far removed from the "reach of government . . . are often in a perfect state of war." These men make way for the second stage of development, "the true American freeholders; the most respectable people in this part of the world; respectable for their industry, their happy independence, the great share of freedom they possess, the good regulation of their families." [29] But these virtuous farmers, valued by Jefferson no less than by Crèvecœur as the bulwarks of democratic government, were not the men who caught the popular imagination. Rather, it was the men whom Crèvecœur and others described, in words remarkably like those of Hobbes's description of man "in a state of nature," who were mythologized into the first American heroes. Hobbes had imagined man's life outside of society as being "solitary, poore, nasty, brutish, and short." To him and to his readers it was a state horrible but hypothetical. In America, however, the hypothesis became truth; and in moving from the hypothetical to the actual, freed men's imaginations to see solitariness not just in terms of horror, but in terms of heroism and high romance.

The popular imagination was free to do what it chose with the Westerner, but the "popular imagination" is complex, and it immediately revealed an ambivalence in regard to him. The "Europeanized" part of the popular imagination seized upon the Westerner in one way, the "native American" in another. Furthermore, although both attitudes were deeply ambivalent about the value and the virtue of living outside of society, the poles of their ambivalences were different and distinct. The Europeanized imagination assimilated the Westerner into the Romantic ideal of the noble savage and made of the Western backwoodsman, trapper, or mountain man, a noble savage in

[29] J. Hector St. John de Crèvecœur, *Letters from an American Farmer* (New York, 1957), p. 51.

whiteface. At the same time, the side of the Europeanized imagination that believed in civilization as a good saw this noble savage or simple backwoodsman as a pathfinder who cleared the way for the march of civilized society across the American continent. These two concepts—that of unrestrained nature as ennobling, and of civilization as a good—although largely antithetical, generally appeared in unembarrassed juxtaposition in the same works. Even those writers who felt that the two were in opposition were often unable to examine their inconsistency, or to let go their belief in both at once.

Leatherstocking, Daniel Boone, Davy Crockett, and other Western heroes, all express this ambivalence toward civilization and the "natural man." [30] Leatherstocking is closest to the Romantic ideal of the noble savage, the man who drinks nature's wisdom at its source and is uncorrupted by the meanness of civilization. At the end of his life he says of himself, "I have been a solitary man much of my time, if he can be called solitary who has lived for seventy years in the very bosom of nature, and where he could at any instant open his heart to God, without having to strip it of the cares and wickednesses of the settlement . . ." [31] But Cooper's deep allegiance was to civilization, and if Leatherstocking is nature's nobleman, he is the only one of his race. Leatherstocking's "Americanness" is evident not only in Cooper's genuine ambivalence about the value of settlement, but in his concept of solitariness. The possibility of choosing to live beyond civilization altogether, the desirability and pleasure of it, is what is "American" about Leatherstocking. His choice to be absolutely autonomous, which does not stem from madness, pride, or criminality, is what makes him an American hero. It is not when he wants to escape the "cares and wickednesses of the settlements" that he is showing his

[30] My discussion of Far Western literature owes a great deal to Henry Nash Smith, *Virgin Land* (New York, 1950), Chs. 5–8.

[31] James Fenimore Cooper, *The Prairie* (New York, 1965), pp. 289–90.

Americanness, but when he seeks a final "refuge" against society on the Western prairie; when he seeks wilderness for its own sake.

The legends surrounding Daniel Boone also have two faces: Boone is seen as what he in fact was, a trail blazer and empire builder; and also as a fleer, like Leatherstocking, from the sound of the settler's axe. In the many accounts of his life he was sometimes described as "a creature of Providence, ordained by Heaven as a pioneer in the wilderness, to advance the civilization and the extension of the country," and sometimes as one who, as a contemporary interviewer reported of him, *prefers the woods* to the settlements.[32]

Byron's eulogy of Daniel Boone, in the Eighth Canto of *Don Juan,* makes clear how Romanticism saw him and his environment:

> The General Boon, back-woodsman of Kentucky,
> Was happiest amongst mortals anywhere;
>   For killing nothing but a bear or buck, he
> Enjoy'd the lonely, vigorous, harmless days
> Of his old age in wilds of deepest maze.
>   · · · ·
> He was not all alone: around him grew
>   A sylvan tribe of children of the chase,
> Whose young, unwaken'd world was ever new,
>   Nor sword nor sorrow yet had left a trace
> On her unwrinkled brow, nor could you view
>   A frown on Nature's or on human face;
> The free-born forest found and kept them free,
> And fresh as is a torrent or a tree.
>
> And tall, and strong, and swift of foot were they,
>   Beyond the dwarfing city's pale abortions,
> Because their thoughts had never been the prey
>   Of care or gain: the green woods were their portions;

---

[32] Quoted in Smith, *Virgin Land,* pp. 61 and 57.

No sinking spirits told them they grew grey,
  No fashion made them apes of her distortions;
Simple they were, not savage; and their rifles,
Though very true, were not yet used for trifles.

Motion was in their days, rest in their slumbers,
  And cheerfulness the handmaid of their toil;
Nor yet too many nor too few their numbers;
  Corruption could not make their hearts her soil;
The lust which stings, the splendour which encumbers,
  With the free foresters divide no spoil;
Serene, not sullen, were the solitudes
Of this unsighing people of the woods.

So much for Nature. . . .

So much for the Romantic view of nature. The American West was more often desert, plains, or mountain than green and pleasant shade; and most nineteenth-century American accounts of the Far West are agreed that it was not "serene" but solitary indeed, and wild and savage as well. The "savage solitude and bleak desolation" of the Great American Plains made them "unlike any other region of earth":

The prevalent impression made on the stranger's mind by the Plains is one of loneliness of isolation. You press on, day after day, without seeing a house, a fence, a cultivated field, or even a forest—nought but a few shy wild beasts at intervals, or undelightful birds, and rarely a scanty, niggard stream, with a few mean, low, scrubby trees thinly strewn along its banks—often one of them only; and, as you go farther west, even these disappear, or are only seen in thin patches, miles apart. . . . For days, if with the mail, for weeks by any other conveyance, you travel westward, still westward, with never a mountain, and scarcely a hill, with never a forest, with seldom a tree, with rarely a brook or spring, to break the monotony of the barren, mainly grassless, dewless landscape, out of which the sun rises at morning, into which it settles at night.[33]

[33] "The Plains, as I crossed them Ten Years Ago," *Harper's New Monthly Magazine*, 38 (1869), 789–95.

An 1856 article entitled "Frontier Yarns" gives a similar description of the unByronic "benignity" of the West, and ends by saying that "the whole face of the country is so miserably rugged and unprepossessing that, but for the tiny delicate flowers that bloom, one can scarce say how, among its sandheaps, I could almost term it an accursed land; for, amid these solitudes, nature has no voice . . ." [34]

The Westerners who heard no voice from nature, nor gathered serenity down from the trees, were by contemporary accounts sullen, taciturn, and savage. I am speaking of those in the vanguard of civilization—of the trappers and guides and mountain men—who lived in savage solitude most of their lives. The accounts of these men dating from the eighteen thirties to sixties, before their transformation into dime novel heroes, are fairly similar whether their authors are writing travel narratives or novels, and whether they are sympathetic towards them or intensely antipathetic.

The first novel that mentions the mountain men is *The Shoshonee Valley*, published in 1830. Its author sees the trappers as brutish, describing them very much as Crèvecœur had described the men of the first stages of frontier settlement thirty or forty years before; yet his description of them is not essentially different from those by writers who sought to eulogize the trappers. They are "strange, fearless, and adamantine men" who have renounced society, "casting off fear, and all the common impulses and affections of our nature . . . finding in their own ingenuity, their knife, gun and traps, all the Divinity, of which their stern nature and condition taught them the necessity . . . [In this way they] became almost as inaccessible to passions and wants, and as sufficient to themselves, as the trees, or the rocks with which they were conversant." The trappers have, furthermore, "an instinctive fondness for the reckless savage life . . ." [35]

[34] "Frontier Yarns," *Putnam's Monthly Magazine*, 8 (1856), 449.
[35] Quoted in Smith, *Virgin Land*, p. 89.

Almost all accounts of mountain men emphasize their hatred of law, of settlement, and of "dull routine." But they also emphasize the self-sufficiency of these men; and in any American description of anything resembling self-reliance, a tone of admiration inevitably creeps in.

An account of a Western journey made around 1850 describes the character of the mountain men when they are caught amongst the settlements. The author, in search of a guide to take him across the Great Plains, found a

trapper and plainsman, who was more than willing to "git away from the settlements" and make venture in new fields. This guide was a noteworthy character in his way. His name was James Mitchell; but he was almost universally known as "Surly Jim," a sobriquet which he had acquired by reason of his morose temper and repellent ways. I have never seen on a human countenance such an expression of grim and pervading discontent as he carried when I first met him, and he could certainly behave ugly enough when he chose; but I am convinced that his surliness was simply the spontaneous and irrepressible expression of his disgust at being crowded out of his hunting-grounds and scarcely less dear solitude, by the slowly rising tide of population. As soon as we had left civilisation behind us, the crust vanished like frost before the morning sun, and I have seldom had a more cheerful, entertaining, and good natured companion than Mitchell proved himself during the trip about to be described.[36]

Another traveller describes a trapper he met as "a morose and misanthropic sort of character . . . he seldom spoke, and when he did, he expressed himself like one conscious that, in drawing upon his words, he was consuming a slender stock which might fail and leave him bankrupt at a moment's warning." [37]

In 1846 Francis Parkman, the future historian, made a journey along the Oregon Trail. He described the mountain men he met as "half-savage men who spend their

[36] "A Wild Western Adventure," *Chamber's Journal*, 55 (1878), 461.
[37] "Frontier Yarns," p. 499.

reckless lives in trapping among the Rocky Mountains, or in trading for the Fur Company in the Indian villages. They were all of Canadian extraction; their hard, weather-beaten faces and bushy mustaches looked out from beneath the hoods of their white capotes with a bad and brutish expression, as if their owners might be the willing agents of any villainy. And such in fact is the character of many of these men." [38]

Brutish and uncivilized, "savage" as most Eastern writers found the mountain men, a kind of simplicity and idealism enshrouded them, too, that had nothing whatever to do with the Byronic innocence of nature's children.

In these descriptions one begins to make out the shape of the new hero, who can be described most simply as the man who lives outside of community. The writers who first wrote about him were discovering a new literary type but not an altogether new man; rather, these heroes are the new men of the old experience, the fundamental American experience of emigration to the wilderness. In this description of the burial of a mountain man, a new freshness, which one feels to be the freshness of a true perception, creeps into a rather stale account of Western adventure:

When the interment was fully ended, one among our number—a young man who had been a special favorite with the old guide—said quietly, as if talking to himself, "He was a good old hoss." It wasn't much, and a man who hadn't traveled among the mountains might have found something for ridicule in the remark; but it was all that our leader, had he been living, would have said for another, or asked for himself. It was no great eulogy; but it meant everything. It meant that the friend whom we had just covered from our sight would have shared the last morsel in his pack, or given the contents of his flask to a comrade in need, even though he had foreseen the suffering which would ensue from his generosity. It meant that the trapper would have died fighting in his

[38] Francis Parkman, *The Oregon Trail* (New York, 1950), p. 58.

tracks sooner than desert the wounded man who looked to his strong arm for aid. It was the last farewell of a heart, grieving, as a frontierman's alone can grieve, over the final severance of that rough companionship, which is dearer to the hunter of the Rocky Mountains than is "the love of woman." The words, indeed, were scanty, but the feeling which prompted them was deep and genuine.[39]

The self-sufficiency, the loneliness, the rough comradery, the inarticulateness, the lurking sense of violence and sudden death, are all American; but especially American is the utterly unsentimentalized sense of men's lives played out against the silent, vast indifference of nature, through which they pass leaving no trace or sign.

In part, the character of the Far West—desert, plains, and rugged mountains—itself desentimentalized the American conception of wilderness. In part it was the greedy seizure of land which characterized the American aspect of the westward movement; not the orderly march of civilization, as in the Europeanized version, but the voracious appetite of Manifest Destiny, a kind of aggregate individualism that had always been the American analogue of community.

In *Virgin Land,* Henry Nash Smith wrote that in the stories about Kit Carson, the first mountain man portrayed as a *hero* in popular fiction, the "logic of the Far Western materials" made itself felt for the first time. He quotes a description of Carson from one of the earliest versions of his life, *Kit Carson, The Prince of the Gold Hunters.*

Far in the background . . . rolled the waving grass of a boundless prairie; amid the silent wilderness of which, towered the noble figure of the hunter-horseman, half Indian, half whiteman in appearance, with rifle, horse and dog for his sole companions, in all that dreary waste; though to the right a yelling pack of wolves were seen upon his track, and on his left the thick, black smoke, in curling wreaths, proclaimed the prairie fire, while in the clear,

[39] "Frontier Yarns," p. 501.

gray eye that looked from the thrilling picture forth, there seemed to glance a look of proud indifference to all, and the conscious confidence of ennobling self-reliance.[40]

Kit Carson's self-reliance, his "proud indifference to all," borders on selfishness and self-obsession, just as the national purpose behind Manifest Destiny borders on mere aggregate greed. That is, the ambivalence of the European Romantic imagination toward "nature," which resulted both in a belief in the natural, almost divine, origins of society, and at the same time in the divinity of the "natural man," was not the American ambivalence. The true American dichotomy was between nationalism, the pull of the American continent to fulfill itself which around 1840 began to be called Manifest Destiny; and the solitary man existing outside of society and the nationalized ego, who relied on the self alone and finally lived for the self alone. This dichotomy arose not out of the European idea of nature, but out of the American experience of wilderness.

The business of Manifest Destiny was the commercial exploitation of the American continent. There was an idealistic side of Manifest Destiny too, left over from the Puritans' belief that God had placed the continent at their backs as once He had placed the rainbow in the sky, and from the American political ideology that on this continent there was to be a new birth of freedom. This sense of "mission" had first assumed a religious, then an economic, then a political, and finally, with Manifest Destiny, a geographic character. But the men who blazed the trail for Manifest Destiny, who were in the vanguard of the wilderness seekers, were not men who were driven by a sense of communal mission. They opened the continent for all to follow, but their motive was not that of the common good, and their emotional

[40] Quoted in Smith, *Virgin Land*, pp. 57–58.

appeal was not at all to feelings of nationalism. Their appeal was in part that of the criminal or outlaw, and in many romances about the West, they degenerated merely into that. But it was not the criminal side of the outlaw which appealed to Americans; it was the self-reliant side. The outlaw, historically, was not the man who *broke* laws but the man who lived beyond the jurisdiction of law. It was the outlaw as any man or Everyman who became the hero.

The native American outlaw was the man who lived outside the confines of government because government simply had not yet reached him, and this was an experience that many Americans had shared, along the westward moving frontier, for over two hundred years. The result of this historical accident was that such men were in fact liberated from the impositions of government and from the restrictions of any will imposed from outside the self. This accident grew into a national ideal. It was an ideal that had to come to terms with many brutalities, for Manifest Destiny led to the waste of vast natural resources, the slaughter of species, and the genocide of the Indian.

Land was being "used up," and so were its natural resources—forests, soil, and animals. The great Western march of civilization, which had begun on the Atlantic shore, was the great destroyer too. An 1869 article on the plains said that drought is the "master scourge" of the plains; but that man is next. Prairie fires, "kindled far more frequently and wantonly by white men than by Indians," have caused "timber to visibly diminish over the course of the last fifty years . . . while the thin screens of timber along many streams have for miles been swept away by the relentless axe of camping teamster or emigrant." [41] The killing off of the great herds of buffalo is also caused by the "passion for slaughter" of civilized men. "The wolf and the

[41] "The Plains," p. 791.

Indian, though persistent in their warfare, are not wantonly destructive—*they* kill to eat, and stop when their appetites are glutted, their wants fully supplied. Civilized man alone kills for the mere pleasure of destroying, the pride of having killed." [42]

The slaughter of Indians began almost with the first year of American settlement. In 1774, Thomas Jefferson reported an incident of mass murder committed against a tribe of Indians by British troops in the Ohio Valley. Among the murdered were, in Jefferson's words, "the family of Logan, a chief celebrated in peace and war, and long distinguished as the friend of the whites." [43] Logan sought revenge against the whites in a battle which the Indians lost. When peace was made, Logan refused to take part in signing the treaty, explaining his refusal in these words:

I appeal to any white man to say, if ever he entered Logan's cabin hungry, and he gave him not meat; if ever he came cold and naked, and he cloathed him not. During the course of the last long and bloody war Logan remained idle in his cabin, an advocate for peace. Such was my love for the whites, that my countrymen pointed as they passed, and said, "Logan is the friend of white men." I had even thought to have lived with you, but for the injuries of one man. Colonel Cresap, the last spring, in cold blood, and unprovoked, murdered all the relations of Logan, not even sparing my women and children. There runs not a drop of my blood in the veins of any living creature. This called on me for revenge. I have sought it: I have killed many: I have fully glutted my vengeance: for my country I rejoice at the beams of peace. But do not harbour a thought that mine is the joy of fear. Logan never felt fear. He will not turn on his heel to save his life. Who is there to mourn for Logan?—Not one. [44]

Logan's statement is both an appeal for some acknowledgment of his humanity and a recognition that in the eyes

[42] "The Plains," p. 793.
[43] Thomas Jefferson, *Notes on the State of Virginia* (New York, 1964) pp. 60–61.
[44] Jefferson, *Notes on the State of Virginia*, p. 61.

of the white man he has none. The white man has dehumanized him. In a sense, what was most American about the treatment of the Indian was this process of dehumanization. He, like his lands, was considered to have no value beyond commodity. Indeed, the Indian was looked upon as a negative commodity—something of no value at all, that was better gotten rid of at once; while land, having for the settlers no ancestral, cultural, or historical associations, was viewed entirely as commodity. This attitude towards the American land and the American native was the common heritage of all Americans; it was the wilderness heritage.

One hundred and fifty years after the death of Logan, Francis Parkman described a "young Kentuckian" who joined his party somewhere along the Oregon Trail. "One of his [the Kentuckian's] chief objects was to kill an Indian; an exploit which he afterwards succeeded in achieving, much to the jeopardy of ourselves, and others who had to pass through the country of the dead Pawnee's enraged relatives." [45] No other comment is made. It was manifestly the Indian's destiny, like the land's, to be "used up." One feels in Parkman's indifference to this the identity of Westerner and Easterner; one is reminded, by this son of Boston, of how homogeneous the American experience was.

But the identity of Westerner and Easterner was most marked in their feeling about the individual in relation to society, since both the experience of immigration and of wilderness were assimilated into the "American mind" as destructive of the ideal of community. With the possibility of escape from society and from the past, there had grown up an ideal of its desirability; and from man having been able philosophically to posit his own existence outside of so-

---

[45] *Oregon Trail*, p. 216. Melville reviewed *The Oregon Trail* in the March 31, 1849, *The Literary World*. In his review he objected to Parkman's "disdain and contempt" for the Indian. See his review in Jay Leyda, *The Melville Log: A Documentary Life of Herman Melville*, 2 vols. (New York, 1969), I, 294–95.

ciety, it became an almost moral compulsion to place one's own welfare above that of society's; to see society as a whole as the "other," and one's self as a separate nation. The level of sophistication from East to West was different, as were the terms and circumstances of the separations; but the underlying concept was the same. Emerson writing to Carlyle about American society as having degenerated, in many places, "to an almost godless state," concludes with an altogether American solution to the problem: "I begin to think even here it behoves every man to quit his dependency on society as much as he can . . ." [46] This is more literate but not very different from the advice of an old mountaineer to a young trapper: "If you see a man's mule running off, don't stop it—let it go to the devil; it is n't yourn." [47] Individualism was so strong a strain in the American mind, society so weak, that society could only be apprehended as an aggregate of individuals. Even a social experiment like Brook Farm, which was an expression of a minority belief in community, foundered on the rock of Yankee individualism; and the *Dial*, organ of the Brook Farmers, said this about another proposed utopian community: "A true community can be founded on nothing short of faith in the universal man, as he comes from the hands of the Creator, with no law over his liberty but the eternal ideas that lie at the foundation of his being. . . . The final cause of human society is the unfolding of the individual man, into every form of perfection, without let or hindrance, according to the inward nature of each." [48]

In *Moby Dick* Melville shows the same inability to posit a truly collectivist community aboard his whaling ship, which

---

[46] *The Correspondence of Thomas Carlyle and Ralph Waldo Emerson,* 1 (Boston, 1883), 85.

[47] Quoted in Smith, *Virgin Land,* p. 91.

[48] Quoted in Vernon L. Parrington, *Main Currents in American Thought,* 2 vols. (New York, 1954), II, 340.

here obviously symbolizes the United States: "How it is, there is no telling, but Islanders seem to make the best whalemen. They were nearly all Islanders in the Pequod, *Isolatoes* too, I call such, not acknowledging the common continent of men, but each *Isolato* living on a separate continent of his own. Yet now, federated along one keel, what a set these Isolatoes were!" (Ch. 27). The metaphor of the many separate continents—as if Melville cannot bear to give to each American anything less than an entire continent— would be ludicrous if it were not so clearly the expression of a genuine quandary: how to reconcile independence with federation. Yet Melville, unlike any other nineteenth-century American writer, understood and expressed the type of the unfederated *Isolato* whose self-reliance had run amuck—run to madness. Melville makes it very clear in *Moby Dick* that the rapacity of the whaling industry is the analogue of the rapacious plunder of the continent; and he sets at the opposite pole of this unleashing of the national ego not a tame and civil self-reliance, but the naked unleashing of the self. For "crazy Ahab" is an *Isolato* too. In the chase after the white whale he and his crew embody both the lawless release of the national ego in its quest after booty and, in the name of the individual ego, the equally bloody release of their most willful, most violent, and most infantile selves.

The Christmas celebration reinforces the Englishness of Scrooge's story. Not only is every aspect of human life important on this day, but on Christmas of all days solitude is most horrible, selfishness most despicable. But that Scrooge is both solitary and selfish does not mean that he is not a part of the continent, or that his life has no effect upon other lives. Underlying the message of the three Spirits is the fact that every life affects for good or evil every other life. Scrooge would be as implicated in Tiny Tim's death, were it to take place, as he is in the lives of those other two children of Man, Ignorance and Want. In that sense, there is no merely personal life for Dickens or for Scrooge; when Scrooge falls, a piece of England is washed away.

Bartleby is the American hero who has chosen to withdraw from society. He is the Kit Carson of the East, a man of walls rather than of mountains. His environment is no less a "silent wilderness" or "dreary waste" than Carson's; and he too confronts the viewer with a "clear gray eye" from which "there seemed to glance a look of proud indifference to all, and the conscious confidence of ennobling self-reliance!" Bartleby's "face was leanly composed; his gray eye dimly calm. Not a wrinkle of agitation rippled him. . . . And more than all, I remembered a certain unconscious air of pallid—how shall I call it?—of pallid haughtiness, say, or rather, an austere reserve about him, which had positively awed me . . ." The closeness of the two descriptions is striking: Kit Carson's "proud indifference" is Bartleby's "austere reserve"; Carson is a man of unrestrained action, Bartleby of unrestrained inaction; Carson is the slayer of buffalo and Indian, Bartleby is a self-slayer. That is, their aggressive strategies are opposite, one directed outward, one inward, but their aggressiveness is about equal.

Their environments are also identical oppositions. The silent wilderness and dreary waste of Carson's "boundless prairie" is the same, writ large, as Bartleby's suffocatingly walled-in world. Melville makes the identity of the tomb-like confinement of Bartleby's surroundings with the isolation of illimitable space quite explicit. Bartleby "seemed absolutely alone in the universe. A bit of wreck in the mid-Atlantic." And Carson's "sole companions," his "rifle, horse and dog" can hardly be less companionable to him than are Bartleby's bequirked fellow clerks and "safe" employer.

It is a commonplace of modern life that the loneliness of cities can be as terrible as that of deserts. But for Scrooge,

London is lonely only until he opens his heart to its inhabitants. For Bartleby the city offers no way out of his prison of loneliness. Several settings reveal Melville's feelings about the possibility for human connection in New York. The office setting is entirely repressive of human relationships; the only street scene offered in contrast to Wall Street is Broadway. What is significant about the narrator's picture of Broadway is not its cheerfulness, but the fact that it offers no glimmering of companionableness. No one stops; no one talks to or acknowledges anyone else; yet the narrator deliberately opposes it to Bartleby's office isolation. "I remembered the bright silks and sparkling faces I had seen that day, in gala trim, swan-like sailing down the Mississippi of Broadway." It is an entirely conglomerate, not companionable, procession. Compare with it this description of London streets:

[Scrooge] dressed himself "all in his best," and at last got out into the streets. The people were by this time pouring forth, as he had seen them with the Ghost of Christmas Present; and walking with his hands behind him, Scrooge regarded every one with a delighted smile. He looked so irresistibly pleasant, in a word, that three or four good-humoured fellows said, "Good morning, sir! A Merry Christmas to you!" And Scrooge said often afterward, that of all the blithe sounds he had ever heard, those were the blithest in his ears.

Scrooge's city provides opportunity for friendly communion on every street corner. But Broadway is not Broadway for Bartleby alone; it is friendless and soulless not only for the mad clerk. The narrator does not seem to have much richer possibilities for human connection than Bartleby. Except for his business relationships we see him, too, always alone and friendless. At church, in his carriage driving dismally around New Jersey and Astoria, in the street on Sunday, he is alone. Solitude is not the hero's exclusive prerogative; it is the shared experience of everyone in this story.

The setting most noticeably absent from "Bartleby" is that

of any home. When the narrator realizes that Bartleby lives in his office, he offers to take him home with him for a time. What is significant is the imprecision of the word "home." " 'Bartleby,' said I, in the kindest tone I could assume . . . 'will you go home with me now—not to my office, but to my dwelling.' " The narrator's difficulty expresses a cultural dilemma. " 'Home,' in England an intimate and emotion-laden word, in America became almost interchangeable with 'house.' " Americans changed homes so frequently that they had lost the sense of the difference between what was merely a house and what was really a home. In cities "boarding-houses," in frontier areas hotels, were almost as much lived in by families as private homes, and Americans came to regard hotels "not merely as places for a night en route but as dwelling-places: 'a home away from home.' " [49] Office, hotel, house, home, dwelling: only the first two had retained specific meanings in America. Compare with this the ecstatically incantatory use of the word "home" in *A Christmas Carol,* when the child Scrooge is to be released from his boyhood loneliness and taken back into the circle of his father's love: " 'I have come to bring you home, dear brother! . . . To bring you home, home, home!' 'Home, little Fan?' 'Yes! . . . Home, for good and all. Home, for ever and ever.' "

The setting of ultimate importance in "Bartleby" is his grave in the Tombs. The crime for which Bartleby is sent to prison is "vagrancy"—having no home. But he is also a killer. The narrator himself is witness to the fact that Bartleby's quiet no-saying is an act of aggression. The first time Bartleby says "I would prefer not to" the narrator "sat awhile in perfect silence, rallying my stunned faculties." The second time he is "turned to a pillar of salt." The third time he feels that he is being "browbeaten in some unprece-

[49] Boorstin, *The Americans,* p. 144.

dented and violently unreasonable way." (That is, the violence is entirely psychological—he is beaten on the brow or mind by the violence of un-reason.) The fourth time, the narrator realizes that Bartleby's will is opposed to his, and that Bartleby's is stronger. This is both acted out and punned upon:

> I closed the doors, and again advanced towards Bartleby. . . . I burned to be rebelled against again. I remembered that Bartleby never left the office.
> "Bartleby," said I, "Ginger Nut is away; just step around to the Post Office, won't you?" . . .
> "I would prefer not to."
> "You *will* not?"
> "I *prefer* not."
> I staggered to my desk . . .

Bartleby not only always prefers not to; he never affirms anything. The narrator is forced to infer what it is that Bartleby prefers, and in so doing he uses the word "yes."

> "You are decided, then, not to comply with my request—a request made according to common usage and common sense?"
> He briefly gave me to understand, that on that point my judgment was sound. Yes: his decision was irreversible.

The narrator says "yes" twice more. Each time it is at a point when he has decided to humor Bartleby in his "strange wilfulness"; each time, he is lying to himself—"For all men who say *yes,* lie [Melville wrote]; and all men who say *no,*—why, they are in the happy condition of judicious, unincumbered travellers in Europe; they cross the frontiers into Eternity with nothing but a carpet-bag,—that is to say, the Ego. Whereas those *yes*-gentry, they travel with heaps of baggage, and, damn them! they will never get through the Custom House." [50]

Bartleby "acquiesces" only once—when he is about to

[50] *The Letters of Herman Melville,* ed. Merrell R. Davis and William H. Gilman (New Haven, 1960), p. 125.

cross the frontier into eternity and enter the Tombs. Melville's no-sayer, who travels with only his ego in his bag, is like Bartleby on his way to the grave with his will intact; and both are like the American frontiersman described in *Old Hicks:*

. . . a frontiersman, with his buckskin suit, pistols, rifle, and knife, is always ready, if you give him plenty of ammunition, to go wherever his horse is able to carry him.

He certainly, of all men, most religiously observes the Biblical precept, "Think not of what ye shall eat, or what ye shall wear for the morrow!" As long as he can use his rifle he has no apprehension on these scores, and never dreams of cumbering himself with anything in the shape of luggage . . .[51]

Bartleby has preserved his ego with the ammunition of his will, the frontiersman with his guns. But with a gun, the frontiersman can kill other men; with his naked will, Bartleby can kill only himself. The Western hero can play out the heroic role as it was developed, romanticized, and finally mythologized in America—the hero as the man beyond the reach of government and law. The Western hero-moved-East, however, must play out the heroic role within the confines of civil society, which he perceives as a prison. That is, an expectation of life whose ideal is unconfined and lawless freedom and self-assertiveness must come to terms with a reality of civil restraint, law, and other people's self-assertion too.

The will, either stymied or unleashed, is important to every character in "Bartleby." For the narrator, freedom is freedom to conduct business, and in this his society abets him. The only time he rebels against government is when it impinges upon his freedom to make money.

The good old office, now extinct in the State of New York, of a Master in Chancery, had been conferred upon me. It was not a

[51] Webber, *Old Hicks,* pp. 23–24.

very arduous office, but very pleasantly remunerative. I seldom lose my temper; much more seldom indulge in dangerous indignation at wrongs and outrages; but I must consider the sudden and violent abrogation of the office of Master in Chancery, by the new Constitution, as a premature act; inasmuch as I had counted upon a life-lease of the profits . . .

Ginger Nut, like the narrator, will fulfill himself through cash; and the two English-born clerks relieve their imprisoned wills in alternate fits of temper or drunkenness. They are all either men who have joined the aggregate fortune hunt that was part of the American destiny, or men who have submitted their wills to other men—in this story, only the two Englishmen. But Bartleby prefers not to submit his will. Settlement is prison.

Settlement is prison, and yet it is never his prison-like surroundings, or even the Tombs itself, which he protests against; and the grave is apparently what he has all along been seeking. Insofar as Bartleby chooses to withdraw from society, he follows the American heroic ideal. But Bartleby chooses to do more than withdraw from society; he chooses to withdraw from life. It is in his choice of death that he departs from the ideal. What is characteristic of the heroic setting in America is the utterly unsentimentalized sense of men's lives being played out against the silent, vast indifference of nature. It is to this, too, that Bartleby prefers not to submit his will. It is not at the walls, or at the wall-like faces of the Wall Street inhabitants, that he registers his most radical protest—it is at their blank indifference to *him*. Captain Ahab, addressing the indifferent lightning that has struck his ship's mast, cries, "In the midst of the personified impersonal, a personality stands here." So Bartleby. Faced by the dead walls of brick and flesh which surround him, he chooses to assert his personality and die; and not even to die as a man, but as an unborn child. That is, he chooses to die not just out of protest at his particular set of walls, but out of protest at the human condition, which is the condition of the indifference of the universe to man. So he does not merely die; he unlives his life. He regresses backward into the womb of time, into the "heart of the eternal pyramids"; back, also, into the foetal position, "strangely huddled at the base of the wall, his knees drawn up, and lying on his side . . ."

But that the universe is indifferent to man was not just an American discovery. It was a possibility that shook both Europeans and Americans in the nineteenth century. And if Bartleby, like Ahab, prefers to die rather than passively to accept its indifference, is that, too, an expression of the American mind?

CHAPTER THREE

THE ENGLISH AND
AMERICAN FOLK HERO
—A CONTRAST

1   THE ENGLISH FOLK HERO

In about 1848 Dickens began writing his autobiography, but broke off when he found himself with memories too painful to pursue. Shortly afterwards he used many of those memories, often the same words, in *David Copperfield*. The auto-biographically founded novel left him freer than actual autobiography to evade or conceal certain things both from himself and from his readers. It also left him freer to make his hero's life more representative of his time and place than his own was. The personal history of David Copperfield is to a far greater degree "Victorian" than Charles Dickens's, whose career was in every way extraordinary; and David's life conforms, much more closely than Dickens's own, to the lives of other Victorian folk heroes. In his fictional representation of himself, Dickens suppresses the irregularities, culturally considered, of his own life. He rewrites his life in conformity with a more general cultural ideal, and so turns himself into a hero of his time.

But how can one discuss a folk hero in an age when there

was no "folk"—no stable, undifferentiated, unselfconscious mass? What I am describing is really a middle-class hero, the modern analogue of the folk hero; a hero with whom the great bulk of the middle classes could identify. If such a hero can be found anywhere in nineteenth-century literature, it will be in the novel, the literary form written, for the most part, by and for the middle class. Such a hero is the man or woman whose life would seem possible, intelligible, and significant to nineteenth-century novel-readers; with whom they could identify and by means of whose experiences and feelings they themselves could grow. This hero is like the person in the nineteenth-century romantic lyric whom Robert Langbaum calls the "pole of sympathy": "the means by which the writer and reader project themselves into the [novel], the one to communicate, the other to apprehend it as an experience." [1] Further, this hero is for the most part "democratic": a man of the people who rises, through his own effort or virtue, into a position of some power or ease in the world.

There were many members of the middle class who could not accept such men as heroes, who were disturbed by the fact that a man could rise through his own effort because of the increasing democratization of nineteenth-century life. Such men, who had perhaps so risen themselves, nevertheless deplored "the general tendency of things throughout the world . . . to render mediocrity the ascendant power among mankind." [2] They too wanted "great" men to worship, but men who had become great through no democratic process. In another fifty or seventy-five years men of such anti-democratic bias would look to the "strong" man, to a totalitarian leader who, paradoxically, had risen often from the lowest ranks of the middle class—Fuehrer, Duce,

[1] Robert Langbaum, *The Poetry of Experience* (New York, 1963), p. 52.
[2] John Stuart Mill, *On Liberty* in *The Essential Works of John Stuart Mill* (New York, 1961), p. 314.

Generalissimo, Commissar. But in mid-nineteenth-century England, worshippers of "great" men such as Carlyle, Tennyson, Arnold, and Ruskin, tended to look to the past for their heroes: to hereditary princes, princes of the Church, poets, philosophers, and priests. They were in part reactionary, looking back to the values of a world they had never known but which they imagined to have been more heroic than their own. But they were responding, also, to a need for guidance in a world that had lost many traditional signposts: they were looking for human heroes to take the place of dead gods.

The notion that great men are needed in an age of waning faith as examples for common men to follow blended rather oddly into another sort of notion about the function of a heroic ideal. This was that common men need "common" heroes, men not too far removed from themselves with whom it is possible for them to identify, rather than extraordinary men who seem to them almost as remote as gods. J. A. Froude, for example, felt that the middle class needed the example of great men of their own class, and that the age therefore needed biographies of professional men, merchants, and workers. "Far off we seem to see a time when the lives, the actions of the really great—great good masters, great good landlords, great good working men—will be laid out once more before their several orders, laid out in the name of God, as once the saints' lives were; and the same sounds shall be heard in factory and in counting-house as once sounded through abbey, chapel, and cathedral aisle—'Look at these men; bless God for them, and follow them.' " [3]

The call for middle-class heroes was implicitly answered

[3] Quoted in Walter Houghton, *The Victorian Frame of Mind* (New Haven, 1957), p. 318. For a fuller discussion of this subject see pp. 317–20. Carlyle and Ruskin, giving this idea a characteristic slant, felt that "captains of industry" must be heroes to their working men and thus establish a new kind of "chivalry."

by the great novelists—Charlotte Brontë and Mrs. Gaskell, Thackeray, Trollope, George Eliot, especially Dickens—who represented men and women of uncommon moral and intellectual value in every walk of middle-class life. And it was explicitly answered by a host of biographies of merchants and industrialists and engineers, most notably those written by Samuel Smiles.

Walter Houghton cites as another source of Victorian hero-worship the feeling of "impotence and timidity" widespread at the "upper levels of social and intellectual life" that impelled those in its grip to long for a heroic life.[4] Arnold and Tennyson often wrote out of such feelings, and although we don't generally associate Dickens with them, his late heroes are for the most part men of precisely this sort: Eugene Wrayburn, Charles Darnay, Arthur Clennam, Pip. These men also long for high romance; but they settle—more, we feel, in obedience to their creator's indomitable will than to their own—for hard work. Dickens's solution to the cultural problems of impotence and doubt, like many other Victorians', was to steep oneself in work. The work he chose for his heroes was not at all romantic, was generally not even imaginative or intellectual. It was the work that the Victorians found closest at hand—the work of merchant and lawyer and engineer and industrialist; the work that Samuel Smiles apotheosized in book after book.

"Quite rightly the mid-Victorians chose engineers as their folk-heroes."[5] Engineering brought technology to the aid of trade, furthering progress by means of the newest frontier of human endeavor, scientific invention. Very often the engineer was truly *of* the folk, the son of a poor farmer or artisan who, joining hard work with inventive skill, pulled himself out of poverty, sometimes into great wealth.

The inventor's power consists, in a great measure [wrote Samuel Smiles], in quick perception and accurate observation, and in

[4] Houghton, *The Victorian Frame of Mind*, pp. 317–20.
[5] Asa Briggs, *The Making of Modern England* (New York, 1965), p. 395.

seeing and foreseeing the effects of certain mechanical combinations. He must possess the gift of insight, as well as of manual dexterity, combined with the indispensable qualities of patience and perseverance,—for though baffled, as he often is, he must be ready to rise up again unconquered even in the moment of defeat. This is the stuff of which the greatest inventors have been made.[6]

This is clearly the stuff of which heroes are made. Smiles turns the inventor's story into a mythic struggle of man against the malignant forces of nature itself, a nature which would impede human progress by hiding the secrets of mechanical laws. The inventors are nonetheless heroes although they have been heretofore unsung. In fact, they are all the more heroic because they are the advance guard of their age, bringing the marvels of the new technology to their fellow men. And they are specifically the heroes of modern life; without their skills, "society, as it is, could not exist."

Smiles does more than discover a new kind of middle-class hero, a folk hero whose origins are in the common people; he attacks, often fairly directly, the aristocratic hero. He puts into the mouth of a "distinguished living mechanic" this criticism of aristocratic heroes: "I do not begrudge destructive heroes ["Kings, warriors, and statesmen"] their fame, but the constructive ones ought not to be forgotten; and there *is* a heroism of skill and toil belonging to the latter class, worthy of as grateful record,—less perilous and romantic, it may be, than that of the other, but not less full of the results of human energy, bravery, and character."[7] Kings, warriors, and statesmen: he is indicting an entire class in order to praise the class from which the modern hero comes. This new hero sets out to find his fortune not in battle or council-hall or castle, but in commerce or

[6] Samuel Smiles, *Industrial Biography: Iron-Workers and Tool-Makers* (Boston, 1864), p. 228.
[7] *Industrial Biography*, p. vi.

counting-house or factory. He proves himself not in war but in peace and through "progress."

There is another condition of the democratic hero's life that is new. The young hero of old folk tales does not create his own fortune but discovers the fortune that is rightfully his, that was his father's legacy to him. But industrial and commercial heroes did indeed create their own fortunes. In nineteenth-century England the lives of the engineers, of the "tool makers and iron workers," proved again and again that men *could* make their own fortunes without the help of inherited wealth, without the help of their fathers. But in this instance actuality had outdistanced ideology or belief. The weight of *sentiment* in the middle class, no less than in the upper, was against the autonomy of self-created wealth. And the middle class, caught between an old ideal and a new reality, straddled the dilemma not only in its pieties but in its way of life. Although the Industrial Revolution broke the monopoly of the power of inherited property, the middle class remained loyal to the idea and the ideal of the patriarchal family; although the Industrial Revolution moved England's strength from the land to the cities, the merchant's dream remained, throughout the nineteenth century, a country estate. It was a dream which he often fulfilled by leaving his business in other hands, when he had grown rich enough, and moving to the country. "From time immemorial a place in the country had been the crown of a merchant's career, and from the first circle the impulse was communicated through all the spheres down to the solid centre of the ten-pound franchise and the suburban villa." [8] Caught up in this paradox, Smiles demonstrates his desire to mitigate the changes which he celebrates by attaching each of his heroes firmly to his family, and by finding the sources of his heroes' successes in their fathers' consents.

[8] G. M. Young, *Victorian England: Portrait of an Age* (New York, 1964), p. 85.

In story after story of coal and iron makers, the young hero chooses his career because of his father's influence or guidance; in no story is the father averse to the career his son has chosen, or the son disrespectful toward the father he will often so far outdistance. Dud Dudley, inventor of iron-smelting by pit-coal, although illegitimate, was much aided by his father Lord Dudley because he was the "special favorite of the Earl his father." John Roebuck's father intended his son to follow his own business of cutlery manufacture "but the youth was irresistibly attracted to scientific pursuits, in which his father liberally encouraged him." Neilson, inventor of the hot-blast furnace, "had much of his father's tastes for mechanical pursuits." Henry Maudslay was put into a carpenter's shop "where his father had worked." James Naysmyth, whose father was an eminent landscape painter, became an inventor because, Smiles says, mechanics was one of his father's hobbies. Smiles allows that only one of his inventors, Henry Cort, "seems to have raised himself by his own efforts"—probably because "nothing is known" of his parents and early life.[9]

Dickens's own career closely fit the new heroic pattern which I have been describing. He rose, through his own effort and genius, from obscurity to fame, wealth, and power. Furthermore, his ideal morality was very much that of his age: duty and self-restraint, hard work, the sanctity of the family, progress. These values unite him in spirit much more with the urban bourgeoisie than with the landed gentry. Although his ideals were sometimes anti-bourgeois, although his sentiments seem often closely allied to those of the small gentry, although paradise, for him, is almost always found in the country, his principal values were closer to those of men of affairs whose affairs were in the cities. He was progressive as they were progressive: anti-aristo-

[9] Smiles, *Industrial Biography*, pp. 69, 170, 190–91, 246, 334, 148.

cratic, anti-traditional; progressive in the cause of independent thought, individual effort, social mobility, and self-help. In the same way that the new hero was democratic Dickens was democratic: he believed in the goodness and romance and importance of the common people; he believed not in birth and privilege but in ability and hard work; above all, he believed in the power of the unaided individual to affect his own destiny. In all these beliefs, his closest contemporary analogue was the inventor-industrialist.

In *Victorian People,* Asa Briggs discusses the reasons why England did not become a "business society" in the mid-nineteenth century. He says that resistance to the power of the businessman, and to his creed of "progress" and "success," came from three directions. It came from the small gentry, whose traditional power was so strong that (and here Briggs is quoting a contemporary source) "the danger is never lest they shall have too little, but always lest they should have too much power, and so, even involuntarily, choke down the possibilities of new life from below." It came from the new civil servants, generally public school or university men, who were either of the gentry themselves or aped the code of the gentry. And it came from labor, which valued class solidarity above individual mobility. A fourth source of opposition, Briggs says, came from within the ranks of businessmen themselves, many of whom were "deferential rather than rebellious, snobbish rather than independent." [10] It was this characteristic of the middle class that at times drew down Dickens's finest scorn.

As to the suffrage, I have lost hope even in the ballot. We appear to me to have proved the failure of representative institutions without an educated and advanced people to support them. What with teaching people to "keep in their stations," what with bring-

[10] Briggs, *Victorian People* (New York, 1955), pp. 11–12.

ing up the soul and body of the land to be a good child, or to go to the beer-shop, to go a-poaching and go to the devil; what with having no such thing as a middle class (for though we are perpetually bragging of it as our safety, it is nothing but a poor fringe on the mantle of the upper); what with flunkyism, toadyism, letting the most contemptible lords come in for all manner of places, reading The Court Circular for the New Testament, I do reluctantly believe that the English people are habitually consenting parties to the miserable imbecility into which we have fallen, *and never will help themselves out of it.* [11]

Thus, the middle class, which was to have been England's hope, which was to have encouraged progress and independence both of thought and of action, apparently does not exist. The crux of Dickens's criticism is that the middle class has no real ideology of its own. In its self-hatred, it struggles to lose its own identity in rapturous rebirth as part of the gentry. Its vitality, its essential democracy, its self-trust and self-respect, its earnest hard work, are forgotten and even repudiated once its members have achieved apotheosis as country gentlemen. Forgotten, too, are the very conditions of nineteenth-century life which permitted them to rise, as well as the fact that it was their response to those conditions which made them, potentially, a force for change in the world: the breakdown of a rigid class system, the growing belief in self-development and self-fulfillment, the conviction that character and talent are more important than birth, and that individual effort is as worthy of reward as hereditary status. It was their rejection of these values that provoked Dickens's anger against his own class—and yet he was susceptible to some of the very weaknesses and snobberies for which he blamed them. In the rest of Briggs's description of the businessman who had turned against his money-making interests we recognize some of the contradictions of Dickens's own life.

[11] Charles Dickens, *The Letters of Charles Dickens,* ed. Walter Dexter, 3 vols. (Bloomsbury, 1938), II, 695.

The moment quietly arrived in private histories when a new family became an old one and when its members basked in the branches of family trees and forgot that there had been ladders to climb on the way. Self-help was a more convenient philosophy for first than for second generations, and Disraeli saw clearer than Smiles that "the industrious ten-pounder, who has struggled into the privileged order of the Commons, proud of having obtained the first step of aristocracy, will be the last man to assist in destroying the gradation of the side by which he or his posterity may yet ascend." If it was not easy for a successful businessman to become a "gentleman" in his own lifetime, he could have reasonable hopes that his children, educated in the new public schools and marrying sons or daughters of the gentry, would eventually become "ladies" and "gentlemen." He could spend his declining years, if he so wished, "in hunting up genealogies" and spreading his wings "for sublime apotheosis among the county families." [12]

We are reminded that Dickens hunted up a genealogy for his family, too.

Even during the active years of their careers, not all businessmen were progressive, let alone ethical, nor did Dickens believe them to be so. Good men ran their businesses ethically; bad ones ran them unethically and furthermore were in a position of dangerously unlimited power over their employees. And no one was more aware of the helplessness of the industrial and commercial laborer, or described his plight more poignantly, than Dickens. But his solutions to the problems of the exploitation of labor were neither what would now be considered progressive or liberal, or were even then considered to be so. The solution he most often presented in his novels to the problem of the exploitation of the working man was benevolent paternalism, the good will of the masters.

But it is not the businessman in relation to his workers that is pertinent to this discussion; it is the businessman in relation to society as a whole. Compared with the whole of

[12] Briggs, *Victorian People*, p. 12.

society, the businessman was—had to be—a force for progress, even for subversion. He was not bound by tradition but by market conditions or industrial techniques; he brought the newest technology to the advancement of manufacture; he encouraged social mobility by his own example, by the example of self-help and self-reliance and self-restraint. That is, he was progressive in ways that Dickens admired and approved. Above all, business society was less tied than the landed or professional gentry to the "horrid respectability," the "little, finite, systematic routine" that Dickens felt was strangling England; the "mere form and conventionalities" that were usurping "in English government and social relations the place of living force and truth." [13] The businessman, at least for as long as he remained in business, simply could not afford mere form and conventionalities. For these reasons, Dickens felt in sympathy with businessmen and could imaginatively project himself into them more easily than into other professional groups, including artists. And he felt close to them emotionally as well.

A great ironmaster or manufacturer or engineer or inventor was able, like Dickens, to rise from obscurity to wealth in a single working lifetime. The Crystal Palace, built to house a great mid-century industrial exhibition and dedicated to peace and progress, was designed by a man whose career exemplified the new hero, "a type of creator as new and as characteristic of the Age as the building he had designed." [14] His name was Joseph Paxton, and his career, the "epitome of self-help," showed how a "common gardener's boy" could rise by his own merits to the highest rank of society: from gardener to engineer to railway director and promoter of newspapers and magazines. [15] But if Paxton rose

[13] Dickens, *Letters*, II, 700.   [14] Quoted in Briggs, *Victorian People*, p. 36.
[15] Robert F. Jordan, *Victorian Architecture* (Harmondsworth, 1966), p. 126, and Briggs, *Victorian People*, p. 36.

through self-help, demonstrating that society was flexible enough to make room for brains and hard work, he was not, as Asa Briggs calls him elsewhere, "self-made." [16] This phrase is crucial to the difference between the English folk hero of the mid-nineteenth century and the American; crucial not so much to who he was, but to the way in which he was understood and mythicized.

The *Oxford English Dictionary* notes that the phrase "self-made man" is of American origin, and gives as its earliest use the title of a book published in New York in 1858, *Self-Made Men* by C. C. B. Seymour.[17] Among the lives of sixty-two self-made men whom Seymour summarizes, there is not one American author; the only English author included is Charles Dickens.[18] Dickens himself had used the phrase four years before in *Hard Times* to describe the mill-owner, Josiah Bounderby. In this portrait Dickens shows the difference between the English understanding of the term and the American. In America the phrase is invariably a term of praise; to Dickens, it is problematic, self-contradictory, misleading. Bounderby is "a man who could never sufficiently vaunt himself a self-made man." He boasts that he was "born in a ditch": "Here I am, and no one to thank for my being here, but myself." Self-satisfied and self-sung, Dickens insists that he is *not* self-made. And in fact, Dickens means to prove through Bounderby that there is no such creature as a self-made man; that the man who says he is self-made is merely ungrateful to the parents who did make him. We do not make ourselves: we are made, for good or ill, and to

[16] Briggs, *Victorian People*, p. 36; *The Making of Modern England*, p. 398.

[17] In fact the *OED* is in error. According to *A Dictionary of American English*, ed. William A. Craigie and J. R. Hulbert (Chicago, 1944), the first use of the term in the United States was in 1832 when Henry Clay used it in a speech in Congress. And Dickens used it in *Hard Times* in 1854.

[18] In another nineteenth-century American compendium of success stories, *The Royal Road to Wealth: How to Find and Follow It* (New York, 1882), by Nelson Sizer, Dickens is again included and described in terms intelligible to Americans as a "writer of the people and from the people," p. 466.

deny it is to add ingratitude and untruth to our other sins, as Bounderby does. At the end of *Hard Times* Bounderby's mother (whose existence he had all along denied) turns up to tell the truth about his origins in a story that could have fallen right from the pages of Samuel Smiles.

"My dear boy knows, and will give *you* to know, that though he come of humble parents, he come of parents that loved him as dear as the best could, and never thought it hardship on themselves to pinch a bit that he might write and cipher beautiful . . . And my dear boy knows, and will give *you* to know, sir, that after his beloved father died when he was eight years old, his mother, too, could pinch a bit, as it was her duty and her pleasure and her pride to do it, to help him out in life, and put him 'prentice. And a steady lad he was, and a kind master he had to lend him a hand, and well he worked his way forward to be rich and thriving." (Book III, Ch. 5)

The emphasis here, as in Smiles, is upon parental influence first and hard work afterwards.

Rouncewell, the Ironmaster in *Bleak House,* is more truly "self-made" than Bounderby, but Dickens, entirely approving of him, doesn't call him so. And Rouncewell stands for other things than Bounderby did. In *Hard Times* Dickens was indicting the heartlessness of the British economic system in its dealings with the laboring class. In *Bleak House* he is indicting the heartless snobbery and willful blindness of all levels of society in their relation to all of the poor. There are individual persons in *Bleak House* who rescue one or two out of the mass of the wretched, as John Jarndyce does, but there is no organization for the relief of England's poor as there is for foreign infidels—The Society for the Propagation of the Gospel in Foreign Parts. The only part of society which seems able to offer the poor any means to help themselves—that can give them work—is industry, represented by Rouncewell. The energy and power of the northern industrialists is contrasted with the moribund aristocracy, represented by the Dedlocks, "whose family greatness seems to consist in their never having done anything to distinguish themselves, for seven hundred years." Rouncewell is no philanthropist; he does nothing, so far as we know, which is directly addressed to the problem of the poor. But he creates jobs and he fosters class mobility; and if there is any hope for the poor it lies in making jobs available to them so that they may help themselves. Above all, Rouncewell shows the industrial interest to be subversive of traditional landed power. Dickens's treatment of Rouncewell as subversive of the aristocracy is extremely complex.

Rouncewell, the son of Sir Leicester Dedlock's housekeeper, wishes to remove Lady Dedlock's maid from her employ because his son Watt wants to marry the girl. He is perfectly respectful during his confrontation with the Dedlocks on this matter, but they immediately understand that his request is an implicit threat to their class. Rouncewell intends to educate the girl for a year or two so that she may rise to his son's station—rise out of the station, as Sir Leicester agitatedly perceives, "unto which [she had been] called." Sir Leicester feels the Ironmaster's request as a blow "to the whole framework of society"—and so it is. Rouncewell is letting the new life from below break into the very drawing rooms of the aristocracy. This is revolution of a kind; and the Ironmaster has already shown himself to be a revolutionary in the chapter earlier in the novel which describes his break with Sir Leicester in his youth:

[Rouncewell's talent for invention when yet a boy set him against becoming a steward at Chesney Wold; and this] propensity gave Mrs. Rouncewell great uneasiness. She felt it with a mother's anguish, to be a move in the Wat Tyler direction: well knowing that Sir Leicester had that general impression of an aptitude for any art to which smoke and a tall chimney might be considered essential. But the doomed young rebel (otherwise a mild youth, and very persevering), showed no sign of grace as he got older; but, on the contrary, constructing a model of a power-loom, she was fain, with many tears, to mention his backsliding to the baronet. "Mrs. Rouncewell," said Sir Leicester, "I can never consent to argue, as you know, with any one on any subject. You had better get rid of your boy; you had better get him into some Works. The iron country farther north is, I suppose, the congenial direction for a boy with these tendencies." (Ch. 5)

Young Rouncewell rebelled against his patrimony—a stewardship at Chesney Wold; but his parent and his patron failed him, too, opposing themselves to what "nature and accident" had made him. Thus the rebel was forced into rebellion by the very persons who should have protected him from it. This is an old story; many another revolutionary has justified himself in this way. But Dickens never supports revolutionaries, either those who rebel against society or those who rebel against their fathers. Although he returns obsessively, in novel after novel, to the theme of selfish parents and wronged children, he never permits the children to avenge themselves upon their parents, nor does he ever support society's victims when they try to attack the social order. Rouncewell is of course a revolutionary only metaphorically. But in the vast revolution that was changing the face of England, the Industrial Revolution, he is an officer—a Captain of Industry. This is reinforced by the name he gives his son. Watt is named in part for Wat Tyler, the famous rebel, and in part for James Watt, the inventor of the steam engine, who brought to England and all the world a more far-reaching revolution than a military insurrection could have achieved.

The problem of Rouncewell's revolutionary character clarifies itself around his paternity. Rouncewell is somebody's son; but more importantly, he is somebody's father. He is one of the fathers of the new England, who offer young Englishmen the opportunity to work and improve themselves. He does not dispense charity to ghosts and ancient virgins and impotent hangers-on such as those who cluster around the childless and dying Dedlocks. Furthermore, Rouncewell's revolution not only changed the face of the modern world; it shifted its center of power from the land to the cities, as Dickens himself helped to shift the modern novel's center of interest from the country to the metropolis.

Dickens is close to great businessmen like Rouncewell ideologically, and he is close to them emotionally as well. In the ideology of the great industrialists he found the social representation of his own inner struggle; the struggle to justify his power and to reconcile himself to his success. Habakkuk believes that the "ingrained traditionalism" of the nineteenth-century manufacturer often impeded the growth of his own business because of his "unwillingness to accept the social consequences of rapid growth." [19] He may have been unwilling to face its emotional consequences as well. Like Dickens, the industrialist had to come to terms not only with his own success, but with his successful supersedence of his father in a society which was still intensely ambivalent toward such success and such supersedence. The English merchant's or manufacturer's desire to associate himself with the gentry—to buy land and leisure and, if possible, a genealogy—was primarily a desire to associate himself with traditional sources of power and prestige. But behind this lay a desire to obliterate, or at least mitigate, his own success; to connect himself with a past; to merge his personal success with that of a family—even if he had to create the family himself. Dickens showed the same desire when he purchased a country estate and dug up a family crest which he called "my father's."

Much Dickens family history is given the Rouncewells. Charles Dickens's paternal grandmother, like Watt Roun-

---

[19] H. J. Habakkuk, *American and British Technology in the Nineteenth Century* (Cambridge, 1967), p. 114.

cewell's, was housekeeper in a great house. But old Mrs. Rouncewell's son, unlike old Mrs. Dickens's, was a man of great force of character and earnestness, and he was a great success. He rose by steady degrees from "constructing steam-engines out of saucepans" to Ironmaster, to owning bank, factory, and great house. His going into iron at all— joining forces with the industrial north instead of remaining in the agricultural south—was considered an act of rebellion by his mother's master. It was therefore without the baronet's patronage or approval that Rouncewell started out in life. It was without his mother's approval too; and later in life, immensely successful in spite of them both, he refuses any share in his mother's legacy. A father now, it has become one of his "cares and pleasures" to educate his children so as to "make them worthy of any station." That is, in the Rouncewell family history, the rise from servant class to gentry was a steady one. After a good education Watt is employed in his father's flourishing business; and if the family continues to live out the Victorian success story, Watt's sons will go to public school and university, and perhaps sell out of business altogether.

In the Dickens family, the housekeeper's son got employment as a minor civil servant through the patronage of Lord Crewe, his mother's employer. But John Dickens did not prosper. As his own family grew, he fell deeply into debt, and instead of educating his oldest son so that he would be worthy of any station, he allowed him to become "a common labouring child." And to the child who had been thus declassed, it seemed that his father "would hardly have been more [satisfied] if I had been twenty years of age, distinguished at a grammar school, and going to Cambridge." [20] When John Dickens was finally imprisoned for debt, it was the old housekeeper's legacy that paid his debts

[20] John Forster, *The Life of Charles Dickens*, 3 vols. (Philadelphia, 1897), I, 51.

and got him out of jail. Finally, in later life it was his own son, Charles Dickens, who employed him in his flourishing business enterprises, who paid his debts, and who at last entirely supported him.

In Rouncewell, Dickens is less interested in the psychology of the son whom nature and accident have made more successful than his father than he is in the psychology of the father who takes pride and pleasure in the progressive, vital nature of his work. Daniel Doyce, the inventor in *Little Dorrit,* also takes pride in his work for its potential good to mankind, and pleasure in the work itself. He has made inventions "of great importance to his country and his fellow creatures." Like so many of Smiles's engineers, Doyce had humble beginnings; like them, he found his true vocation with his parents' help. He was the "son of a north-country blacksmith, and had originally been apprenticed by his widowed mother to a lock-maker . . . had 'struck out a few little things' at the lock-maker's, which had led to his being released from his indentures with a present, which present had enabled him to gratify his ardent wish to bind himself to a working engineer," and had at last become an engineer himself (Ch. 16). The Government, represented by the Circumlocution Office, does not want Doyce's inventions; wants to be "left alone." But Doyce believes that his inventive gift was "not put into his head to be buried. It's put into his head to be made useful. You hold your life on the condition that to the last you shall struggle hard for it. Every man holds a discovery on the same terms." Doyce is talking about a vocation, not a job; he might use the same words to describe the dedication of an artist. Together with Clennam, Doyce becomes a thriving businessman, and Clennam comes to be called "Doyce and Clennam," as if the partnership had indeed made them one person. Their initials, thus, are D. C.; like David Copperfield's, they are Charles Dickens's initials reversed. And the combination of inven-

tive genius and business sense is reminiscent of Dickens's
own, as well as of David Copperfield's—another novelist
with a good head for business.

The only artist in Dickens's novels who takes as much
pleasure in his work as these businessmen, and in the good
that it can do, is David Copperfield. And David describes
his dedication to his work and the pleasure he takes in it in
terms that Rouncewell might use about iron-mongering, or
Doyce about inventing:

> I laboured hard at my book, without allowing it to interfere
> with the punctual discharge of my newspaper duties; and it came
> out and was very successful. . . .
> Having some foundation for believing, by this time, that nature
> and accident had made me an author, I pursued my vocation with
> confidence. Without such assurance I should certainly have left it
> alone, and bestowed my energy on some other endeavour. I
> should have tried to find out what nature and accident really had
> made me, and to be that, and nothing else.
> I had been writing, in the newspaper and elsewhere, so pros-
> perously, that when my new success was achieved, I considered
> myself reasonably entitled to escape from the dreary [parliamen-
> tary] debates. (Ch. 48) [21]

What is of most importance in Dickens's feelings about the
virtual interchangeability of a writing career and certain
kinds of commercial careers is that in making the identity
he is not underestimating the importance of art. Rather, he
is emphasizing its power as a social force; its real power in
the world. His was an age when the writer was listened to to
an extent that now seems almost incredible. Queen Victoria
looked to Tennyson for comfort; G. M. Young believes that

---

[21] In *Industrial Biography,* Smiles also makes an identification between poet and
inventor. Writing of the life of Joseph Bramah he remarks: "The inventive faculty
is so strong in some men that it may be said to amount to a passion, and cannot be
restrained. The saying that the poet is born not made, applies with equal force to
the inventor, who, though indebted like the other to culture and improved oppor-
tunities, nevertheless invents and goes on inventing mainly to gratify his own instinct" (p. 228).

Carlyle had an immense "atmospheric effect" upon Victorian values; Dickens's work was considered by almost all—and called by Thackeray—a "national benefit." [22] And Dickens consciously and carefully used his writing as a force for good in the world. So great did his contemporaries consider his power for effecting good that a Nonconformist preacher called his novels one of the "three great social agencies" of the time.[23] When his reputation as a novelist was established, Dickens turned also to a wider audience and a more explicitly didactic form—magazine and, very briefly, newspaper publication. His first editorial in *Household Words* shows how conscious he was of his great power:

> We aspire to live in the Household affections, and to be numbered among the Household thoughts, of our readers. We hope to be the comrade and friend of many thousands of people, of both sexes, of all ages and conditions, on whose faces we may never look. We seek to bring into innumerable homes, from the striving world around us, the knowledge of many social wonders, good and evil, that are not calculated to render any of us less ardently persevering in ourselves, less tolerant of one another, less faithful in the progress of mankind, less thankful for the privilege of living in this summer-dawn of time. . . .
>
> We have considered what an ambition it is to be admitted into many homes with affection and confidence . . . We know the great responsibility of such a privilege; its vast reward . . . The hand that writes these faltering lines, happily associated with *some* Household Words before to-day, has known enough of such experiences to enter in an earnest spirit upon this new task, and with an awakened sense of all that it involves.[24]

When Dickens used his power and success as a social force, as an agency for doing good, he clearly exulted both in the "great responsibility" and in the "vast reward" they

[22] Young, *Victorian England*, p. 55; Edgar Johnson, *Charles Dickens: His Tragedy and Triumph* (New York, 1952), p. 490.

[23] Young, *Victorian England*, p. 55.

[24] *Household Words* 1, No. 1 (30 March 1850), 1.

brought him. It was when he faced his power and success in relation to his father's weakness and failure that they became sources not of strength and pleasure, but of self-doubt, guilt, and fear. From *David Copperfield* to *Great Expectations* one can trace his growing ambivalence and finally his overwhelming guilt over this problem, a problem born with him out of the circumstances of his own family, and reinforced by the values of the Victorian world within which he found such power, and which had such power over him as well.

II   THE AMERICAN FOLK HERO

In England, career was to a great extent determined by birth. Business and some professions were open to the lower orders of the middle class, and through these careers such men could sometimes rise to wealth and power. But government and the higher civil service, and some professions, were still dependent upon education and birth. The folk hero, as I have said, was the man who rose by means of the new technology; the man who brought nature to the service of the nation and his own success. In the United States, where all careers were open to the middle class, there were a number of paths to wealth and power. The American folk hero, therefore, was less defined by career than by character. And heroic characteristics in America were always those clustering around the primacy of the self: self-reliance, self-expression, self-fulfillment. The American folk hero was, above all, self-made.

Benjamin Franklin first grasped the importance of this characteristic of the new American hero, and first understood the self-made man's revolutionary implications. He self-consciously reshaped his life, in his writing, to make himself the epitome of the self-made man. With characteristic understatement, he demonstrated that the father's precedence over the sons could be overturned with triumphant success: "From the poverty and obscurity in which I was born and in which I passed my earliest years, I have raised myself to a state of affluence and some degree of celebrity in the world." [25] This quiet statement was revolutionary in its import, and would be revolutionary in its impact upon the world. John Adams believed that Franklin's reputation

was more universal than that of Leibnitz or Newton, Frederick or Voltaire; and his character was more beloved and esteemed than any or all of them. His name was familiar to government and people, to kings, courtiers, nobility, clergy, and philosophers, as well as plebians, to such a degree that there was scarcely peasant or citizen, a valet de chambre, coachman or footman, a lady's chambermaid or a scullion in a kitchen who was not familiar with it and who did not consider him a friend to humankind. When they spoke of him they seemed to think he was to restore the golden age. His plans and his example were to abolish monarchy, aristocracy, and hierarchy throughout the world.[26]

But just as the idea of the self-made man did not spring full-born out of Franklin's imagination—it was already part of the folkways of Franklin's time—so Franklin himself had not caused the abolition of monarchy, aristocracy, and hierarchy in America. That had been accomplished by a silent revolution which had begun a hundred and fifty years before, almost with the first settlement of America. In the same way, the Revolutionary War itself was not only a military and political upheaval; it was the culmination of a change in the entire hierarchal order of society in America. As John Adams perceived and pointed out, "The Revolution was effected before the War commenced. The Revolution was in the Minds and Hearts of the People. A Change in their Religious Sentiments of their Duties and Obligations." And the duties and obligations of Americans had

[25] Benjamin Franklin, *The Autobiography and Other Writings*, ed. L. Jesse Lemisch (New York, 1961), p. 16.
[26] Quoted in Carl Van Doren, *Benjamin Franklin* (New York, 1938), pp. 30–31.

moved not only from England to America, and from King to people; it had moved also from society to the self

The assumptions behind the concept of the self-made man were based upon certain assumptions about the nature of new conditions in the new nation: the freeing of the individual from subordination to a rigid social system; the freeing of society itself from inherited class and status; the belief that every man is entitled to pursue happiness in his own way; that character and effort are more than birth; that instinct is more than book knowledge. God reveals himself to the individual man, truth reveals itself to the individual man, practical wisdom reveals itself to the individual man; and social and political institutions stand between the individual man and God, truth, and, especially, success. By the mid-nineteenth century Americans were self-governed; their political theories were self-evident; their philosophers were self-reliant; their poets were self-celebrating; and their heroes—presidents, businessmen, engineers, inventors, pioneers—were self-made.

When he wished to, Dickens was able to represent his own success through business success because in the successful businessman's career he saw not only an analogue to his own success, but in the world of the middle-class businessman he saw many of his own values expressed—as that world saw its values expressed in Dickens's novels. In America, where almost any man could rise to success, hypothetically if not in fact, a serious writer could not. A writer in America neither had power within his society, nor did he have the ear of the powerful, as so many of the great English social critics had—even though, as many of them believed, they had neither sufficient power nor sufficient attention.

There was a great deal of urgent, practical work to be done in America—not redone, or done better, as in Europe, but done for the first time, and done in haste in order to make possible the ordinary business of life. And as the English middle class made folk heroes of their engineers and inventors because they were men who brought the newest technology to the conquest of nature and the aid of material progress, so did the Americans. But Americans went even further in their romanticization of inventors than the English did. In the lives of American inventors, as they were recorded by Americans, there is a curious element beyond any ordinary heroism of courage or intelligence. There is the heroism of genius; of men divinely touched, almost maddened, by their creative powers.

Accounts of American inventors were not told primarily in terms of money. Like artists, they were seen as following the bent of their genius for its own sake. The bent of the inventor's genius is toward utility: he expresses his fancy in objects rather than in words, and in objects whose ultimate aim is to tame nature. *Success in Life,* published in New York in 1850, begins a chapter on inventors with this anecdote:

A father was heard to say, "I would rather my son would only know enough to come in when it rains, than to be a mechanical genius."

"Why so?"

"Because men of genius are poor as church mice all their lives."

This was a mistake, for genius frequently meets with its due reward. But supposing the man of inventive talent does not become rich, if he possess means enough to make him free from actual want, he may be quite as happy, and even more so, than a rich man without genius. The pleasure he has in invention, he would not exchange for all the luxuries that wealth could purchase; yet he has his trials, and very severe ones they are, when he happens to be greatly in advance of his age. Let him bear up nobly under the scorn or the persecution which the men who disturb long-settled errors, or advance new opinions, are apt to encounter. . . .[27]

Here is all the terror of genius: risk of fortune, servitude to the gift or the god, and the promise of great good to man-

[27] L. C. Tuthill, *Success in Life* (New York, 1850), pp. 21–22.

kind. Many men of mechanical genius "dabbled in the arts" before finding their true vocations. Condescending and naive as this sounds, it was no doubt often true; men who desired success avoided the arts in nineteenth-century America, and turned their gifts into channels of greater reward and social esteem. According to the author of *Success in Life*, Benjamin Franklin, while a "printer's boy," "takes a strong inclination for *poetry*, and *writes* some little pieces. It is astonishing how many men of genius, in every art and profession, have scribbled verses in their younger days." Eli Whitney's imagination "was an active faculty," like that of "most men of inventive genius," "prompting them occasionally to poetical composition." [28] Robert Fulton was a landscape and portrait painter before he became a poet-inventor: "Few men are endowed with inventive genius, and without this endowment it is worse than useless to spend life in forming plans and making models. . . . Fulton was one of the 'few,' with the capacity to theorize, and to render the theory practical; that is, to invent and execute." [29] Another account of Fulton's life adds persecution and ostracism to the other trials endured by the poet of progress:

It seldom happens that a man of [inventive] genius receives the full measure of homage to which he is entitled. He is apt to be ridiculed as a visionary, and persecuted as a plagiarist during his life, and forgotten after his death. These hard conditions seem to be the penalty which the man pays for overleaping his neighbor in intellectual greatness; a sort of iniquitous compensation which the rabble insists on establishing. If there is one man more than another who fortunately can not complain of this cruel injustice, it is Robert Fulton. Every American must experience a thrill of satisfaction in knowing that the greatest benefactor of his country lives also in its best recollection. In every considerable city of the New World the streets are named after him . . . It is not only their name, but their present perfection, that they owe to this worthy son of the land of freedom. Without his application and industry, without his early perception and steady pursuit of the useful ends

[28] Tuthill, *Success in Life*, pp. 56, 113.   [29] Tuthill, p. 99.

of steam power, America might yet be, to a great extent, an impenetrable and unwieldy forest.[30]

Dickens might have written this as parody; but a kind of idealism shines through its smug boasting nonetheless.

Elias Howe, inventor of the sewing machine, was born in 1819, the same year as Herman Melville. His career, lovingly described in *The Royal Road to Wealth,* is the classic life of the inventor-hero. The son of a poor farmer, Howe goes to Boston to work in the shop of a "mechanical inventor." One day a "capitalist," a "well-dressed and fine looking man" enters the shop and mentions that "a fortune was in store for the man who should invent a sewing-machine." A few years later Howe decides to invent such a machine out of the "pressure of poverty." "It was then that he caught the inventor's mania, which gives its victims no peace till they have accomplished the work to which they have abandoned themselves." He finds a backer and goes to work. "So far as we know, neither of the parties indulged in any dream of benevolence. . . . The greatest doers of good have usually proceeded in the same homely spirit. Thus Shakespeare wrote, thus Columbus sailed, thus Watt invented, thus Newton discovered." Thus Howe, who soon becomes rich and famous. The sewing machine's good to mankind is immeasurable; a Professor Renwick declares "under oath" that it has saved labor amounting to nineteen millions of dollars per annum.

The canting materialism of this story is entirely lost upon its teller, who sees in the "trials and triumphs of this man, the old story of poverty, hardship, with the ridicule and selfishness of the world."

Nearly every great invention has been born of necessity in the vale of poverty, if not of suffering. Fulton, Goodyear, Morse, and Howe passed through a similar "Red Sea" and "wilderness" to the

[30] Charles C. B. Seymour, *Self-Made Men* (New York, 1858), pp. 460–61.

land of hope and promise. He who has the fortune or misfortune
to think much in advance of his fellow-men, rarely finds one who
can or will appreciate and help him. Inventors not only have to
eat the "bread of carefulness," but often their care is taxed to the
uttermost to get bread . . .[31]

The best American poet is clearly the ex-poet, the poet
metamorphosed into his mature role, that of poet inventor.

Inventors were the American poet-heroes; but there was
also, in America, a poetry of money itself. In 1842 Dickens
wrote indignantly from America that when he told Americans that they would have no literature of their own unless
they acted to secure an international copyright, the "universal answer (out of Boston)" was: "We don't want one. . . .
Our people don't think of poetry, sir. Dollars, banks, and
cotton are *our* books, sir." [32] Americans learned to satisfy
their esthetic needs in the ecstatic contemplation of cotton
fields, forests, mineral veins, grazing land. Cotton and
wheat and furs and cattle and ores and lumber were being
taken out of the land and converted into cash, and somehow this was apprehended by Americans as high romance.

In England, there were other kinds of romance to follow
the adventure of money-making—the romance of importance on the land, of marrying one's children into the leisure class, of entering society, and so on. In the United
States there was much less that the rich merchant could do
with his money that would bring him more prestige than
the money itself did, and very little to look forward to that
was more glamorous than the making of it had been. Large
fortunes began to be accumulated in America in the nineteenth century, and all the writers of the so-called American
Renaissance were born in the optimum years for millionaires' births—between 1801 and 1860. In fact, Melville, the
son of a merchant, born in New York City in 1819 fulfilled

[31] Sizer, *The Royal Road to Wealth*, pp. 476–96.
[32] Edgar Johnson, *Charles Dickens*, p. 421.

all of the conditions that Pitirim Sorokin, in his study of American millionaires and multimillionaires, found to have been the optimum conditions of birth for an American millionaire.[33] With such possibilities for getting rich open to everyone, at least in theory, and with not much to contend with money for prestige and power, it is no wonder that the making of money seemed a heroic activity to Americans.

The ideal of a contemplative life seemed ludicrous in a land where the results of activity were not only lucrative, but were urgently needed. Early in the days of the Republic the study of the classics became the symbol for all such useless tasks.

"We occupy a new country. Our principal business should be to explore and apply its resources, all of which press us to enterprize and haste. Under these circumstances, to spend four or five years in learning two dead languages, is to turn our back upon a gold mine, in order to amuse ourselves catching butterflies." [34] To call this materialism would be to turn our backs upon the conditions of that world and apply to it the conditions of our own. European observers of America often did call it materialism, but few Americans did. At least until the 1870's or '80's, most Americans believed that their principal business should be the exploration and exploitation of the resources of their country. American writers were more apt to suspect themselves of being butterfly-catchers than to suspect that the rest of their countrymen were crass materialists. And even when the writer defended his right to catch butterflies, he seldom questioned *their* right to mine gold. Emerson, Hawthorne, Melville, Whitman, all at one time or another expressed

[33] Pitirim Sorokin, "American Millionaires and Multi-Millionaires," *Journal of Social Forces,* 3 (1925), 627–40.

[34] Quoted in Daniel J. Boorstin, *The Lost World of Thomas Jefferson* (Boston, 1960), p. 221.

their fear that they were, as Hawthorne put it, "writer[s] of story books," "idler[s]," and "fiddler[s]."

In the minds of many Americans, the activity of writing was in itself suspect. Although the period of the Founding Fathers had been dominated by great writers—Franklin, Paine, Adams, Jefferson, Hamilton—once the ferment of ideologies was over, writers came to be held in mounting mistrust. They seemed to men of action to ignore their country's most essential need, which was to deal directly with the material existence of the continent. During the presidential campaign of 1828 the antagonism between the man of action and the man of letters was given succinct statement: "John Quincy Adams who can write, And Andrew Jackson who can fight." Jackson was further eulogized as the "unlettered man of the West, the nursling of the wilds, the farmer of the Hermitage, little versed in Books, unconnected by science with the tradition of the past. . . . What wisdom will he bring with him from the forest? What rules of duty will he evolve from the oracles of his own mind?" [35]

Many American writers, no less than American businessmen, would not have balked at this description of a hero. Cooper, Emerson, Thoreau, or Whitman could have written it. Many of the central beliefs of transcendentalism are embodied in it: self-reliance; the belief in the divinity of the individual soul and its ability to apprehend God directly; its contempt for books and its belief in the Western wilderness. And Melville's own description in *Moby Dick* of Andrew Jackson as a democratic hero raised up by the "democratic God" could be appended to it with almost no disjunction of feeling or of style: "Thou who didst pick up Andrew Jackson from the pebbles; who didst hurl him upon a warhorse; who didst thunder him higher than a throne! Thou

[35] Quoted in Richard Hofstadter, *Anti-Intellectualism in American Life* (New York, 1962), p. 159.

who, in all Thy mighty earthly marchings, ever cullest Thy selectest champions from the kingly commons . . ." (Ch. 26).

The writer did no real *work:* that had always been the crux of the complaint against him. To men who saw the whole United States as a glorious open-air factory waiting for the "hands" to come in; men to whom the "very earth is a chemical laboratory; the forest an assemblage of powerful hydraulic engines; Action, Effort, Productiveness, the law of the Universe, 'The Music of the Spheres' is not idle or useless" [36]—to such men the poet's music was bound to seem both idle and useless. Speaking to a young men's mercantile association in Indianapolis in 1844, Henry Ward Beecher satirized poets and writers, so-called "men of genius":

So far as my observations have ascertained the species they abound in academies, colleges, and Thespian societies; in village debating clubs; in coteries of young artists, and young professional aspirants. They are known by a reserved air, excessive sensitiveness, and utter indolence; by very long hair, and very open shirt collars; by reading of much wretched poetry, and the writing of much, yet more wretched; by being very conceited, very affected, very disagreeable, and very useless:—beings whom no man wants for friend, pupil, or companion.[37]

Utterly indolent "and very useless"—this is the crux of Beecher's criticism too. Many American writers not only ironically agreed that they were useless, but set out to prove it. If declaring oneself a writer was tantamount to declaring oneself a loafer, then the writer would loudly proclaim that he was just that. This Whitman did, for example, when he said in the very opening stanzas of *Leaves of Grass,* "I loafe and

[36] Sizer, *The Royal Road to Wealth,* p. 11.
[37] Quoted in Irvin G. Wyllie, *The Self-Made Man in America: The Myth of Rags to Riches* (New York, 1954), p. 35.

invite my soul, I lean and loafe at my ease"; and the self-portrait which he had reproduced in the first edition of *Leaves of Grass* exactly fits Beecher's derisive description of the poet. Thoreau declared that time spent in watching the changing of the seasons at a Massachusetts pond was business enough for any man. Hawthorne lived "idly" for ten years, writing tales in his mother's attic. Melville summed up his many statements about the artist's need for leisure in a single sentence in *Moby Dick:* "To insure the greatest efficiency in the dart, the harpooneers of this world must start to their feet from out of idleness, and not from out of toil."

Melville realized that this notion of rest was foreign to the majority of Americans who looked upon leisure as indolence and uselessness, and had done so since Puritan times. Middle-class Englishmen were heirs to a Puritan tradition that was, if anything, stronger and more lasting than the American. But in England there were other traditional values, older and quite as prestigious as the Puritan ethic. A living aristocracy still supported the ideal of leisure; and the ideal of the Renaissance man was still strong among the upper English gentry, was part of their traditional definition of themselves as "gentlemen." The practice of art, the pursuit of scholarship, the enjoyment of leisure, all had precedents and traditions that went further back in time than Puritanism, and these ideals existed side by side with a Protestant work ethic very much like that which was in more or less undisputed command in America. In 1863 Melville cut an editorial from the London *Times* and pasted it in his note-book:

Leisure is the nurse of art and scholarship, the gradual untier of knots, the guide that ushers into the depths and mysteries of knowledge, the gradual former of that discrimination and perception which distinguishes the man of high education. Irregular and anomalous education which can take a hasty advantage of the odd moments and the spare attention of a busy life, cannot be expected to produce these effects, because it has in truth, not the whole man, but only a fragment of him at its command. It takes a sharp mind under such circumstances even to skim the surface; the secrets of the depths below are the prize of a gradual struggle, which it requires time even to commence, for we do not even see our difficulties till we have been a considerable time looking about us.

Underneath this clipping Melville wrote, "How un-American is all this, and yet—how true." [38]

Not everyone in America disregarded the artist. But the serious reading public was not large, it was for the most part Eastern, and it was rather heavily female. Such as it was, however, it was eager to encourage a native American literature. Emerson's Phi Beta Kappa address, delivered at Harvard in 1837, gave voice to the feelings of literate Americans as to the state of literature in America and the status of the American man of letters. Called "The American Scholar," it was really a call for an American poet. The occasion which it celebrated, Emerson said, was

a friendly sign of the survival of the love of letters amongst a people too busy to give to letters any more. As such it is precious as the sign of an indestructible instinct. Perhaps the time is already come when it ought to be, and will be, something else; when the sluggard intellect of this continent will look from under its iron lids and fill the postponed expectation of the world with something better than the exertions of mechanical skill. Our day of dependence, our long apprenticeship to the learning of other lands, draws to a close. The millions that around us are rushing into life, cannot always be fed on the sere remains of foreign harvests. Events, actions arise, that must be sung, that will sing themselves. Who can doubt that poetry will revive and lead in a new age, as the star in the constellation Harp, which now flames in our

---

[38] Quoted in Merton M. Sealts, Jr., *Melville's Reading: A Check-List of Books Owned and Borrowed* (Madison, Wis., 1966), pp. 22–23.

zenith, astronomers announce, shall one day be the polestar for a thousand years? [39]

The American writer who answered Emerson's call most literally was Walt Whitman, the most innovative poet of the nineteenth century, and innovative largely in the service of his country, whose themes, "events and actions" could only be sung, he felt, in new poetic forms. In some ways Whitman's response to the call—at least the Whitman who had heard democracy singing and had given it a voice—was not typical. Most typically, the American writer turned his eyes inward upon his own psyche; turned away from society in order to explore and examine the workings of the self. Tocqueville's observation about the effect democracy has upon its citizens can be applied directly to the effect American life had upon its writers. In a democracy "everyone shuts himself up tightly within himself and insists upon judging the world from there." "Thus not only does democracy make every man forget his ancestors, but it hides his descendents and separates his contemporaries from him; it throws him back forever upon himself alone and threatens in the end to confine him entirely within the solitude of his own heart." [40]

And such literary criticism as there was in America recognized the sovereignty of the self in American literature. An essay written twenty years after Emerson's address praised Melville for just that: "Mr. Melville was not only a young man, but a young American, and a young American educated according to the standard of our day and country. He had all the metaphysical tendencies which belong so eminently to the American's mind—the love of antic and extravagant speculation, the fearlessness of intellectual conse-

[39] Ralph Waldo Emerson, "The American Scholar," in *The Selected Writings of Ralph Waldo Emerson* (New York, 1940), p. 45.

[40] Alexis de Tocqueville, *Democracy in America*, 2 vols. (New York, 1945), I, 4, 106.

quences, and the passion for intellectual legislation, which distinguish the cleverest of our people." [41] But both the call for an American literature, and sympathetic response to it, were very limited; and the degree of success, the degree of fame, power, and money, available to native American writers was very meager. What kind of person would answer Emerson's call, then?

In part, he would have to be one who had already set himself in opposition to the dominant values of his day, who defined himself less as spokesman for his culture than as rebel from it; a man who must have asked himself, with Thoreau, why he should be "in such desperate haste to succeed, and in such desperate enterprises? If a man does not keep pace with his companions, perhaps it is because he hears a different drummer." [42] For whatever else he was, he would have to be a man who could deal with achieving only a limited amount of success, as success was defined in America. Any person, therefore, who set out to be a writer in America had to be prepared to accept failure, and no one understood this better than the writers themselves. In a letter to his English publisher in which he was talking about American indifference to the matter of an international copyright, Melville described the writer's position in America.

Who have any motive in this country to bestir themselves in this thing? Only the authors.—Who are the authors?—A handful. And what influence have they to bring upon any question whose settlement must necessarily assume a political form?—They can bring scarcely any influence whatever. This country & nearly all its affairs are governed by sturdy backwoodsmen—noble fellows enough, but not at all literary, & who care not a fig for any authors except those who write those most saleable of all books nowadays—ie—the newspapers, & magazines. And tho' the number of cultivated catholic men, who may be supposed to feel an interest

[41] Jay Leyda, *The Melville Log*, 2 vols. (New York, 1951), II, 564.
[42] Henry David Thoreau, *Walden* (New York, 1966), p. 215.

in a national literature, is very large & every day growing larger; yet they are nothing in comparison with the overwhelming majority who care nothing about it. This country is at present engaged in furnishing material for future authors; not in encouraging its living ones.[43]

Encouraged or not, American writers went on writing, and what they wrote was in part licensed by the very absence of a significant reading public. The "passion for intellectual legislation"—that is, the independence of mind—which Melville's anonymous critic felt was fostered by the quality of life in America, joined with the scant attention paid to what the writer thought and wrote, gave to the American writer a greater freedom of subject and permitted him a wider range of speculation than his English counterpart had, whose feeling of public responsibility was comparatively very heavy. Having so small an audience, the American writer had the less reason to please what audience he had, and all the more reason to please himself.

And many nineteenth-century American writers pleased only themselves for many years, waiting long for whatever "success" they achieved in their own lifetimes. Some, like Poe, Thoreau, and Dickinson, received almost no recognition during their lifetimes. Hawthorne struggled long to gain fame, Whitman longer. But of them all, Melville had least long to wait.

The story of Melville's "success" and subsequent fall from fame is a curious one. Almost forgotten by the time of his death, not rediscovered until the twentieth century, his work was popular both in England and America during the early years of his career. His first novel, *Typee,* achieved almost instant popularity and some notoriety. If Melville's popularity declined with his next eight novels, it was a decline in which he in large measure participated. His rea-

---

[43] *The Letters of Herman Melville,* edited by Merrell R. Davis and William H. Gilman (New Haven, 1960), p. 134.

sons—complex and neurotic—for cooperating in his own failure will be discussed in a later chapter. But that he feared success; that he intentionally turned away even from such success as was open to him as a writer in America, is clearly revealed by the pattern of his published work.

Typee and *Omoo,* Melville's first two novels, were not only popular, but were well-received critically both in England and in the United States, where the best reviewers, always on the look-out for native genius, immediately recognized his talent.[44] Yet Melville himself held the two books which had made him famous in low esteem: "What 'reputation' H[erman] M[elville] has is horrible," he wrote to Hawthorne five years after *Typee* was published. "Think of it! To go down to posterity . . . as a 'man who lived among the cannibals'!"[45] He intended to make his third novel, *Mardi,* another South Seas adventure story, but it very quickly veered into mingled fantasy, allegory, and treatise. That Melville had deliberately set out *not* to please his readers in *Mardi* is evident from the contradictory remarks he made about it to his English publishers. In an early letter about the book he wrote, "I doubt not that—if it makes the hit I mean it to—it will be counted a rather bold aim; but nevertheless, it shall have the right stuff in it, to redeem its faults, tho' they were legion."[46] Less than three months later his ambivalence is even more marked:

I believe that a letter I wrote you some time ago . . . gave you to understand, or implied, that the work I then had in view was a bona-fide narrative of my adventures in the Pacific, continued from "Omoo"—My object in now writing you—I should have

---

[44] Hawthorne said that *Typee* was "worthy of the novelty and interest of its subject"; Margaret Fuller wrote that "it compares very well with the best contrivance of the learned Dr. Johnson"; George Ripley called it the "work of an artist"; and Walt Whitman called it "A strange, graceful, most readable book. . . . As a book to hold in one's hand and pore dreamily over of a summer day, it is unsurpassed." *Melville Log,* 1, 208, 209, 210, 211.

[45] *Letters,* p. 130.   [46] *Log,* 1, 269.

done so ere this—is to inform you of a change in my determinations. To be "blunt" the work I shall next publish will be downright & out a "Romance of Polynesian Adventure"—But why this? The truth is, Sir, that the reiterated imputation of being a romancer in disguise has at last pricked me into a resolution to show those who may take any interest in the matter, that a *real* romance of mine is not Typee or Omoo, and is made of different stuff altogether. This I confess has been the main inducement in altering my plans—but others have operated. . . . As for the policy of putting forth an acknowledged *romance* upon the heels of two books of travel . . . That, Sir, is a question for which I care little, really.[47]

Melville must have had a pretty clear idea about the critical reception his "real" romance would have. His wife, who had made the fair copy of *Mardi* for the publishers, wrote anxiously to her mother: "I suppose by this time you are deep in the fogs of Mardi—if the mist ever does clear away, I should like to know what it reveals to you—there seems to be much diversity of opinion about Mardi as might be supposed. Has father read it? When you hear any individual express an opinion with regard to it, I wish you would tell me—whatever it is—good or bad—without fear of offence—merely by way of curiosity." [48]

Mardi's bad reviews stung Melville into some acknowledgment of what he recognized in himself as a deep ambivalence toward his own talent: "You may think, in your own mind [he wrote to his publisher], that a man is unwise,—indiscreet, to write a work of that kind, when he might have written one perhaps, calculated merely to please the general reader, & not provoke attack, however masqued in an affectation of indifference or contempt. But some of us scribblers, My Dear Sir, always have a certain something unmanageable in us, that bids us do this or that, and be done it must—hit or miss." [49]

He quickly wrote two more travel narratives, *Redburn* and

[47] *Log*, I, 275.   [48] *Log*, I, 302.   [49] *Letters*, p. 86.

White Jacket, designed "merely to please the general reader," which they did. But that they did not please him he made clear in a letter to his wife's father:

They are two *jobs,* which I have done for money—being forced to it, as other men are to sawing wood. And while I have felt obliged to refrain from writing the kind of book I would wish to; yet, in writing these two books, I have not repressed myself much—so far as *they* are concerned; but have spoken pretty much as I feel.— Being books, then, written in this way, my only desire for their "success" (as it is called) springs from my pocket, & not from my heart. So far as I am individually concerned, & independent of my pocket, it is my earnest desire to write those sort of books which are said to "fail."—Pardon this egotism.[50]

The ambivalence toward success and failure, in fact the desire for failure, could not be more marked—nor more self-aware. Melville not only knew that his indifference to public opinion was partly an "affectation"; he also knew that he could not control his own impulse—the "something unmanageable" in him—to repulse interest, even to "provoke attack."

A certain kind of success, however—that of being understood by those whose opinion he valued—Melville acknowledged as open-heartedly as Dickens himself could have done. Hawthorne's praise of *Moby Dick* has not survived; but Melville responded to the older man's approval with an outburst of deep feeling. "A sense of unspeakable security is in me this moment, on account of your having understood the book . . . It is a strange feeling—no hopefulness is in it, no despair. Content—that is it; and irresponsibility; but without licentious inclination. I speak now of my profoundest sense of being, not of an incidental feeling." In the same letter he adds, "So, now, let us add Moby Dick to our blessing, and step from that. Leviathan is not the biggest fish;—I have heard of Krakens."[51] The Kraken was *Pierre*—of all

[50] *Letters,* pp. 91–92.   [51] *Letters,* pp. 142, 143.

Melville's books the one that most damaged his reputation, a "dead failure," "the craziest fiction extant." [52]

Melville began *Pierre* even before *Moby Dick* was through the press, as if he already feared the artistic success of what he knew was a masterpiece. The magnitude of *Pierre*'s perversity guaranteed its failure: a brother-sister marriage, a murder, two suicides, a death from outraged propriety, turgid plot, uncertain prose. But at the same time that Melville feared success he defended himself against failure: a month before *Moby Dick* was completed he wrote, "All Fame is patronage. Let me be infamous: there is no patronage in *that.*" [53]

Melville stopped writing prose in 1857, with the publication of *The Confidence Man.* His poetry, which he worked on until his death, followed a pattern of failure similar to that of his prose writing. In 1866 he published *Battle-Pieces and Aspects of the War,* a collection of short and fairly distinguished poems that was ignored by critics and public alike. The next ten years he spent writing *Clarel: A Poem and Pilgrimage in the Holy Land*—18,000 lines of rhymed iambic tetrameters dealing with philosophic and religious questions which, published at his own expense, is still largely unread. The pattern of ambivalence re-emerges: success is feared, and what is successful is quickly followed by what will be sure to "provoke attack"; at the same time, the terrible humiliation of failure is followed by whatever will prove Melville's indifference to and scorn for public approval by being made deliberately unreadable. Nothing reveals Melville's ambivalence toward this complex matter of success more clearly, however, than his brief career on the lecture platform, nor could anything offer a greater contrast to Dickens's spectacular success onstage.

In 1857, having decided not to "write any more at

[52] *Log,* I, 458 and 455.   [53] *Letters,* p. 129.

present," Melville tried lecturing as a means of earning money. A letter survives from the Clarksville, Tennessee, Literary Association inviting Melville to lecture:

We . . . are instructed to tender you the earnest invitation of our Society to address them at whatever time during the coming Fall or Winter as may best suit your convenience. We are anxious that it is the impression with our Northern Brethren that Literary men meet with poor appreciation in the South, but we can assure you, there are many amongst us who have delightedly perused your productions, and who are eager to render personal, that charming acquaintance they have formed with you through the medium of your genial pen. Presuming that your steps have never wandered this far West, we indulge the hope that this opportunity of seeing our portion of the Union and our forms of society will induce you to accept the invitation.[54]

To this call Melville responded with a lecture entitled "Roman Statuary." A cousin, Henry Gansevoort, commented upon Melville's choice of subject: "His forte is narration or description in other words a wild, bold word painting—When he essays philosophy he seeks to ascend by waxen wings from his proper sphere only to find his mind dazzled his wings melted and his fall mortifying—" [55] There is no record of what Clarksville thought of statuary. A Boston journal, however, thought that its audience "would have preferred something more modern and personal"; Cleveland blamed the "prevailing *practicality* of pioneer society" which renders them "destitute of that cultivation of nature and taste necessary to a fine and general appreciation of Art" for the lecture's meager attendance. A Charlestown, Massachusetts, paper reported that "Mr. Melville's fault was . . . in the selection of his subject . . . No man could reasonably hope to interest a common audience upon such a subject." Rochester agreed: "The audience generally, were

<hr>

[54] *Log*, II, 583.   [55] *Log*, II, 585.

disappointed; and we think that the lecturer erred in his choice of a theme." [56]

Melville began his second lecture season with a talk entitled "South Seas." The *Berkshire County Eagle* reported that it was in "the style of Mr. Melville's best books, quaint, simple and polished; redolent of the spicy odors of the South Seas, and sparkling with original thoughts." The cousin who had been critical of the first lecture subject reported of the second: "It was in Cousin Hermans true vein. He was emphatically himself, and the lecture was to me like a quantity tied together—of his vivid and colloquial sketches." Melville himself seemed either not to notice the difference between the reception of the two lecture subjects, or not to care. In answer to an inquiry about his lectures from a prospective client he answered simply that he had two lectures, "The South Seas" and "Statues in Rome." [57]

Obviously there was a large element in Melville's obscurity and failure that was not culturally determined, but self-determined. And the sources of what was self-willed in Melville's failure, like the sources of what was self-willed in Dickens's extraordinary success, must be looked for not in their cultures, but in their lives.

[56] *Log*, II, 586, 589, 592, 593.   [57] *Log*, II, 597, 601, 602.

CHAPTER FOUR

CHARLES DICKENS

I BIOGRAPHICAL

John Dickens was the son of servants. He himself rose out of the servant rank into the petty civil service through the patronage of his parents' employer, Lord Crewe; and he solidified his status in the middle class by marrying the sister of a fellow clerk in the Navy Pay Office. His eldest son and second child was the novelist Charles Dickens.

Gifted and precocious, Charles was clearly his father's favorite. From the time that he was about five until he was nine, the Dickenses lived comfortably in Chatham, near Rochester. Charles remembered long walks with his father past Gad's Hill Place, the home he would eventually buy; he remembered his father setting him on tables to show off the little boy's talent for singing and story telling before friends; he remembered school; he remembered listening to other children playing outside while he stayed indoors, reading "as if for life." But now began the calamity that was to darken the next few years of Dickens's childhood with a despair that he would never forget, and to which he would return, in different ways, in novel after novel.

Good-natured and expansive, John Dickens was spending more than he could afford, and when he moved his family to London it was to a "mean small tenement" next door to a washerwoman. In London his financial difficulties led to his imprisonment for debt. Meanwhile, Charles suffered the loss of his parents' care, the loss of schooling, and the loss of status. He became a "poor little drudge" at home and at last, for wages of six or seven shillings a week, he became a drudge in a blacking warehouse. Two themes run through his heartbroken recollections of that time: the loss of his education; the dread of losing caste. When he wrote of "all that he had lost" in losing Chatham, it was principally his education that he meant: "What would I have given . . . to have been sent back to any other school, to have been taught something anywhere!" Until he was forced to sell them, only the books his father had bought and kept in the "blessed room" in Chatham had kept alive his "hope for something beyond that place." [1] When his mother devised a fruitless scheme for making money by opening a school for the children of colonial nabobs, Charles hoped that if it succeeded "perhaps even I might go to school myself." [2] Of the time in the blacking warehouse—a period of about six months—he wondered in tones that convey his brooding anguish how it could have been that he, "a child of singular abilities," was not sent to "any common school." And his bitterest indictment of his parents was that they were all this time "quite satisfied. They could hardly have been more so if I had been twenty years of age, distinguished at a grammar school, and going to Cambridge." [3] The loss of the education that was to have permitted him to become a distinguished man; the horror of poverty which was also the terror of loss of class: these were the two sides of the nightmare.

I know I do not exaggerate, unconsciously and unintentionally, the scantiness of my resources and the difficulties of my life. I

[1] John Forster, *The Life of Charles Dickens*, 3 vols. (Philadelphia, 1897), I, 36, 29. Referred to hereafter as *Life*.

[2] *Life*, I, 43.   [3] *Life*, I, 51.

know that if a shilling or so were given me by any one, I spent it in a dinner or a tea. I know that I worked, from morning to night, with common men and boys, a shabby child. . . . I know that I have lounged about the streets, insufficiently and unsatisfactorily fed. I know that, but for the mercy of God, I might easily have been, for any care that was taken of me, a little robber or a little vagabond.[4]

The place to which declassing may ultimately lead is revealed in the last sentence—the criminal underworld from which there is literally no return. In the nineteenth century even more than in our own, there was a mortal fear in this connection. The chasm between the criminal class and the middle was bridgeable in one direction only.

Even in the warehouse world, the child clung to his class status: he was still the "young gentleman." But in such company the signs and even the memory of his education and therefore of his gentility would, he feared, quickly leave him; indeed, he could feel them slipping away. His worst suffering came when he watched his sister Fanny receive a prize at the Royal Academy of Music where she was a scholarship student. When he thought how he himself "was beyond the reach of all such honorable emulation and success the tears ran down my face. I felt as if my heart were rent. I prayed, when I went to bed that night, to be lifted out of the humiliation and neglect in which I was. I never had suffered so much before." [5]

Less than a year later John Dickens was released from prison through a legacy left him by his mother, and almost inadvertently released Charles from his prison in the warehouse. "I do not write resentfully or angrily," Dickens wrote, in words that ring with resentment and anger, "but I never afterwards forgot, I never shall forget, I never can forget, that my mother was warm for my being sent back." [6]

---

[4] *Life,* I, 57.   [5] *Life,* I, 66.   [6] *Life,* I, 68.

The nightmare ended thus abruptly, bringing with it a "relief so strange that it was like oppression." Dickens was twelve years old when he entered Wellington House Academy, and his education was resumed.

Concerning the father's imprisonment in the Marshalsea and the son's in the warehouse, the family placed a taboo of silence that never was lifted. Charles—a boy overflowing with high spirits—attended school for two years more and then his formal education ended forever. In later years Dickens would occasionally imitate, "good humouredly" according to his friend and biographer John Forster, his father's response to questions about the education of his famous son.

"Pray, Mr. Dickens, where was your son educated?"
"Why, indeed, sir—ha!ha!—he may be said to have educated himself."

And a schoolmate at Wellington House commented that as far as education went, Dickens "was quite a self-made man." [7]

John Dickens found his son a clerkship in an attorney's office; from there, Charles followed his father into the world of shorthand reporting and journalism. By 1834 he was top reporter for the *Morning Chronicle* in which he had begun to publish the Boz sketches. At about this time Dickens began paying his father's new debts, referring to his father's incorrigible looseness with money as "the damnable shadow" cast over his life. [8] A year later, not yet twenty-three years old, he was earning more than his father had ever done as a government clerk. From about this time on, he would assume responsibility for his father until John Dickens died. In 1836 *Pickwick* began to come out, and

[7] *Life,* I, 89, 83.
[8] Edgar Johnson, *Charles Dickens: His Tragedy and Triumph* (New York, 1952), p. 98.

Dickens leaped to fame. But a dozen years later he wrote that "famous and caressed and happy" as he then was, in his dreams he still often wandered back to that time of his life when his world seemed suddenly to have ended.[9]

In the agony of those years of neglect and abandonment, Forster wrote, Dickens himself "used to find, at extreme points in his life, the explanation of himself." [10] Dickens seems to have meant, Forster is saying, that he located in that time the source of those extremes of mood or emotion for which he could find *no* explanation; that he attributed to those experiences what was unexplained, and inexplicable even to himself, in his character. Those years, Forster wrote, had set Dickens's will, had made him rely upon himself alone, had given him "a cold isolation of self-reliance." What they had done, in effect, was to make him suppress in himself that part of his father which had allowed such calamity to overtake the child. In the fragment of autobiography in which he attempts to understand those days, Dickens returns again and again to his father's betrayal of him in an effort to understand how the tender father who had loved and nursed and been proud of him could also have abandoned him. In the list of his father's faults and virtues which he drew up in the autobiographical fragment, two faults cancel out all of the virtues: "ease of temper" and "straitness of means." And it is those two inadequacies— poverty and lack of will power—which Dickens himself determined he would never yield to. His extraordinary need for order and dominance, which everyone who knew him felt, was an expression of his fear of the disorder and ruin which helpless dependence upon others can bring about. That those two traits of his father's, laxness with money, weakness of will, were present in him, however repressed, Forster attests:

9 *Life*, I, 53.   10 *Life*, I, 72.

[Dickens] had otherwise, underneath his exterior of a singular precision, method, and strictly orderly arrangement in all things . . . something in common with those eager, impetuous, somewhat overbearing natures, that rush at existence without heeding the cost of it.

To this observation, Forster appends a footnote:

Anything more completely opposed [than Dickens himself] to the Micawber type could hardly be conceived, and yet there were moments (really and truly only moments) when the fancy would arise that if the conditions of his life had been reversed, something of a vagabond existence . . . might have supervened. It would have been an unspeakable misery to him, but it might have come nevertheless. The question of hereditary transmission had a curious attraction for him, and considerations connected with it were frequently present to his mind. Of a youth who had fallen into a father's weaknesses without the possibility of having himself observed them for imitation, he thus wrote on one occasion: "It suggests the strangest considerations as to which of our own failings we are really responsible, and as to which of them we cannot quite reasonably hold ourselves to be so." [11]

Forster has connected John Dickens's two failings—ease of temper and straitness of means—both with Micawber and with Dickens himself. And as the above passage reveals, Dickens has done so too. In another place Dickens wrote of the "wayward and unsettled feeling which is part (I suppose) of the tenure on which one holds an imaginative life." This feeling he had "often only kept down by riding over it like a dragoon." [12] He had had to ride down the wayward and unsettled feeling in order not to be like his father, and in the struggle itself—which is to say, in his ambivalence concerning the traits which were like his father's and his fear of giving into them—he located the source not only of his success, but of his creative gift. In another sense, Dickens founded his strength upon his father's weakness.

[11] *Life*, III, 179–80.   [12] *Life*, III, 187.

Had his father been stronger, there would have been less need for the son to have been strong; the less strong, hence, the less disciplined and creative, the son would have been. On several levels, then, Dickens built what was best and strongest and most "gifted" in himself on what had been weakness in his father; and so his ambivalence toward his father rested on several levels at least.

Thus Dickens's self-reliance was in part the other side of an overwhelming fear of dependence. He hung onto his own will as if for life; he was self-made because, reliant upon others, he feared that he would be undone. Behind all these fears lay his father's old betrayal of him. But the anger consequent upon the fear was complicated by his love for his father, and by the memory of his father's love for and pride in him. And it was further complicated, as we have seen earlier, by a strong and widely held social ambivalence toward self-creation. These things produced in Dickens immense personal ambivalence toward his own power and will. Only when he was in a position of power was he safe; but his very power dramatized his father's weakness and further defeated him; and any display of his own power defeated his father in himself. Finally, his very fear of becoming too much like his father was one source of his enormous strength; in part it was by defeating his father in himself that he developed such power over himself, over his art, and over the world.

These two fears—of poverty and of lack of will power— are generally shared by people of precarious social standing and little means who wish to rise in the world. If they let go of any of their advantages—having nothing else to fall back upon—they will drop back into the pit of the lower class. The vices traditionally attributed by the well-to-do to the laboring class ever since the rise of capitalism and the Protestant ethic, the sins that the industrious middle class in particular had always accused it of, were laziness and moral laxity, indigence and crime. These were precisely the failings that the child Dickens feared he might become guilty of: "I know that, but for the mercy of God, I might easily have been, for any care that was taken of me, a little robber or a little vagabond." [13] They were the crimes which his father's neglect had exposed him to and from which, once committed, no escape was possible. Here again, the structure of Dickens's emotional identity resembles that of the successful parvenu, the bourgeois hero.

In less extreme form, the forces which in these ways shaped Dickens shaped a large part of the nineteenth-century middle class. Much of the middle-class world was taking fears very similar to Dickens's—fear of the implacable opposition of landed, traditional interests to its rising power and to its very life—and turning them into strengths: into conscience and moral rectitude, into industriousness, frugality, energy, self-reliance and self-help. And like Dickens, too, the middle-class world was ambivalent toward its own aggressive energy; especially, it was ambivalent toward one object of its aggression—the class which God had placed above it as parents are placed above children, the aristocracy and the landed gentry. Like Dickens, the rising middle class had to break through the old, rigid social exclusions, and to defeat the monopoly of landed power and the power of privilege, in order to survive. In its ambivalence toward what it had been forced to do, it acted often to protect the very persons and class to which it had been opposed during its upward struggle by adopting their values, by internalizing their contempt for itself, and finally by selling out of the bourgeois world and buying into theirs. In all these things, Dickens was like the most mobile portion of the middle class and it in turn was like Dickens. He ex-

[13] *Life,* I, 57.

pressed, because he had himself experienced, the psychic struggle behind the social revolution that the new middle class was waging against and with the gentry.

II DAVID COPPERFIELD

In *The Personal History, Adventures, Experiences, and Observations of David Copperfield* Dickens used many of the experiences of his own personal history and turned them into public history. He told his own story—the progress of a novelist—changing it for various reasons: for concealment, for narrative and dramatic effect. He also changed it in the service of his culture; in order to turn himself into a hero of his time.

There is a change in the novel after David's rescue by his great aunt and the resumption of his childhood, and the change has to do with Dickens's conception of his hero and the kind of heroic tradition of which he is a part. Many readers have noticed that the magic of the first quarter of the novel is in part the magic of fairy tale: that the early chapters are full of wicked stepparents and good fairies, of testings and trials and heart-stopping rescues. But these chapters have more than the trappings of fairy tale; they have the ideology of fairy tale too, the ideology of the pre-industrial world. David's early life follows the pattern of the lives of mythic and fairy tale heroes which are built around an aristocratic and patriarchal ideal in which a young man neither makes nor finds himself, but seeks his fortune and finds his father, or seeking his father, finds a fortune—for they turn out to be the same. He finds the wealth and position that are truly his; all he must do is prove that he is the king's son by means of a mark, by means of his courage, by means of his gentleness, and the powers of the air will protect him and lead him to the inheritance that has been waiting for him all along. But if this is an ideal of a golden age, it is also the ideal of childhood; the nursery is our remnant of the golden age when the riches of love and ease did not have to be earned, but came to us as our birth-right.

In turning the story of David's childhood into a myth of the pre-industrial world, Dickens was not being anachronistic: the psyche keeps no time. He was being true to the family romance which sees every father and mother as king and queen, and children as little princes, cherished or disinherited, loved or betrayed and abandoned. In a sense, David grows up with the world—or the world with David. His childhood is England's pre-industrial past; his youth is his initiation into the modern world; his maturity is his acceptance of the terms of the industrial world through his own effort and hard work. But David's childhood, like Dickens's own, was broken into by the modern world too soon—and one is reminded that even the story of the child as prince is based upon certain social and economic conditions: that behind the fairy godmothers, the kings and queens, there were coffers filled with gold and silver; and that outside the palace walls were poor folk, laboring hinds, and little robbers and little vagabonds. This Dickens never forgets, and the magic of the early chapters of *David Copperfield* is grounded in social and economic realities as well as upon psychological truths.

The greatest shift between the first quarter of the novel and the rest—the part before David's reinstatement in school and after—is in its concept of the heroic. The child David is a hero in the old, pre-industrial tradition. His quest is to find his father, his name, and his father's legacy to him. The adult David is a modern, bourgeois hero. Dickens seems to feel that the older myth is truer to childhood than the newer, truer to the feelings of childhood, and truer to the legitimate expectations of childhood. Dickens himself, when he talked about it, ascribed his adult strength and will and success to the bleak years of his parents' betrayal of him, as did David Copperfield. But in the novel we see the real source of the child's survival of his childhood trials as well as of the adult's overcoming of his adult trials. The child David survives the warehouse, the neglect and loneliness of his life in London, and his terrifying trek to Dover, because of his happier infancy. The magic spell that protects David on the road to Dover—the memory of his mother's "girlish beauty that I recollected so well and loved so much"—was woven in his infancy, and David's strength is derived from the loving remembrance of a cherished childhood, not from the sorrows of abandonment.

Judging from Dickens's fragmentary autobiography, his own mother, busy with child-bearing and rearing, very early ceased to be his principal protector. It was therefore his father's betrayal which seemed to have impressed him most deeply, because it was upon his father's pride in him that he had most heavily relied. Dickens remembered, too, that when his father at last rescued him from the blacking warehouse, his mother was "warm" for sending him back. And again and again it is to his father's betrayal of him that Dickens returned, trying to account for it in various ways, as we have seen. In *David Copperfield* he returns to the theme of a father's betrayal and abandonment of his son by means of David's various surrogate fathers, who are all partial portraits of John Dickens, and who betray David in various ways and to varying degrees. But Dickens cannot deal directly with a father's betrayal of his son in *David Copperfield* since David has never had a father.

It is not necessary to either of the heroic concepts in *David Copperfield*—the pre-industrial or the bourgeois—that the hero be fatherless. One therefore feels that Dickens had a personal reason for giving David no father; that he did not want to face too directly his ambivalence toward his own father through David's feelings for his. Whatever cruelty or neglect or stupidity is practised upon David by his surrogate fathers—by Murdstone, Micawber, Mr. Dick—they are not true paternal cruelties. And in whatever ways David has to surpass and supersede these surrogate fathers in order to become a successful man, it is not his actual father whom he surpasses and supersedes. In these ways he protects his father. On the other hand, whatever strengths David may have derived from a strong or loving father are denied him too—and so he owes his strength, his success, his fame, to no man. In this sense, he can magnify his own achievement; he can seem to have created himself.

The early part of *David Copperfield* shows Dickens normalizing his life in accordance with traditional English values; the latter part, which tells of the development of David's adult career, shows Dickens making his life conform to the ideal of the modern folk hero and the new values of the middle class. Samuel Smiles mitigated the success of his basically self-made engineers and industrialists by attaching them firmly to their fathers; and successful Victorian businessmen tended to do the same. They often first traced their success to their parents' training and consent, and then they used their business success to buy their way into the gentry, as a kind of rewriting of the past; almost as an attempt to assert that they did not rise *to* wealth but *out* of wealth. Dickens does precisely these things in *David Copperfield*. The two extremes of Dickens's life—the poverty and the power—are lopped off in the novel. David has less far to travel on the road to success than Dickens had, and he travels less far along it. Beginning life firmly entrenched in the middle class rather than in a precarious borderline between it and poverty, his success is far less spectacular than Dickens's was. David was thus able to identify himself more closely with his father than Dickens could do, while still facing his own success.

David was born into the minor gentry; we know this from the title of the novel. He is David Copperfield the Younger of Blunderstone Rookery—that is, he bears his father's name and lives on his father's land. He is deprived of his patrimony by his mother's weakness of character and her second husband's hatred of him. It is Murdstone's hatred of David much more than his desire for David's money which makes him attempt to deprive David of caste; he dislikes him so much that he stops his education and sets him to work as a "little laboring hind in the service of Murdstone and Grinby." Here David works with boys who are themselves of the lowest rank of society, whose fathers are laborers—bargemen and watermen. And David's fear, like Dickens's, is that he will sink to their level, or lower. "I know that I worked from morning until night, with common men and boys, a shabby child. . . . I know that, but for the mercy of God, I might easily have been, for any care that was taken of me, a little robber or a little vagabond." After some time David forms a "desperate resolution." He will find his only living relative, a paternal great-aunt, and throw himself upon her mercy. When he presents himself to Aunt Betsey, he recites a list of grievances which are significant in themselves and in their order of mounting outrage: "I am David Copperfield, of Blunderstone, in Suffolk—where you came, on the night when I was born, and saw my dear mama. I have been very unhappy since she died, I have been slighted, and taught nothing, and thrown upon myself, and put to work not fit for me" (Ch. 13). He was hated, denied his father's legacy, taught nothing, abandoned, and finally declassed or put to work beneath his station.

Aunt Betsey is David's only living link with his father. And like Murdstone and Micawber and Mr. Dick, she is, in a sense, another of David's surrogate fathers. She is strangely masculine: a woman, but head of a family; married, but using her own name, as men do; and dressing and looking altogether more like a man than like a woman. Betsey's sexual identity is at least ambiguous. David sees her first "wearing a gardening pocket like a toll-man's apron, and carrying a great knife," and he repeatedly describes her in masculine terms:

My aunt was a tall, hard-featured lady, but by no means ill-looking. There was an inflexibility in her face, in her voice, in her gait and carriage, amply sufficient to account for the effect she had made upon a gentle creature like my mother, but her features were rather handsome than otherwise, though unbending and austere. . . . Her dress was of a lavender colour, and perfectly neat, but scantily made, as if she desired to be as little encumbered as possible. I remember that I thought it, in form, more like a riding-habit with the superfluous skirt cut off, than anything else. She wore at her side a gentleman's gold watch, if I might judge from its size and make, with an appropriate chain and seals; she had some linen at her throat not unlike a shirt-collar, and things at her wrists like little shirt-wristbands. (Ch. 13)

It is she who restores David to his proper sphere; she who sends him back to school, as Dickens's father did him. In a sense she is David's most satisfactory "father," as much an ideal father as an ideal fairy-godmother. Why is it a woman who is the link with David's father?

All we know about David's real father is that he was a gentleman, that he did not have to work, and that he was good to his wife. We also know that David feels that he has harmed this good father; that the "doors of our house were—almost cruelly" locked against his grave. David feels that it is he himself who has locked the doors against his father in order to take possession of his father's wife. And to punish himself for this, the child's fantasy creates an avenging father, who exacts punishment upon his son for his wish. The avenging father is Murdstone, who rises from under the wronged father's gravestone. For this reason, Murdstone harms David wilfully; wilfully brings the horrors of the warehouse upon David as Dickens's father unwillingly had done. "I think Mr. Murdstone's means were straitened at about this time, but it is to little purpose. He could not bear me, and in putting me from him, he tried, as I believe, to put away the notion that I had any claim upon him—and succeeded" (Ch. 10).

One of John Dickens's reasons for forgetting his son's claim upon him—"straitened means"—has been assigned to Murdstone and immediately withdrawn as being insufficient cause. In the other details of behavior that Murdstone shares with John Dickens, one begins to see a pattern and a motive emerging which shed a different light upon John Dickens's betrayal of his son than that which Dickens provides in the autobiographical fragment. There is a scene in which Murdstone stands David up before his friends to provide them with entertainment, and although it is entertainment at the child's expense, it is reminiscent of John Dickens's showing off of his little son before friends. That is, Dickens attributes to Murdstone John Dickens's pride in himself, only reinterpreted as masked dislike; and the dislike is derived from rivalry over the child's mother.

Rivalry for the love of Clara Copperfield is the source of Murdstone's dislike of David, and of David's of him. Murdstone is paying David back for the love Clara feels for her son, as David very clearly perceives. In another sense, David's own conscience has conjured up Murdstone from under his father's gravestone to punish him for having successfully taken his real—his dead—father's place. Dickens returned many times to the theme of fathers who neglect or harm or destroy their sons, explaining their behavior in various ways. In *David Copperfield* he transforms the father into a stepfather, and locates the source of his hatred in sexual rivalry for the mother. The closeness of some of the details to certain details in Dickens's own life suggest that Dickens had found another source—besides "straitness of means and ease of temper"—for what had seemed to him, as a child and as a man, behavior more easily grounded upon hatred than upon love and pride. It is John Dickens's pride in his young son which Dickens here transforms into Murdstone's seeming pride in David. At the moment when Murdstone is about to consign David to his hell in the warehouse, the moment after his friend Quinion, through whose agency David will go to Murdstone and Grinby's asks what is being done with the boy, Murdstone gives David a strange, ambiguous look: "That old, double look was on me for a moment, and then his eye darkened with a frown, as it turned, in its aversion, elsewhere." The double look represents the father's duplicity—his apparent protectiveness which masks his real hostility. It is an important moment in itself, but it is even more important in its echo from a happier time. In the light of his present perception, David reinterprets the past, and discovers that his stepfather had always meant him harm; that the love and protection he had once promised had always been a sham, had in fact been masked hatred. The "double look" hearkens back to David's first excursion with Murdstone, in the happy days before his mother's remarriage, when Murdstone set the boy to entertain his friends (among them Quinion) in the same way that John Dickens must have exhibited his own "sharp" little boy. It was on that day that David first noticed the double look. "He had that kind of shallow black eye—I want a better word to express an eye that has not depth in it to be looked into—which, when it is abstracted, seems, from some peculiarity of light, to be disfigured, for a moment at a time, by a cast" (Ch. 2). The jollity of their day turned around David, whom his future stepfather calls Brooks of Sheffield because "Somebody's sharp."

There was much laughter at this, and Mr. Quinion said he would ring the bell for some sherry in which to drink to Brooks. This he did, and, when the wine came, he made me have a little, with a biscuit, and, before I drank it, stand up and say, "Confusion to Brooks of Sheffield!" The toast was received with great applause, and such hearty laughter that it made me laugh too, at which they laughed the more. In short, we quite enjoyed ourselves. (Ch. 2)

It was perhaps in some such way as this that Dickens himself read back meaning into his father's old pride in him, and so explained the apparent outward hostility of his father's later behavior.

Micawber is one side of John Dickens, the improvident, optimistic side, which had abnegated the proper duties of a father; and David is, significantly, Micawber's boarder, not son. Indeed, in the time of his financial troubles John Dickens treated his "very small and not-over-particularly-taken-care-of boy," as Dickens once described himself, more like a confidential friend than like a young son. The evil stepfather Murdstone is that side of the father powerful enough to protect a child, and therefore morally culpable for having cast him off. Mr. Dick is the side of John Dickens which was entirely helpless and foolish, Murdstone's opposite in kindness as well as in strength. It is the evil father alone who is related to the beautiful young mother, and he is related in some way to David's guilty possession of that mother. A connection is made between sexuality and danger which will recur later on in the novel. Whenever sexual love is at issue, death and punishment are not far away. All these unsatisfactory father figures represent Dickens's continuing attempt to understand his father, and to understand him in relation to himself—especially in relation to his own abandonment. Aunt Betsey is also a father figure, but one who, being a woman, is not a rival for his mother's love. Above all, she is a father figure who can protect David from the implications of his own self-creation.

In the sense that Betsey gives David back his patrimony she stands in place of his father. But when she loses all her money, and he must make his own fortune; when he becomes richer than she and must support her; then it is not a father whom he supersedes and supports and protects, but only a woman. She is thus able to protect David from the implications of his own success—the necessary supersedence of his father in order to make himself. Most important, she protects him from the guilt attendant upon that super- sedence by *requiring* it of him. He must make his own for- tune not only for his sake but for hers, for she is now only a dependent woman. Betsey's function in *David Copperfield* becomes clearer when she is compared with her counterpart in *Great Expectations,* Miss Havisham. Like Betsey, Miss Ha- visham has been abandoned by the man she loved; like Bet- sey, she raises a girl to avenge her sex; like Betsey, she is rich and eccentric. Like Betsey she plays the role of fairy godmother to the hero. But in *David Copperfield,* the god- mother is truly a good fairy; in *Great Expectations,* she is a false one, and only deludes Pip into thinking that she means him well. Pip believes—mistakenly—that Miss Havisham is the source of his change in fortune. But Pip is bitterly and deliberately disappointed in his expectations. In the sun- shine of David's world, reality always turns out to be better than appearance; but Pip's reality turns out to be immeasur- ably worse, especially in the matter of Miss Havisham's du- plicity as to the source of Pip's fortune. Aunt Betsey's chief function in relation to David is to stand in place of a father to him so that when the time comes when David must surpass and supersede his father, it is only a woman whom he is superseding—and in the Victorian world, such super- sedence is of no consequence. But when Miss Havisham steps aside, Pip is left facing the ex-convict, Magwitch. Miss Havisham thus does not serve to protect the hero from the consequences of his own ambition but to punish, expose, and humiliate him by means of his expectations, especially by means of his father.

Once David has been adopted by his aunt he feels that he

has made "another beginning." But he has actually returned to the old beginning; retreated, for a time, from
harsh economic reality back into the fairy world of his earliest childhood. There he remains until his aunt loses her
money and he is finally and forever expelled from paradise
and set to work. During this time Aunt Betsey, like a good
parent, prepares David for what is to come. She begins to
shed her fairy-tale characteristics and to represent instead
the real world—the modern, striving, middle-class world.
First she educates him so that he may be made "happy and
useful"; and then she outlines a morality for him to follow.
She wants him to be

"A fine, firm fellow, with a will of your own. With resolution. . . .
With determination. With character, Trot. With strength of character that is not to be influenced, except on good reason, by anybody, or anything. That's what I want you to be. That's what your
father and mother might have been, Heaven knows, and been the
better for it. . . . That you may begin, in a small way, to have a
reliance upon yourself, and to act for yourself." (Ch. 19)

She is training him to be what his father was not—strong-
willed and self-reliant. She is giving him her sanction, which
is really his father's sanction, to suppress his father's traits
in himself. Moreover, she is initiating him into the middle-
class ethic of self-reliance, self-trust, self-help.

David is not yet ready for these lessons, and the profession he chooses while still protected by his aunt's money is
one that is pointedly useless. Steerforth explains just how
anachronistic the profession of proctoring is:

"What *is* a proctor, Steerforth?" said I.
"Why, he is a sort of monkish attorney," replied Steerforth. "He
is, to some faded courts held in Doctors' Commons—lazy old nook
near St. Paul's Churchyard—what solicitors are to the courts of
law and equity. He is a functionary whose existence, in the natural
course of things, would have terminated about two hundred years
ago. I can tell you best what he is by telling you what Doctors'

Commons is. It's a little out-of-the-way place, where they administer what is called ecclesiastical law, and play all kinds of tricks with obsolete old monsters of acts of Parliament, which three-fourths of the world know nothing about, and the other fourth supposes to have been dug up, in a fossil state, in the days of the Edwards. . . . On the whole, I would recommend you to take to Doctors' Commons kindly, David. They plume themselves on their gentility there . . ." (Ch. 23)

In exactly the oppostite spirit from the one which is characteristic of his maturity, David passively enters that world, "did not feel indisposed" toward it. It is this mood of ease and pleasure which David associates with his love for Dora—a privileged, paradisiacal mood: "What an idle time! What an unsubstantial, happy, foolish time! Of all the times of mine that Time has in his grip, there is none that in one retrospection I can smile at half so much, and think of half so tenderly" (Ch. 33). These are the feelings of a golden age when idleness was sanctioned by God, when love was free from guilt. When Betsey tells David that his patrimony is lost, he is plunged back, suddenly, into the memory of the warehouse and to the lessons of that time. Now he must turn "the painful discipline of [his] younger days to account, by going to work with a resolute and steady heart." He is thrown out of the idleness of Doctors' Commons and enters the life of journalism and Parliamentary debating— moved from the golden age into the iron.

In his description of his mastery of shorthand reporting we meet the new David, the striving, competitive, bourgeois hero with the self-trust, courage, earnestness, and industriousness to overcome all obstacles in order to become successful:

I feel as if it were not for me to record, even though this manuscript is intended for no eyes but mine, how hard I worked at that tremendous shorthand, and all improvement appertaining to it, in my sense of responsibility to Dora and her aunts. I will only add to what I have already written of my perseverance at this time of my life, and of a patient and continuous energy which then began to be matured within me, and which I know to be the strong part of my character, if it have any strength at all, that there, on looking back, I find the source of my success. I have been very fortunate in worldly matters; many men have worked much harder, and not succeeded half so well, but I never could have done what I have done, without the habits of punctuality, order, and diligence, without the determination to concentrate myself on one object at a time, no matter how quickly its successor should come upon its heels, which I then formed. . . . My meaning simply is that whatever I have tried to do in life, I have tried with all my heart to do well, that whatever I have devoted myself to, I have devoted myself to completely, that in great aims and in small, I have always been thoroughly in earnest. I have never believed it possible that any natural or improved ability can claim immunity from the companionship of the steady, plain, hard-working qualities, and hope to gain its end. There is no such thing as such fulfillment on this earth. Some happy talent, and some fortunate opportunity, may form the two sides of the ladder on which some men mount, but the rounds of that ladder must be made of stuff to stand wear and tear, and there is no substitute for thoroughgoing, ardent, and sincere earnestness. (Ch. 42)

This is after paradise indeed; nothing comes of itself, neither love nor money; everything is earned, and hard-earned. Here are the middle-class virtues, the rules for success, self-consciously and seriously expounded. And when David has become a successful novelist, he describes the labor of authorship in very much the same terms as this. The same virtues that made of him a successful shorthand reporter made him a successful novelist.

I laboured hard at my book, without allowing it to interfere with the punctual discharge of my newspaper duties, and it came out and was very successful. I was not stunned by the praise which sounded in my ears, notwithstanding that I was keenly alive to it, and thought better of my own performance, I have little doubt, than anybody else did. It has always been in my observation of human nature that a man who has any good reason to believe in himself never flourishes himself before the faces of other people in order that they may believe in him. For this reason, I retained my modesty in very self-respect, and the more praise I got, the more I tried to deserve it. . . . Having some foundation for believing, by this time, that nature and accident had made me an author, I pursued my vocation with confidence. Without such assurance I should certainly have left it alone, and bestowed my energy on some other endeavour. I should have tried to find out what nature and accident really had made me, and to be that, and nothing else. (Ch. 48)

Again, the virtues of the early industrial world are expounded: hard work, punctuality, success. Again, the work of art does not require a different milieu or a different ethic from the work of business. And still later on, in David's last description of himself as a novelist, he again locates the source of his strength in his childhood tragedy which is finally apotheosized as his rebirth into the industrial age, with all the industrial and industrious virtues he then learned. Here, too, is the socialization of the individual will which, while practising it, quieted David's—and Dickens's—guilt about his own success.

[Agnes] knew (she said) how such a nature as mine would turn affliction to good. She knew how trial and emotion would exalt and strengthen it. She was sure that in my every purpose I should gain a firmer and a higher tendency, through the grief I had undergone. She who so gloried in my fame, and so looked forward to its augmentation, well knew that I would labour on. She knew that in me, sorrow could not be weakness, but must be strength. As the endurance of my childish days had done its part to make me what I was, so greater calamities would nerve me on, to be yet better than I was, and so, as they had taught me, would I teach others. (Ch. 58)

Here is the final apotheosis of "labour," "affliction," "grief," and "sorrow" into an active social force. It was the aspect of his art that Dickens felt was a force for good and progress in the world which mitigated in his own mind his enormous personal success. That Dickens felt the need for such mitigation is evident in the suppression of his own immense personal will in his fictional hero. Although any of David's descriptions of his practice of his craft might have been applied by Dickens to himself, his own indomitable will is absent from David's character. David said about his career as a shorthand reporter: "I have tamed that savage stenographic mystery. I make a respectable income by it. I am in high repute for my accomplishment in all pertaining to that art, and am joined with eleven others in reporting the debates in Parliament for a Morning Newspaper" (Ch. 43). Dickens wrote about the analogous period in his own life that he "went at it with a determination to overcome all the difficulties, which fairly lifted me up into that newspaper life, and floated me away over a hundred men's heads." [14] The difference between the two descriptions is in the amount of revealed will; here and throughout *David Copperfield* the determination and will which were so great a part of Dickens's character are subdued and normalized. The determination not to be victimized, which David feels very strongly in childhood and which Dickens felt throughout his life, does not appear at all as a motive for success in David's adult life. It is not a sufficiently socialized motive; furthermore, it is faintly shameful, a mode of "selfishness" which Dickens obviously did not feel to be heroic. In very young manhood, David's motives for success stem almost entirely from love: from loving gratitude to his aunt; above all, from his adoration of Dora which, although slightly silly, is perfectly respectable. Later, under the influence of the high-minded Agnes, his motive for desiring success becomes social and ethical, and David's personal will almost entirely disappears. For David does not entirely share Dickens's social or cultural dilemma: he is not an imposter in the genteel world, as Dickens sometimes felt that he was. Da-

[14] *Life,* 1, 47.

vid's father had not been declassed and sent to prison and rescued through a servant's legacy. David's world is not built on the terror that he may after all be self-made, for David has received the sanction of the past, the laying on of hands from father to son.

Again, these deviations from Dickens's own life are made in the service of his culture, as well as in the service of his own psychic needs. They are made in part to avoid his own supersedence of his father, his own defeat of his father in himself, and the guilt attendant upon such supersedence and defeat in a novel dealing with his own triumphant success as a novelist and with the sources of that success. Dickens succeeds in turning David's will into the will to help others. But there is a residue of guilt remaining still in David's feelings about his success in relation to his father which is revealed in the ambiguity of Dickens's treatment of David's two marriages. The old guilt David had felt for his childish possession of his mother was exorcised, as we have seen, through Murdstone's cruel punishment of him; but that it was only partly exorcised is proved by the fact that it is played out again, this time more heavily masked and hidden even from David. It shows itself not in his relationships with his surrogate fathers but with his two wives, Dora and Agnes.

After the blissful first year, David begins to refer to his marriage to Dora as "the mistaken impulse of an undisciplined heart." The phrase "undisciplined heart" is repeated over and over again, always in association with Dora. David's old warehouse experience, on the other hand, he refers to as the "painful discipline of my younger days." ("What I had to do was to turn the painful discipline of my younger days to account, by going to work with a resolute and steady heart.") He ends a long disquisition on the kind of work habits and "earnestness" this discipline had taught him by saying, "How much of the practice I have just reduced to precept, I owe to Agnes, I will not repeat here. My narrative proceeds to Agnes, with a thankful love." Thus Agnes is associated with the disciplined heart; Dora with lack of discipline. What does discipline really mean applied to the "heart"—that is, to love?

Annie Strong, who invented the phrase, says that when she loved her handsome young cousin her heart was undisciplined, but that her decrepit old husband is the object of her disciplined affection. The difference is clearly centered upon sexuality. If David moves from undisciplined to disciplined love as he moves from Dora to Agnes, he is therefore moving from sexuality to some "higher" form of love. It is with no idle gesture that the angelic Agnes is always pointing upward: "Ever pointing upward, Agnes, ever leading me to something better, ever directing me to higher things!" The raised hand is a directional signal—a warning off the flesh; but it is also a chastisement. Discipline is often a form of punishment.

In one sense, Agnes is David's reward for having lived through marriage with Dora, and the overt reason for Dora's death is to free David to marry the well-earned Agnes. Dora has bequeathed Agnes to her husband as the deserved successor of the child-wife:

"Dearest husband!" said Agnes, "Now that I may call you by that name, I have one thing more to tell you."
"Let me hear it, love."
"It grows out of the night when Dora died. She sent you for me."
"She did."
"She told me that she left me something. Can you think what it was? . . . She told me that she made a last request to me, and left me a last charge."
"And it was—"
"That only I would occupy this vacant place."
And Agnes laid her head upon my breast, and wept, and I wept with her, though we were so happy. (Ch. 62)

In the sense that Dora has bequeathed Agnes to David, she is rewarding him; this is the overt meaning of the bequest.

But in the sense that Dora has ordered Agnes as her successor, David is being punished—this is the hidden meaning. Agnes is David's discipliner or punisher, and he is weeping not only out of happiness. But what is David being punished for?

On one level, perhaps the most important, Dora is Clara Copperfield come back to life. The beautiful child-wife is another incarnation of the beautiful child-mother; she is even guarded by the same dragon, Miss Murdstone. But an adult David can defeat dragons, and David succeeds in consummating his marriage with his child-wife. By marrying his mother through marrying Dora, David is at last able to take his father's place in his mother's bed, and so he becomes guilty of fantasy-incest. The child who feared that he had killed his father in order to win his mother was punished by being exiled from his little kingdom by Murdstone, the fearsome, guilt-born incarnation of the murdered father. The man who possesses his mother in the form of Dora is punished for his fantasy-incest by seeing his young wife actually waste away and die. He is made to pay further for this heart incest by being given to Agnes, the discipliner or punisher of the undisciplined heart. In fact, the very word "incest" is derived from a Sanscrit word signifying "undisciplined" or "unpunished." [15] The word "incest" is an archaic form of the word "unchaste," and the meaning of the verb chaste is "to correct or amend by discipline." The

[15] Ernest Jones, "Psychoanalysis and Folklore," in *Jubilee Congress of the Folklore Society: Papers and Transactions* (London, 1930), pp. 22–37. The entire passage from the Jones article is applicable here: "It is perhaps the outstanding discovery attaching to the name of Freud that every young child goes through a stage of intense incestuous attachment which leaves an ineffaceable mark on all its later development. In connection with it two invariable reactions occur, fear, hate, and, soon afterwards, guilt. The dread of punishment, as distinct from the normal fear of punishment or enmity, is in the unconscious always associated with this primary theme, whatever be the context in which it occurs consciously. The sense of sin is born in connection with incest wishes, all sin is apprehended as incest by the unconscious, and therefore all guilt and moral punishment remain throughout life inextricably intertwined with these primary ideas. *The very word 'incest' is derived from a Sanscrit word signifying 'undisciplined,' 'unpunished.'* " [My italics.]

deeper meaning of the phrase "undisciplined heart" is now clear: it means "unchaste heart" or "incestuous heart." The disciplined heart, then, is the chaste heart; and as David's love for his first wife was implicitly unchaste and incestuous, his punishment is his second wife, who is both chaste and punishing. And in back of incest lurks, of course, parricide. Before the child can sleep with his mother he must kill his father, as David all along feared that he had done, both as a child and as a man. It is thus, ultimately, the crime of parricide for which David pays by his marriage to Agnes who, in a less ambiguous form, will reappear in *Great Expectations* as the terribly "disciplining" Estella.

The two sources of David's guilt, both relating to his father—his childhood desire for his mother and his adult desire for security, success, and dominance—are almost impossible to separate from one another; indeed, they exist in a causal relationship. David's fantasies create their own realities, and his reality sustains and fulfills his prophetic fantasies. His guilt about his father's exclusion from the ecstatic parlour of his infancy and from his mother's bedroom, within which David himself sleeps, creates the avenging stepfather, Murdstone. The now flesh-and-blood Murdstone expells David from paradise and throws him into the real hell of the nineteenth-century laboring class. From the conditions of the real world Dickens fashions adequate symbols for his hero's inner life; the child's world is to the adult's as the golden age was to the industrial age, as we have seen; and the pathos of the declassed gentleman's son is the pathos of all mistreated children—the pathos of all the world's rightful little princes denied the kingdom of their parents' loving care.

But the symbols do not remain adequate in David's adult life, primarily because Dickens does not face David's adult inner life with clarity. Nor does he permit David to do so. David is protected from the knowledge of his own ambition by having the goal of romantic love substituted for the will

to succeed and dominate; protected from the emotional injuries of the warehouse experience by the intervention of a
"new beginning" which, we are told, obliterates the other
childhood; protected from facing his father's defeat in his
own success through the intervention of a woman, Aunt
Betsey. He is protected in the service of a fairly uncritical
acceptance of certain values of his culture, and it is the very
uncriticalness of Dickens's acceptance of these values which
makes David often sound, in his rather crass celebrations of
the bourgeois virtues, like a page from Samuel Smiles.

In 1851, a year after *David Copperfield* was published,
John Dickens died. His death caused Dickens to reconsider
the relations between fathers and sons, and especially of the
sons' responsibilities toward their fathers, at the same time
that his intellectual maturing was causing him to reappraise
the relations of individuals to society, and especially of society's responsibilities toward its individual members. The
older Dickens grew, the "better man" he thought his father
to have been—the worse, perhaps, himself. The older he
grew, the worse he found society to be in all its political,
economic, and social manifestations—the more innocent,
therefore, individual men and women caught helplessly in
its meshes. In his consideration of the relationship of English institutions to individual Englishmen, his understanding and his heart immeasurably deepened during
these years. In his consideration of sons in relation to their
fathers, his understanding seemed to rigidify and his heart
to suffer a constriction: in its infinite compassion, to find
less and less pity and understanding for sons, and least of
all for his father's son, for himself.

III GREAT EXPECTATIONS

Dickens had had more than his usual difficulty in selecting a name for David Copperfield. His first discarded name
was David Mag; and "Mag" turned up eleven years later in

Great Expectations as the first syllable of Magwitch's name. In *Great Expectations* Dickens was consciously returning to the themes of his earlier autobiographical novel—returning, that is to say, to the themes of his own life. "To be quite sure I had fallen into no unconscious repetitions," he wrote to Forster, "I read David Copperfield again the other day, and was affected by it to a degree you would hardly believe." [16] However much affected he was, Pip, his new hero, turned out to be an entirely different child and man from David.

David Copperfield is the story of a posthumous boy child living in paradisiacal bliss with his young mother until a stepfather—whom the boy thinks of as in some way his dead father's avenging spirit—displaces him from his mother's side first by sending him away to school and then, after his mother's death, by claiming his property and setting him to work in a warehouse as a common laborer. After much unhappiness, David sets out on a dangerous journey to find his father's aunt, who adopts him and sends him back to school, thus allowing him to resume, for a time, his happier childhood. Several years later this aunt loses all her money and David must enter the world of competitive wage-earning. He works very hard and eventually becomes a successful novelist. His first wife is a beautiful and loving child; his second wife an inspiration and a guide. With her and with their children, David lives happily ever after.

Great Expectations is about an orphan child, Pip, who is born to a blacksmith's forge but is raised to gentility by a transported convict for whom the boy once stole some food. Unaware of their true source, Pip ascribes his great expectations to a rich, half-mad recluse whose adopted daughter,

---

[16] *Life*, III, 362–63.

brought up to wreak revenge upon all men, he loves, and whom he expects to have bestowed upon him at the same uncertain future time when Miss Havisham will reveal herself as his benefactress. Awaiting these events, the now grown-up Pip lives idly and unhappily in London until the convict, Magwitch, comes home and reveals himself. At first repelled by him, Pip learns to love Magwitch, who is recaptured, thus forfeiting Pip's inheritance, and dies. After a nearly fatal illness, Pip learns to hate his own snobbish ingratitude to the blacksmith who was a father to him. He can marry neither of the women he loves, both of whom have married other men, and so leaves England for a number of years in order to become a clerk and then a partner in a small business, with no expectations now but those that may come to him through hard work.

David Copperfield's story spans two worlds: it moves from the innocent, leisured, unearned happiness of childhood to the work and experience of the fallen, adult world. David's expulsion from paradise occurs when his guilty conscience raises Murdstone from out of his father's grave. This happens to him when he is about the same age Pip is when he comes to consciousness in the graveyard. As David's awakening conscience created Murdstone, Pip's creates Magwitch, Pip becomes aware of himself, and at once the convict appears.

Like *David Copperfield*, then, *Great Expectations* opens with the birth of the hero; with the birth of the consciousness of his own identity, and with the birth, too, of his conscience. There is no paradisiacal world in *Great Expectations*, even for children: no time before the knowledge of good and evil, no time before the necessity to work. We are all born into a fallen world, but it is the privilege of childhood—it was the privilege of David's childhood—not to know it. In *Great Expectations*, every child is born into this knowledge—not Pip alone, but Joe and Biddy and Estella and Magwitch—not because that is right, but because it is so—or so it seems to Pip. Pip imagines only his dead brothers to be perfectly idle, "born on their backs with their hands in their trouser pockets." And he describes even their deaths in terms of work: they "gave up trying to get a living exceedingly early in that universal struggle." Mrs. Joe's repeated complaint that she has brought Pip up "by hand" is therefore not an idle one. Labor and the knowledge of good and evil are the results of the explusion from paradise; and work and conscience are two of the central preoccupations of *Great Expectations*.

An ideal of leisure is left over from Eden, from an aristocratic age, and from childhood—children are permitted to play. It is an ideal, too, of Christmas which, of all holidays, is the one meant especially for pleasure, for rest, and for innocent play—the holiday which celebrates the childhood of the world. *Great Expectations* opens on Christmas Eve, although hardly any notice is taken of it, and Pip is put to work in the same sentence which announces the day: "It was Christmas Eve, and I had to stir the pudding for next day with a copper-stick, from seven to eight by the Dutch clock." From seven to eight—the religion of work keeps time to the rhythm of the machine that measures time. It is significant that Pip is called to Miss Havisham's to play, and that he cannot. The first conversation between Pip and Miss Havisham turns upon notions of play and work.

"Who is it?" said the lady at the table.
"Pip, ma'am."
"Pip?"
"Mr. Pumblechook's boy, ma'am. Come—to play." . . .
"I am tired," said Miss Havisham. "I want diversion, and I have done with men and women. Play."

I think it will be conceded by my most disputatious reader that she could hardly have directed an unfortunate boy to do anything in the wide world more difficult to be done under the circumstances.

"I sometimes have sick fancies," she went on, "and I have a sick fancy that I want to see some play. There, there!" with an impatient movement of the fingers of her right hand; "play, play, play!"

For a moment, with the fear of my sister's working me before my eyes, I had a desperate idea of starting round the room in the assumed character of Mr. Pumblechook's chaise-cart. . . . (Ch. 8)

Pip's word for his sister's punishment is "working"; and the play he thinks of, before giving it up, is that of a work-horse. Miss Havisham sends for Estella who immediately perceives that a boy who must labor cannot also play. Miss Havisham tells her to play cards with Pip and Estella protests "With this boy! Why, he is a common labouring-boy! . . . What do you play, boy?"

"Nothing but Beggar my Neighbour, miss."
"Beggar him," said Miss Havisham to Estella. So we sat down to cards. (Ch. 8)

In such play there is no leisure and no joy. Playing cards has become merely a class insignia to prove that one need not work. And the name of the game casts ironic light on the source of the money which supports the upper class in its leisure.

Miss Havisham has stopped the clocks at Satis House; the brewery is empty; she does no work. But she does not play, either. Too near to madness to be free enough to play, too mad to know where her fantasies end and reality begins, her fantasies are not play, but deadly earnest. Pip instantly understands this, and he protects her with preposterous lies from his sister and from Pumblechook, who have no understanding of fantasy or of play. Pip is himself too unhealthy—too "worked"—to see these compassionate lies as play, but adds them to his already overburdened conscience as another sin. The absence of work as something positive, as "a state of complete harmony between man and nature and between man and man," the true Biblical meaning of

rest according to Erich Fromm, is not possible at Miss Havisham's any more than play is there possible.[17] The very garden is ruined, and in its ruin it has not returned to nature
but turned into rubbish, to rank weeds and a "wilderness of
empty casks." And the "pale young gentleman" whom Pip
encounters in the garden proposes to Pip not that they play
but that they fight, and fight according to the rules. "Laws
of the game!" he cries. "Regular rules!" Everywhere the
tempo of life is relentless, and everywhere it is the tempo of
the machine.

If there is no joy in play, there is even less in work. Pip
has always been at work; but when he is finally bound over
to the forge he feels himself "bound" indeed. His indentures are a form of imprisonment—partly because, historically, they turn him into a temporary slave. Pumblechook
reminds him that as an apprentice he is "liable to imprisonment if [he] played at cards, drank strong liquors, kept late
hours or bad company, or indulged in other vagaries . . ."
This list reminds one that this fallen world has fallen into
Puritanism. The Puritan ethic opposed itself to sport and
play, according to Max Weber, because they were a "means
for the spontaneous expression of undisciplined impulses
. . ." "Impulsive enjoyment of life," the Puritans feared,
"leads away . . . from work in a calling." [18]

Pip must learn to accept the conditions of the fallen
world—must learn to *wish* to earn his own bread. But his
earliest dream was to be a "gentleman," and when Jaggers
tells him that this is to come true he exclaims "My dream
was out; my wild fancy was surpassed by sober reality; Miss
Havisham was going to make my fortune on a grand scale."
His is a world where fancy is dead earnest, however, and
dreams have the force of reality, and so Pip must reform his

[17] Erich Fromm, *The Forgotten Language* (New York, 1957), p. 244.
[18] Max Weber, *The Protestant Ethic and the Spirit of Capitalism* (New York, 1958), p.
168.

dreams. At the end of the novel, when Pip has finally accepted the conditions of the fallen world, when he has given up his expectations, what is it that he has become? A small capitalist, a partner in the firm of Clarriker & Co. of which he says "I must not leave it to be supposed that we were ever a great house, or that we made mints of money. We were not in a grand way of business, but we had a good name, and worked for our profits, and did very well" (Ch. 58). That is, he has accepted entirely the Puritan ethic—a just reward for honest toil.

In *David Copperfield* Dickens minimized his own immense success as he minimized the will behind it, but he did not try to obliterate either the will or the success. Toward the end of the novel Agnes says to David, "Your growing reputation and success enlarge your power of doing good, and if *I* could spare my brother . . . perhaps the time could not." Here success and power are very clearly linked to each other, although they are socialized into a source of good in the world. Still later in the novel David himself says, "I had advanced in fame and fortune," and finally, "I hear the roar of many voices, not indifferent to me . . ." David, like Pip, worked for his profits, but his profits were immensely greater than Pip's—"fame and fortune," "success" and "power." Between the writing of *David Copperfield* and *Great Expectations* Dickens had changed his mind about the value of these things. Perhaps he had found them empty triumphs. Perhaps he had decided, too, that fame, fortune, success, and power are potentially criminal. It is not the hero who enjoys them in *Great Expectations;* in fact it is the hero's task—and it is a heroic one—to learn to wish to give them up.

Jaggers has "power"; he is the most powerful person in *Great Expectations.* He has power over the underworld, power within the system of criminal justice, power over Magwitch and Miss Havisham, over Estella and her mother,

especially over Pip. He is Pip's "guardian"—something between a father and a god. He is a father without any emotional tie, without love; he is a god without mercy. In fact he
can be seen as a very primitive sort of local god, who pre-
sides over a certain place (here "Little Britain," which
stands, of course, for Great Britain), and who must be constantly propitiated, prayed to, and especially sacrificed
to—in cash. But sometimes the sacrifice is exacted in blood,
for he is above all a capricious god, and his worshippers are
as flies to his wanton will. He is most often indifferent, very
often wrathful, sometimes vengeful, occasionally pitiful,
never loving. He is very like the oldest personifications of
Jehovah in the earliest books of the Old Testament which
are, like *Great Expectations* itself, steeped in the mysterious
workings of an inexplicable deity. Having such power over
everyone in the novel, Jaggers is in a way the Author of
their being. In fact he has something of an author's power
over their lives, too.

Miss Havisham has "fortune"; it is her money which determined the direction of Pip's dream. In *David Copperfield*
Betsey Trotwood had some small fortune and she used it to
make her adopted son "happy and useful." In the later
novel, Miss Havisham uses her fortune to turn her adopted
daughter into an instrument of her own madness and
revenge.

And it is Magwitch, the transported convict, who has
achieved "fame" for his extravagant "success." "I've been a
sheep-farmer, stock-breeder, other trades besides, away in
the New World," he tells Pip, who answers, "I hope you
have done well." "I've done wonderful well. There's others
went out alonger me as has done well, too, but no man has
done nigh as well as me. I'm famous for it" (Ch. 39).

If *Great Expectations* has a purely social message, it is
somehow embodied in Magwitch and his money, in Pip and
his expectations of unearned wealth. The problem of Mag-

witch's money is an extremely vexed one. Beginning life as a criminal, Magwitch is transported to New South Wales where, in a sense, he is reborn. He begins life there as an honest working man and becomes very rich. Furthermore, he now has a highly respectable motive for earning money—he is repaying a debt. Principally, however, he is working out of love for a boy who is in a way his son. When he returns to England, however, the law again proclaims him a criminal, and he forfeits his money and his life. But he has learned that the daughter he had loved and long ago lost is alive; above all, he has earned the love of his "son," Pip. Some sort of equation has been set up involving money and love which is never fully balanced, partly because the two are finally unequatable quantities, partly because such equations, involving human emotions, are by their very nature ambiguous and unresolvable. But that they are very often equated is too well known to need restatement; that Dickens felt that they were equated by his society is one of the underlying themes of *Great Expectations;* but that he was himself ambivalent about their relationship is shown, I think, in the frequency with which such equations are introduced throughout the novel.

The equation of love and money has another variant in the story of Miss Havisham and Estella—which is of course obliquely related to Magwitch's story as well, since Estella is Magwitch's daughter. She is not Magwitch's heir in part because, having loved her, Magwitch "owed" her nothing. The child of criminals, Estella was rescued by a rich woman from the dire poverty which would have made her a criminal too. Miss Havisham brings Estella up to be the instrument of her own hate—and so Estella, unable either to love or to accept love, is allowed to inherit Miss Havisham's money. Here the equation has balanced itself through money, rather than through love: loss of love is recompensed by a cash gain. Estella's history is of course more complex than this—nevertheless, something resembling this equation underlies it.

Pip and his expectations are at the center of the novel and his story is the least reduceable to formulae of any sort. Embodied in Pip's expectations and their outcome is Dickens's mature attitude about the relationship of money to society in the mid-nineteenth century. Dickens in fact does find a fairly simple solution to the problem of how Pip is to earn a living—but its very simplicity, compared with the complexity of Pip's attitudes toward money throughout the novel, indicates that Dickens remained largely ambivalent and unclear about the complex problem of the just and proper distribution of money among all the members of society. But even the apparent clarity of Pip's relationship to Clarriker & Co. is not without its hidden complexities. All the money in *Great Expectations* is tied, ultimately, to the criminal Magwitch; and all of it passes through the soiled hands of Jaggers, without whose dubious "justice" society, as it exists in the novel, could not carry on its "business."

Pip is born into the laboring class. Because he is exposed to money at Miss Havisham's he begins to long for it—for unearned money, which he equates (as does almost everyone else in the novel) with being a gentleman. Soon this equation of money and gentility is further complicated by the addition of love—Pip falls in love with Miss Havisham's ward who is a lady and therefore unattainable to him, a common laboring boy. Suddenly everything changes. Pip comes into the expectation of money, he moves to the city (which is described almost entirely in terms of a prison, as his indentures at the forge were described as a form of imprisonment, and as his passion for Estella is as well). He becomes a useless idler—therefore, according to his own definition, a gentleman; and he is Estella's suitor. But Magwitch's return and eventual capture lose Pip his fortune and therefore (he believes) his right to Estella. Brokenhearted, broken in health, broken financially, he is rescued by Joe. By now Pip's heart has been disciplined. Giving up his desire for unearned money, giving up all hope of sexual fulfillment, he becomes a clerk in a small firm and there earns, presumably, precisely his "just" reward. In *The Dickens World* Humphry House says that Dickens's ideal businessmen "represent a stage of capitalist development in which the capitalist is normally an active member of a fairly small firm . . . a man whose work bears a relation to his income similar to that of professional people to theirs. Such people as this (together with the professionals) were the basis of the 'respectable' middle class that Dickens represented." [19]

Dickens's other qualification for the respectable middle-class gentleman was that he be educated; and Pip has been educated, too. He has received only two "goods" from Magwitch's money—his education, and his access to respectable employment in the middle class. The education has been a free gift to him from Magwitch, who had specified to Jaggers that Pip was to be educated as a gentleman. In this sense, Magwitch is Pip's father, since a father's gifts do not have to be earned but are the child's right. Pip loses Magwitch's fortune because no man has a right, in Dickens's view, to an unearned income. But the way in which he has earned access to employment in the middle class shows how very complex was Dickens's understanding of the inextricable interdependence of the worlds of crime and respectable business, of criminals and just men, of money and virtue, of poverty and vice. Pip earned his place in the just firm of Clarriker & Co. by the one virtuous deed he did with Magwitch's money—the purchase of Herbert's partnership. And he bought the partnership with the money he had "earned" in childhood by his service to the escaped convict—a service which was itself a criminal act, a theft. The circle is an end-

[19] Humphry House, *The Dickens World* (Oxford, 1960), p. 164.

less one, and Dickens does not address himself to the question of whether, in the endless interlocking links that make up the social order, even Clarriker & Co. is not somehow involved in crime, in the oppression of the poor, in beggaring its neighbors.

Until his employment by Clarriker & Co. near the end of the novel, Pip has always felt like a criminal. In his analysis of *Great Expectations,* Julian Moynahan demonstrates that the apparently will-less and powerless Pip is actually one of the most powerfully destructive persons in the novel.[20] Moynahan shows that Pip's repressed will has the power to create alter egos who commit the crimes for which Pip, thus reasonably, feels guilty. In this way, Moynahan explains what otherwise seems to him to be Pip's inordinate sense of guilt. Orlick the killer, Drummle the brutal wife-beater, act for Pip and out of Pip; they are manifestations of Pip's repressed will. But Pip himself explicitly locates two sources for his feelings of guilt: one is his ingratitude to Joe; the other, his sister's earliest treatment of him. Before he had even come to self-consciousness amongst the gravestones, he had felt guilty for not lying beneath them, guilty even for having been born. His sister treated him as if he were a criminal, and so he felt like one. This was not the fault of Pip's rising will, but of the fallen world which had denied him any childhood paradise of love. More particularly, it was the fault of his sister, Mrs. Joe.

When Magwitch tells the story of his childhood, he makes it clear that society was to blame for turning him into a criminal, and we accept his judgment. "In jail and out of jail, in jail and out of jail, in jail and out of jail," Magwitch says putting his career into a "mouthful of English."

"This is the way it was, that when I was a ragged little creetur as much to be pitied as ever I see (not that I looked in the glass, for

[20] Julian Moynahan, "The Hero's Guilt: The Case of *Great Expectations,*" *Essays in Criticism,* 10 (January, 1960), 60–79.

there warn't many insides of furnished houses known to me), I
got the name of being hardened. 'This is a terrible hardened one,'
they says to prison visitors, picking out me. 'May be said to live in
jails, this boy.' Then they looked at me, and I looked at them, and
they measured my head, some on 'em—they had better a-
measured my stomach—and others on 'em giv me tracts what I
couldn't read, and made me speeches what I couldn't unnerstand.
They always went on agen me about the devil. But what the devil
was I to do? I must put something into my stomach, mustn't I?"
(Ch. 42)

There is no sentimentality, for none is needed; there is no
sentimentality, because there is no evasion of the truth. But
when Joe Gargery tells the story of his childhood to Pip,
and especially when he draws the moral of the story, the effect is sentimental just because we feel that the true nature
of his experience is evaded; that those experiences could
not have given birth to this Joe.

"My father, Pip, he were given to drink, and when he were over-
took with drink, he hammered away at my mother most onmer-
ciful. It were a'most the only hammering he did, indeed, 'xcepting
at myself. And he hammered at me with a wigour only to be
equalled by the wigour with which he didn't hammer at his anwil.
You're a-listening and understanding, Pip?"

"Yes, Joe."

" 'Consequence, my mother and me we ran away from my father several times; and then my mother she'd go out to work, and
she'd say, 'Joe,' she'd say, 'now, please God, you shall have some
schooling, child,' and she'd put me to school. But my father were
that good in his hart that he couldn't a-bear to be without us. So,
he'd come with a most tremenjous crowd and make such a row at
the doors of the houses where we was that they used to be ob-
ligated to have no more to do with us and to give us up to him.
And then he took us home and hammered us. Which, you see,
Pip," said Joe, pausing in his meditative raking of the fire, and
looking at me, "were a drawback on my learning."

"Certainly, poor Joe!"

"Though mind you, Pip," said Joe, with a judicial touch or two
of the poker on the top bar, "rendering unto all their doo, and

maintaining equal justice betwixt man and man, my father were that good in his hart, don't you see?"

I didn't see, but I didn't say so.

"Well!" Joe pursued, "somebody must keep the pot a-biling, Pip, or the pot won't bile, don't you know?"

I saw that, and said so.

" 'Consequence, my father didn't make objections to my going to work; so I went to work at my present calling, which were his, too, if he would have followed it, and I worked tolerable hard, I assure *you*, Pip. In time I were able to keep him, and I kep him till he went off in a purple 'leptic fit. And it were my intentions to have had put upon his tombstone that whatsume'er the failings on his part, remember reader he were that good in his hart." (Ch. 7)

In this way Joe patches together the pitiful shreds of a brutal childhood in order to make them into a standard Victorian story of the dutiful son following in the footsteps of his artisan father. In fact it was Joe who supported his father, but the locution he uses turns his victimization into a privilege. Dickens, we remember, referred to his father's dependence upon him as "the damnable shadow" cast over his life. Not only does Joe forgive his father for preventing him from attending school (and we recall that Dickens's deepest sense of outrage came from his father's neglect of his schooling); he also forgives him for breaking his mother and hammering him. He drowns his proper rage in bathos. And the lesson to Pip ("You're a-listening and understanding, Pip?") is that he must do the same. Why can Magwitch see his persecutors as persecutors, while Joe must insist upon and believe in the essential goodness of his father's "hart"? Because Magwitch has been mistreated by society; Joe by his own father.

Pip over and over again locates the source of his feelings of criminal guilt in ingratitude to Joe, the man who has stood in place of a father to him. Moynahan points out that ingratitude is not a crime and finds the origins of Pip's guilt in the criminal behavior of his alter ego, Orlick. But because ingratitude does not seem a crime to Moynahan, or to us, does not mean that it did not seem one to Pip, or to Dickens. Pip's world—its work ethic, its conviction of sin, its aversion to play and games, its attitude toward parents and children—is fundamentally Puritan. And the Puritans, following Deuteronomy, considered ingratitude toward parents to be literally a crime. The Puritans of Massachusetts had written into their "Laws and Liberties" that "If a man have a stubborn or Rebellious son . . . such a son shal be put to death." [21] And the Puritans of Massachusetts were Englishmen; and England was still, in the nineteenth century, the heir of seventeenth-century Puritan attitudes. In that world view, ingratitude is a crime—above all, ingratitude toward one's father.

Magwitch calls himself Pip's "second father." "You're my son—more to me nor any son." And Pip, despite his loathing, accepts responsibility for that relationship and, ultimately, for Magwitch's life. But he does so, for once, with a remarkably clear sense of the true limits of his culpability. He does not condemn his own aversion to the convict; and he ascribes his overcoming of the aversion in part to a change in the convict himself—to a "softening" in Magwitch. There is an odd equality uniting the ignorant convict and the educated gentleman, far greater than that between Joe and Pip, despite their shared early lives. Pip and Magwitch share an equality more like that of brothers than of father and son, a fraternity that increasingly approaches an identity. Moynahan showed us that Pip is not only Pip; his aggressive and sexual drives are separated out into Orlick (whose name is a rearrangement of the syllables which make up "killer") and Bentley Drummle. On a much more conscious level, he is also Magwitch; or Magwitch is Pip. In

[21] Quoted in George Lee Haskins, *Law and Authority in Early Massachusetts* (New York, 1960), p. 146. See also Deuteronomy xxi.18–21.

a sense, they represent two possible developments of the same seed, or pip, planted in different soils. Magwitch is what Pip might have become, without Joe to save him.

Magwitch is the child of the warehouse experience who was abandoned and is never reclaimed, cut off from any renewal of childhood, cut off from parental protection and love. Pip is the child released from the warehouse experience and saved by a loving father. Both Pip and Magwitch are different from David in that they are born into the warehouse, that is, into a fallen world. But Magwitch, unlike Pip, goes the whole route that David once feared he would travel; goes from being a little laboring hind to becoming a "little robber" and a "little vagabond." "Tramping, begging, thieving, working sometimes when I could—though that warn't as often as you may think, till you put the question whether you would ha' been over-ready to give me work yourselves—a bit of a poacher, a bit of a labourer, a bit of a waggoner, a bit of most things that don't pay and lead to trouble, I got to be a man" (Ch. 42).

Dickens's understanding of the nature of the warehouse experience obviously has changed between *David Copperfield* and *Great Expectations*. To David, being a little laboring hind was tantamount to being a robber and a vagabond; but to Magwitch and therefore to Pip, the difference is immense— not merely a class apart, but a world apart. To labor at no matter what calling is to be a part of the living world; to have no labor to do, to be a criminal, is to be thrown out of the social order altogether and into the underworld; to become an object rather than a person, an object which can be locked up, picked up, carted off, thrown out. To be a robber is to *be* robbed of all the rights of citizenship and of humanity.

Magwitch is the victim of society for whom society has no work, and who must therefore become a criminal. In *David Copperfield*, Dickens could not see beyond his own, and David's, snobbish disdain of the laboring class. But in *Great Ex-pectations* he has moved from snobbery and self-pity to a criticism of society itself. He no longer disdains either labor or the laboring class; he has moved his horror from the condition of having to labor in the laboring class to the social conditions that prevent one from being able to find any labor to do. Magwitch's beginnings are almost identical to Pip's: "I first become aware of myself down in Essex a-thieving turnips for my living. Summun had run away from me—a man—a tinker—and he'd took the fire with him, and left me wery cold." It was this which Pip was spared. A tinker had run away from Magwitch, and taken the fire with him; but the blacksmith comes to Pip, to try to soften his sister's upbringing by hand, and brings the child to the fire at the forge. "When I offered to your sister to keep company [Joe tells Pip], and to be asked in church, at such times as she was willing and ready to come to the forge, I said to her, 'And bring the poor little child. God bless the poor little child,' I said to your sister, 'there's room for *him* at the forge!' " (Ch. 7). Joe Gargery, then, is the father who rescues Pip from the part of Magwitch's fate which was the absence of a father's love—and who rescues him by means of the blacksmith's forge.

Sometime after his father's death, Dickens said of him, "The longer I live, the better man I think him." [22] In the fragment of autobiography written long before John Dick-ens's death, Dickens blamed his father's neglect of himself on two faults, ease of temper and straitness of means, and as long as his father lived, Dickens continued to be annoyed by the consequences of these traits. But in *Great Expectations* ease of temper and straitness of means are not incompatible with great virtue. They are, in fact, attributes of the saintly man who was Pip's first father, Joe Gargery. Joe's passivity

22 *Life*, III, 32.

and poverty in no way harm the child, while his love and protection save him. Dickens seems to be saying now that the blacking warehouse was not the central crisis of his childhood as the blacksmith's forge was not the central crisis of Pip's. The crisis of Pip's childhood has nothing to do with money or class, but with love. Pip's hell is the absence of love, and it is the sister who takes the place of his mother, and who bears his mother's name, who makes that hell. In some such way as this, Dickens reassessed the events of his own past to make his father his deliverer, his mother his would-be destroyer. The central issue in this reconsideration of his past is, again, the source of love. It was love that saved Pip from Magwitch's fate: his father's love, Joe Gargery's.

So bent is Dickens upon making the principal source of Pip's guilt his criminal ingratitude toward Joe that he entirely removes David's reason for feeling guilty toward his father—the desire he felt for possession of his mother. Pip cannot feel desire for Mrs. Joe, whose embattled bosom, stuck full of pins, repels the advance of all living creatures. It is Joe's second wife who is like Clara Copperfield; who is young and gentle and loving; and who is the object of Orlick's (and therefore of Pip's) lust. But Pip represses his lust for Biddy—is not guilty of even fantasy incest with the woman who will become Joe's wife. And toward the child of Biddy and Joe, the child who is also named Pip, the older Pip will see Joe free to become a better father—the father Mrs. Joe prevented Joe from being to him.

Pip's redemption begins when he realizes that he must renounce Magwitch's money partly because it now seems to him criminal to live on unearned money, partly because, in some narrowly moralistic way, Pip doesn't deserve it. But there is a sense in which Pip doesn't get Magwitch's money because he deserves something better than a criminal's patrimony. By means of Pip's association with Magwitch,

Dickens is reassessing once more the blacking warehouse experience. It is through Magwitch and Magwitch's money that Pip is dragged to the borderline of the criminal underworld, and Pip must reject both the man and his money in order to remain a "gentleman." What Pip has *earned* from Magwitch, Dickens seems to feel, is the right to respectable employment. What he has been given unearned, again, is an education. And it is this education which was Magwitch's gift to him, along with the unearned love which was Joe's gift, which together "fathered" Pip, and which made of him a true gentleman.

Dickens's insistence upon Pip's responsibility for what he could not altogether help causes Pip to hide much of his rage from himself. And it is this buried aggression which gives birth to the monsters Orlick and Drummle. By giving Pip's rage objective rather than subjective shape, by turning the elements at war within him into Drummle and Orlick, rather than allowing them to result in ambivalence and ir-resolution and conflict within Pip himself, Dickens avoids the kind of psychological understanding which would lead to forgiveness rather than to punishment; refuses the relative judgment in favor of the absolute. Orlick and Drummle are absolute villains and may be eliminated: they die out of Pip during the nearly fatal illness from which Pip at last emerges worthy of forgiveness because he has literally killed in himself the unworthy, criminal elements. He has at last turned his last shred of rage at the injustices done him against himself alone; and the result of this is his life-long depression. The lesson the post-Freudian world has learned is that by airing and recognizing the sources of aggression or anger or pain, one can bypass punishment and still exorcise the demon. This is precisely what Victorian social re-formers were discovering in their research into the origins of crime and poverty, into sanitation and education and the conditions of labor. But this kind of understanding Dickens, like most other Victorians, had for social problems only.

Between the composition of *David Copperfield* and *Great Expectations,* Dickens's criticism of society had immeasurably deepened. The "little gentleman" David unthinkingly and completely accepted the fact that to be a gentleman's son was intrinsically nobler than to be a bargeman's, or a waterman's, or a blacksmith's. Pip must unlearn this. Casting aside class snobbery, he casts aside, too, all artificial distinctions between man and man; only souls, stripped of tailoring, are weighed. The criminal is not more guilty than the complacent citizen; all of society is implicated in the hunger and pain of each of its abandoned children. That is the meaning of the broad shaft of light which links the thirty-two condemned criminals and their mortal judge in "absolute equality." And for these victims of society Dickens has more compassion than he has for Pip, who must teach himself that although a victim, he is also a kind of criminal; that although he could have been nothing more than what he was made, he is yet responsible for what he is.

The Victorian Age was one of searching social criticism and radical reform. But in its attitudes towards human relationships of a personal kind, especially relationships within the family, it was an age of tenacious clinging to old values, an age of many pieties and much cant, and of much evasion of the truth of human feelings. In this, Dickens was a child of his age. His compassionate understanding of society's victims, especially of its child victims, was unsurpassed; as was his compassionate judgment of children who were victimized by their parents. But his abused children are almost always unaccountably passive in their suffering. Not only may they never rise in rebellion; they often seem scarcely to rise to any consciousness of their mistreatment. In order to protect parents from their children's retaliation, often even from their understanding of the harm that has been done them, Dickens strikes the children blind, or deaf, or idiot; or else with such an overwhelming habit of self-sacrifice that we hardly believe that they are human. Thus Joe Gargery scarcely knows that he was ever the victim of a sadistic father, while Magwitch sees very clearly that he himself is as much the victim of his own criminality as society is.

The patriarchal ideal that still controlled English feeling about the family, and especially about the relationship between fathers and sons, was an ideal and a discipline which, as G. M. Young said, was "not yet enlightened—or distracted—by . . . psychological explorations." [23] And this was true at a time when other traditional sources of authority were being questioned and disputed by the whole tenor of life in the nineteenth century, and by many of the great social critics, Dickens among them. But the personal, familial pieties affected social behavior as well as behavior within the family. That is, the nineteenth century offered to the middle ranks of Englishmen the opportunity to be whatever their intelligence and their enterprise and their labor could make them—as long as what they became did not too overtly threaten the central piety of the age—the traditional structure of the family and, above all, the traditional authority of the father.

The reformed Pip is reformed in his social thinking, not in his understanding of himself. He has called back all of his aggressive energies and directed them against himself instead of against others. The aggression remains, but it is now directed inward. He is therefore depressed—that is the dominant mood of both endings of the novel—but he is also, therefore, non-aggressive. His fear of achieving any dominance, his guilt at having superseded his fathers—Joe and Magwitch—will not allow him to exploit his true gifts; will not even let him find out what nature and accident had

[23] Young, *Victorian England: Portrait of an Age* (New York, 1964), p. 152.

meant him to be, and be that, and nothing else. But neither will it allow him to exploit any other human being. Pip's state of mind, in a highly exaggerated form, is expressive of one side of the English mind in the mid-nineteenth century. The disjunction between what society offered the individual of courage and energy and will, and what the social ideal, still tied to a traditional, patriarchal morality, permitted him to take, colored England of the mid-century. To the normal cultural manifestation of Pip's highly exacerbated state of mind, G. M. Young attributed England's moral soundness: "It was the good fortune of England [in these years] to confront a sudden access of power, prosperity, and knowledge, with a solidly grounded code of duty and self-restraint." [24]

Out of the traditional morality of England's past, the belief that "conventional behaviour grounded on a traditional creed was enough to satisfy all right demands of humanity," in conflict with the immensely increasing opportunity of England's present, came the characteristic bent of the Victorian mind. Out of the traditional morality of Joe's forge, in conflict with Pip's modern, liberated imagination, comes the characteristic bent of Pip's mind. And Joe, and Joe's forge, and Pip's changing attitude toward them, are representative of John Dickens, and of the blacking warehouse, and of Dickens's changing assessment of them—an assessment which, in the years since the composition of *David Copperfield,* had moved yet farther in the direction of the general cultural ideal. It was an ideal which, very broadly speaking, was at once humane and retrogressive. It was humane in having broadened the range of its social sympathies not only to include men and women of all social classes, but to include the declassed as well. It was retrogressive in its personal ideal, basing individual morality upon the repression

[24] *Victorian England,* p. 100.

of certain feelings relating to family and sexual life, and sealing those repressions with the cement of guilt. But it is possible that this retrogression in individual psychology was itself partly responsible for the socially progressive temper of the time; that the social strength of Dickens's England was built upon the repression, to some degree, of each individual Englishman's personal will.

CHAPTER FIVE

HERMAN MELVILLE

I BIOGRAPHICAL

The Melville family was moving downward through the extremely mobile American social structure. Herman Melville's mother was descended from wealthy New York Dutchmen whose family names, Gansevoort and Stanwix, had become American place names. Melville's paternal grandfather had been a revolutionary war hero whose elder son was in and out of debtor's prison throughout Herman Melville's childhood and whose younger son, Melville's father, began his career as a prosperous New York merchant and importer, and died bankrupt in 1832 when Herman was twelve years old. Melville's mother then supported herself and eight children by begging from her brothers, who were also hard-pressed for money in the depression years of the 1830's; and the entire Melville-Gansevoort clan was suffering a decline throughout the period of Herman's youth. After a solid but not spectacular early success, Melville himself was to follow this pattern: constant money worries, genteel poverty, and memories of past glory.

Herman Melville was the third child and second son of Allan and Maria Melville. His father, ambitious, optimistic, socially pretentious, kept increasing his style of living between 1819, the year of Herman's birth, and 1830, when he moved his family to Albany in an effort to escape his creditors and to alleviate his wife's growing nervous depression. In New York City he had moved to three successively more fashionable and expensive homes, kept a private carriage, educated his sons in private schools, and kept a governess for his daughters. In Albany he established a fur-cap shop and factory by borrowing heavily from his father and his wife's brother, buying merchandise on credit which was never repaid. Driving himself too hard, he became ill and then mentally deranged, raving for three weeks before he died. His older brother described his death in typical Melville rhetoric: "Hope is no longer permitted of his recovery, in the opinion of the attending Physicians and indeed,—oh, how hard for a brother to say!—*I ought not to* hope it.—for,—in all human probability—he would live, *a Maniac!*" [1]

Twelve and a half years before his own death, Allan Melville had announced his second son's birth in a letter to Peter Gansevoort, his wife's older brother: "With a grateful heart I hasten to inform you of the birth of another Nephew, which joyous event occurred at ½ past 11 last night—our dear Maria displayed her accustomed fortitude in the hour of peril, & is as well as circumstances & the intense heat will admit—while the little Stranger has good lungs, sleeps well & feeds kindly, he is in truth a chopping Boy—" [2]

Peter Gansevoort was to befriend his nephew through all of his long life and to be more appreciative of his gifts than Allan Melville ever was. The oldest son, Gansevoort, brilliant and precocious, was his father's favorite. Herman was docile but dull. At seven his father described him as "very backward in speech & somewhat slow in comprehension." [3]

---

[1] Jay Leyda, *The Melville Log: A Documentary Life of Herman Melville*, 2 vols. (New York, 1951), I, 52. Hereafter referred to as *Log*.

[2] *Log*, I, 3.   [3] *Log*, I, 25.

Four years later Gansevoort was still being praised for his intelligence, while Herman was still given second place.

Gansevoort is . . . becoming a distinguished classical Scholar at the Grammar School, & is at the head of the Class in most of the English studies . . . Herman I think is making more progress than formerly, & without being a bright Scholar, he maintains a respectable standing, & would proceed further, if he could be induced to study more—being a most amiable & innocent child, I cannot find it in my heart to coerce him, especially as he seems to have chosen Commerce as a favorite pursuit, whose practical activity can well dispense with much book knowledge.[4]

Only sixteen when Allan Melville died, Gansevoort took over the new business his father had been trying to establish in Albany. But in 1837 Gansevoort, too, failed; and he was soon at home, a nervous invalid taking over a year to recover from an injured ankle. Two years later, however, when Herman set sail for the Pacific, Gansevoort was in New York City studying for the law, and when Herman returned almost four years later, he found that Gansevoort had turned his ambition toward politics. With a reputation for being a fiery orator, he was stumping the country for James K. Polk; and when Polk was elected President, the Democrats rewarded Gansevoort with a secretaryship at the American legation in London. He sailed for England in 1845 with the manuscript of Herman Melville's first novel. Harper's had rejected *Typee,* fearing that it was fiction; but Gansevoort succeeded in selling it to the London firm of John Murray, and also in interesting G. P. Putnam in putting out the American edition.

Meanwhile, Gansevoort was embarrassing the legation by his peculiar behavior, and the ambassador was trying to have him reassigned. Twenty years later, the American publisher, G. P. Putnam, remembered a dinner at which

[4] *Log,* 1, 43.

Gansevoort Melville had represented the Minister: "Replying to a formal toast, 'The President of the United States,' the Secretary [Gansevoort] electrified the diplomatic circle by a Tammany speech, winding up somewhat thus: 'I was the one who helped to place Mr. Polk where he now is, and I know that he will not *dare* to recede from 54.40!' " [5] He was both physically and mentally ill. In a pathetic letter to his brother Herman he wrote that

I sometimes fear I am gradually breaking up . . . I think I am growing phlegmatic and cold. Man stirs me not, nor woman either. My circulation is languid. My brain is dull. I neither seek to win pleasure or avoid pain. A degree of insensibility has been long stealing over me, & now seems permanently established, which, to my understanding is more akin to death than life. Selfishly speaking I never valued life much—it were impossible to value it less than I do now. The only personal desire I now have is to be out of debt.[6]

Gansevoort's own description of his illness was corroborated by that sent home by the angry Ambassador:

I confess that I have never before met with precisely his parallel; and, with a rhetorical extravagance of speech and manner, and truthlessness the most extraordinary, he is constantly doing things that I will not venture now to hint at. . . . For the last month he has been confined to his house, with what he represented to me as an affectation of the eyes, and a consequent *loss of sight!* From his physician, however, I learn that his sight is not materially affected, & that his disorder is in some degree connected with the brain, and a state of nervous derangement, which if it should now come would not surprise me. I have never seen him since he came here that he was not in a mood painfully extravagant, as to all Men & things.[7]

Both descriptions of Gansevoort's illness are strikingly reminiscent of Peter Gansevoort's account of Allan Melville's death fourteen years before:

[5] *Log*, I, 201.   [6] *Log*, I, 209.   [7] *Log*, I, 213.

He was unwell, when he last wrote to you. But persisting in giving attention to his business—He devoted himself so closely and assiduously, as to produce a state of excitement, which in a great measure robbed him of his sleep. It is but a few days since he yielded to the wishes of his friends and remained at home. The excitement however could not be allayed and yesterday he occasionally manifested an alienation of mind. Last night he became much worse—and today he presents the melancholy spectacle of a deranged man—[8]

The brilliant Gansevoort, his father's pride, was dead at the age of thirty.

At the time of his father's death, Herman Melville was twelve and a half years old. He was taken out of the Albany Academy and put to work as a clerk in a bank; three years later he was a clerk in his brother's fur-cap store and at the same time attending the Albany Classical School, from which he received a school-teacher's certification two years later. He taught in a one room country school for about six weeks, finding discipline difficult to maintain among thirty pupils, some of whom were as old as he. The next year he moved with his family to the little Hudson River town of Lansingburgh where his mother, still burdened with four unmarried daughters and eight-year-old Thomas, hoped to be able to live more cheaply. At the Lansingburgh Academy Herman studied engineering and surveying in order to find work on the still unfinished Erie Canal, but without success. That summer, at the age of nineteen, he escaped the family money worries by going to sea on a merchant ship bound for Liverpool, which would get him home in time to take over another country school in the fall. In 1840 he decided to try his luck in the West, where his uncle, Thomas Melville, was starting life afresh at the age of sixty-one; but the new life in Illinois was no more successful than the old had

[8] *Log*, I, 51.

been, and, discouraged, Herman returned home. Unable to find work on land, he again escaped to sea—this time aboard a whaling ship bound for the South Seas.

Melville reached home almost four years later to find his family in better circumstances than when he had left. Four grown-up sisters were eager to listen to his tales of South Sea adventures, and family and friends encouraged him to write them down. The finished book, *Typee,* was dedicated to Judge Lemuel Shaw, Chief Justice of Massachusetts, who had been a childhood friend of Allan Melville's, had remained a friend to his widow and children—which to the Melvilles meant that he had lent them money—and to whom Gansevoort had been in debt at the time of his death. Lemuel Shaw was to befriend Herman Melville for the rest of his life, and to partially support him as well, for in 1847, a year after *Typee* was published, Melville married Judge Shaw's only daughter. For the next ten or eleven years Melville attempted to support his wife and four children by writing, but with less and less success and more and more support from his wife's father and his mother's eldest brother, Peter Gansevoort. After 1857, Melville stopped writing prose almost entirely, and turned to poetry, which he published intermittently, mostly at his own expense, for the next twenty years. In 1863 he gave up his Berkshire farm and moved his family to New York City; and in 1866, after years of effort, he received a petty government post— Inspector of Customs in New York City at the salary of four dollars a day. In 1887 sufficient family legacies at last permitted him to retire. When he died four years later, his death was reported in a New York newspaper under the headline, "Death of a Once Popular Author":

There died yesterday at his quiet home in this city a man who, although he had done almost no literary work during the past sixteen years, was once one of the most popular writers in the United States.

Herman Melville probably reached the height of his fame about 1852, his first novel having been printed about 1847 . . . Of late years Mr. Melville—probably because he had ceased his literary activity—has fallen into a literary decline.

Probably, if the truth were known, even his own generation has long thought him dead.[9]

Melville did not leave even a fragmentary account of his childhood, and the Melville family letters were systematically destroyed by Melville himself, by his daughters, and by almost everyone into whose hands they happened to fall.[10] Nor did Melville include much childhood material in his novels. Unlike Dickens, who mined his childhood years, Melville mined his young manhood, principally the years at sea. He was interested in the hero at the moment of making himself, of consciously casting off his past, and not in the years of the parents' greatest influence on the child. But what one does not talk about is often as significant as what one does. Even in America, the child was father to the man.

The undervalued and sensitive child who was born in the shadow of a brilliant and favored older brother; who watched his father fall deeper and deeper into debt until, bankrupt, he went mad and died; and who was taken out of school and put to work in a bank at the age of twelve, obviously had much to think about—or to try to forget. And this child was to watch his brilliant older brother repeat their father's pattern. Handsome, gregarious, ambitious for success, Gansevoort, too, failed in business; and, a dozen years later, died, after a brief illness, mentally deranged and in debt. The lesson to be learned by the younger son and brother would seem to have been that it is dangerous to seek or even to desire success; that to be favored by one's father is an ambiguous, even a treacherous, blessing, since it may lead one to madness and death; that only in passivity,

[9] *Log,* II, 836.   [10] *Log,* "Preface," pp. xiii–xvi.

poverty, and obscurity, are safety. To the circumstances which had taught him these lessons Melville returned obsessively in his novels and stories.

In his novels Dickens, too, returned obsessively to the central trauma of his childhood—his neglect and abandonment. But Dickens's trauma had not had fatal consequences, and so neglect or abandonment does not prove fatal for very many of his fictional children, most of whom find surrogate parents who raise them, however inadequately, to adulthood; and once adults they are able for the most part to become parents, or at least surrogate parents, themselves. Unlike Melville, Dickens assumed that the story of a life, especially the life of a hero, necessarily includes his adult life; that childhood, however poignant and compelling, is merely a preparation for the loving, working, adult life which is to come. Inadequate as Dickens found his own father to have been, inadequate as he shows most parents to be in his novels, their inadequacy does not prevent their sons from becoming men—does not arrest them in adolescence through the fatal example of their fathers' manhood. Most of Melville's heroes *are* so arrested. In terror for their lives of becoming men and fathers, they remain perpetual sons. And because they remain sons, and the sons of fathers lost to them in death, they long for and perpetually seek their fathers, too.

The poles of Melville's ambivalence toward his father, and of his heroes toward their fathers, are thus very radically separated. Added to the son's ordinary love for his father is an extraordinary idealization of him, both because he in some way rejected his young son, and because by dying he became forever lost to him and unknowable. Added to whatever hatred born of fear the young son feels at the spectacle of his father's—to him—immense power, was his consciousness of his father's inordinate failure and impotence, and his consequent fear of becoming like his father and, like him, going mad and dying. To Melville and to his heroes, becoming a man and a father therefore presented almost insurmountable obstacles: the inordinate fear of becoming like his father forcing the son to attempt an almost total self-creation; the inordinate idealization of the father forcing the son either to defy a kind of god, or to become one—such defiance or such achievement equally impossible to sustain. If the son is a heroically aggressive hero such as Ahab or Pierre, he will challenge and assault his idealized father in an effort to become a man himself, in which case he will go mad and die. If he is a passive hero such as Redburn or Ishmael, he will be content to expose his father's impotence and failure without attempting a self-creation, in which case he will survive in safety, but impotent himself, and failed.

The story of such a hero—the story of the undervalued, disinherited, exiled son of a father at once immensely hated and immensely idealized—took symbolic form in Melville's imagination in the story of the Biblical Ishmael. Abraham had two sons, Ishmael and Isaac. God commanded Abraham to banish the illegitimate Ishmael for the sake of Isaac, who was to found a great people, God's chosen people. Exiled, Ishmael was forced to wander out into the desert while Isaac, although beloved, was not safe—was liable to be sacrificed at the behest of his father, and his father's Father. In the ancient world, however, the father was a great patriarch whom God loved, and whom he tested because of his love. And so Abraham's hand was stopped from killing his beloved son in time. But in the modern world, fathers die ambiguously raving, and favored sons are not only brought to the sacrificial altar but are killed as well—and not for love, nor for their father's or his Father's sake, but for nothing. For in the modern world God, if there is a God, sends ambiguous signs down from heaven. And only Ishmael—unloved and disinherited—survives. Not only did Melville apply this story to his own family romance, seeing his father as Abraham, Gansevoort as Isaac, and himself as Ishmael, but he saw in the configuration of Abraham, Isaac, and Ishmael a symbolic romance of America as well.

From the first, Americans had seen themselves as the descendants of Abraham and Isaac. If they kept their covenant with their Lord, He would keep His with them; if they did not they would "perishe out of the good Land." Controversy very quickly arose as to whether the Puritans, in their prosperity, were fulfilling their part of the covenant. That God was keeping His promises most Americans agreed; and Benjamin Franklin, the great myth-maker, quite rightly put his exuberant advice on achieving prosperity into the mouth of "Father Abraham." But Franklin felt that he had raised himself out of the poverty and obscurity in which he had been born only in part through God's help. In part, he had raised himself because God had *not* helped him, because his father could not help him, because his older brother, to whom he was apprenticed, beat and mistreated him. So Franklin fled Godly Boston and went to Philadelphia where, in exile like Ishmael from his father and his Father's chosen people, he created himself.

We have seen that the nineteenth-century American folk hero, unlike the English, was defined not by his occupation but by his character: he was self-made. The character of Ishmael is thus allied with one side of the American self-made man—the side which made itself not through choice but through necessity. In the *Autobiography,* Franklin's mythic retelling of his own life, the son makes himself into a success, outfathering his father. This Melville could not do, as we have seen. Yet Melville's need to make himself was very great, dictated, like Franklin's, by emotional as well as by economic necessity. Melville faced economic necessity very early because of his father's bankruptcy and early death; and this necessity was made more difficult by his family's claims to gentility which were so unsuited to Melville's rather grimly limited economic prospects. Emotionally, the self-making was forced upon him by his father's preference for his oldest son, which had the symbolic effect of orphaning the younger son; and then by his father's early death, which orphaned him in fact. But unlike Franklin and the self-made heroes who followed his model, Melville and his heroes could not make themselves into great successes. Melville's heroes are unable even to become successful adults, husbands, and fathers. What they do become, however, are witnesses of the experience of being unfathered. And as witnesses of their own unfathering they, too, are in the American grain—a grain that, since Melville's day, has risen to greater and greater visibility. Huck Finn and Nick Carraway and Jay Gatsby; beatnik and drop-out and hippy; exiles in Cuba or in Canada, on the road or in the commune; all the young men who light out for all the territories where their fathers' real or imaginary deaths have permitted them to go, or where their own inability to become fathers has forced them to go, are heirs to Melville's Ishmaels. And they, no less than Franklin's heirs, are made in America.

II REDBURN

Redburn is a fictional account of Melville's first trip abroad—the voyage he made as a common sailor aboard a merchant ship the summer he was nineteen. Gansevoort had obtained the berth for his brother, and his mother had instructed him to get Herman "everything within the range of his means that will make him comfortable." Two of his brothers and a friend of Gansevoort's saw Herman off. All of these details are changed in the novel to make the hero poorer and more forlorn than Melville himself had been. Wellingborough Redburn travels to New York all alone, without enough money even to pay his fare to the city; and all the money he has for his equipment is what he can get by selling an old hunting gun that was an older brother's. This "fowling piece," his hunting jacket, and his trousers, stylishly decorated with rows of buttons—all signs of a genteel past—either let Redburn down or get him into trouble with the crew. The gun fetches a quarter of what it is worth; his clothes are unsuitable for sailoring and earn him the contempt of his shipmates. These emblems of class must literally be thrown overboard before Redburn can fit himself for the reality of an ordinary seaman's life, where all distinction is earned, not inherited.

The issue of class is first raised in the novel's full title: *Redburn, His First Voyage. Being the Sailor Boy Confessions and Reminiscences of the Son-of-a-Gentleman in the Merchant Service.* Redburn thus immediately associates himself with his father only to dissociate himself from his father's class—the merchant sailor who is a gentleman's son obviously is not a gentleman himself. We would suspect, further, that a gentleman's son who falls out of the gentry into the class of merchant sailor will have more to forget about his genteel upbringing than to remember, if he is to survive his new lot in life.

In its fall from a patrician past, the Melville family was not typically American. But in its unfitness to guide its children by its own example, it repeated the classic American immigrant experience. The Melvilles seemed immigrants from another time. In 1826 Herman Melville's father wrote a letter of advice to a twenty-year-old nephew who was going to sea:

Endeavour to blend the graces & courtesy of the Gentleman, with the frankness & sincerity of the Sailor . . . The name you bear should also inspirit you to services of the highest estimation in private society, & to deeds of noble daring in public life; descended through a long line of respectable Ancestors, from a Scottish hero, who emblazoned by his achievements an hereditary title, which came down from remote antiquity, & who fell on Floden Field in defense of his Country's freedom; *your* great object with GOD's blessing must ever be, to preserve the Family name unsullied in social intercourse with the World, & render it conspicuous in the naval history of the Nation . . .[11]

Twelve years later, Herman Melville went to sea at the age of nineteen. In the novel he wrote about that voyage, the young man who accompanies the hero to his ship speaks in language very much like Allan Melville's, and the pretentiousness and lies of this "really honest-hearted but foolish friend" result in Redburn's being cheated out of his badly needed advance pay. Penniless, he goes without food his last day ashore, but his hunger is nothing like the grim starvation he encounters for the first time in his life in England. Before coming to Liverpool he had "never seen anything like it":

Poverty, poverty, poverty, in almost endless vistas: and want and woe staggered arm in arm along these miserable streets.
    And here, I must not omit one thing, that struck me at the time. It was the absence of negroes; who in the large towns in the "free states" of America, almost always form a considerable portion of the destitute. But in these streets, not a negro was to be seen. All were whites; and with the exception of the Irish, were natives of the soil: even Englishmen; as much Englishmen, as the dukes in the House of Lords. This conveyed a strange feeling: and more than anything else, reminded me that I was not in my own land. For *there*, such a being as a native beggar is almost unknown; and to be a born American citizen seems a guarantee against pauperism; and this, perhaps, springs from the virtue of the vote. (Ch. 41)

Redburn is naive about the "virtue of the vote" because he has no real understanding of class—no understanding that an English duke is almost as far removed from an English beggar as a white man from a negro slave in the

[11] *Log*, I, 26.

United States, and his very lack of understanding points up the contrast between his family's empty snobbery and the grim earnestness of David Copperfield's terror of poverty. The Redburns have genteel pretensions in a country where class status, unfortified by cash, means very little, and so their snobbery is merely self-congratulatory. But David's genteel birth—apparent in his accent and his manners—impresses the laboring boys amongst whom he is thrown in the wine warehouse, and earns him preferential treatment there despite the fact that his real "earnings" are not more than theirs, and are probably less.

It is clear at the beginning of *Redburn* that the failures of Redburn's father, of his family, and of his own youthful hopes, are what have driven him to sea, as it is clear at the end that what he has learned will not change the pattern of his life as far as failure is concerned. In any case, the focus of the novel is not on career or on any outward manifestation of success or failure, but on a purely existential self-discovery. In fact, Redburn can find himself only in an existential sense, since his principal discovery will be that there is nothing but the self: no legacy from the past, no meaningful paternity, no true community.

Redburn's journey, like many another, is made in order to find his father. He first thinks of going to sea because he remembers "standing with my father on the wharf when a large ship was getting under way," and because his father "had several times crossed the Atlantic." In Liverpool, he hopes to follow in his father's footsteps with the aid of a map and a guidebook which his father had once used and marked. But he cannot follow him—the city has changed too much in twenty-five years. And one has a mounting feeling that Redburn made the journey already knowing this; that a part of him at least hoped to expose his father's impotence. Melville did not have his father's very guidebook when he was in Liverpool, but bought one there like the one his father might have used. By giving Redburn his father's very guide and map, he points the finger accusingly at the father: it is he himself, and not only the dead hand of an impersonal past, who has betrayed his son.

From the very outset of the novel, one feels a certain duplicity about Redburn's quest for his father. It is a journey made not only in the spirit of respectful love, but out of resentful self-pity, too. He uses the difference between his father's past condition and his present one as grist for the mill of his anger; and loving regret gives way increasingly to what one finally feels was his hidden feeling—angry resentment:

> Yes, in this very street, thought I, nay, on this very flagging my father walked. Then I almost wept, when I looked down on my sorry apparel, and marked how the people regarded me; the men staring at so grotesque a young stranger, and the old ladies, in beaver hats and ruffles, crossing the walk a little to shun me.
>
> How differently my father must have appeared; perhaps in a blue coat, buff vest, and Hessian boots. And little did he think, that a son of his would ever visit Liverpool as a poor friendless sailor-boy. (Ch. 31)

In some places the syntax of the sentences makes it almost impossible to tell whether his pity is directed at his father or himself. "What trials and troubles he [his father] had encountered; how he had been shaken by many storms of adversity, and at last died a bankrupt. I looked at my own sorry garb, and had much ado to keep from tears" (Ch. 31).

At last Redburn admits that the guidebook is totally useless in modern-day Liverpool: "the thing that had guided the father, could not guide the son"; "Every age makes its own guidebooks, and the old ones are used for waste paper." When he finds that the ancient pool itself from which (he believes) Liverpool takes its name has been cemented over to hold the new Custom House, then resentment and self-pity give way to an almost gleeful contempt.

Well, well, Wellingborough, thought I, you had better put the book into your pocket, and carry it home to the Society of Antiquaries; it is several thousand leagues and odd furlongs behind the march of improvement. Smell its old morocco binding, Wellingborough; does it not smell somewhat mummyish? Does it not remind you of Cheops and the Catacombs? I tell you it was written before the lost books of Livy, and is cousin-german to that irrecoverably departed volume, entitled, *"The Wars of the Lord,"* quoted by Moses in the Pentateuch. Put it up, Wellingborough, put it up, my dear friend; and hereafter follow your nose throughout Liverpool; it will stick to you through thick and thin . . . (Ch. 31)

Several thousand years out of date, the father is consigned to oblivion now; but Redburn has all along suspected that this would turn out to be the case. Experience has served only to reinforce intuition, which is another way of saying that the young have nothing to learn from the past, and a good deal to forget. The young are therefore thrown continually back upon themselves; all knowledge is really self-knowledge; all fulfillment is really self-fulfillment. Redburn derives an intense, almost ecstatic gratification from this awareness, and he expresses his joy in terms similar to those which David Copperfield uses when his journey to Dover is over, and he is safe in a home again. David is happy because *his* intuition, too, has been confirmed, but it is an altogether different intuition from Redburn's: that he had a father who loved him and was worthy of his love; that the past does stretch into the present and can influence the course of the future; that a human family exists which is better than solitariness. On the night of David's reunion with his father's aunt, he meditates upon his past in the little room into which she has locked him for safekeeping.

The room was a pleasant one, at the top of the house, overlooking the sea, on which the moon was shining brilliantly. After I had said my prayers, and the candle had burnt out, I remember how I still sat looking at the moonlight on the water, as if I could hope to read my fortune in it, as in a bright book, or see my mother with her child, coming from Heaven, along that shining path, to look upon me as she had looked when I last saw her sweet face. I remember how the solemn feeling, with which at length I turned my eyes away, yielded to the sensation of gratitude and rest which the sight of the white-curtained bed—and how much more the lying softly down upon it, nestling in the snow-white sheets!— inspired. I remember how I thought of all the solitary places under the night sky where I had slept, and how I prayed that I never might be houseless any more, and never might forget the houseless. I remember how I seemed to float, then, down the melancholy glory of that track upon the sea, away into the world of dreams. (Ch. 13)

Much about civilization that Dickens cherished, and that was cherished by his culture, is contained in this passage— the intense appreciation of home and of homely comforts, of tradition, of family life, of the simple virtues which are really great moral truths; above all, the security of the individual within the circle of a family. What David has here recaptured is the bliss of his earliest memory of two pairs of outstretched arms—Clara Copperfield's and Clara Peggotty's—within whose loving embrace the child was free to grow. But Redburn's intensest pleasure comes when he is alone, encircled by the bare bowl of the sky and a "certain wonderful rising and falling of the sea." "I felt as if in a dream all the time; and when I could shut the ship out, almost thought I was in some new, fairy world, and expected to hear myself called to, out of the clear blue air, or from the depths of the deep blue sea" (Ch. 13).

The special joy of such feelings comes from the total exclusion of other people, and from the swelling of one's own consciousness to fill the entire void between earth and sky. A little later on, Redburn again describes his ecstatic pleasure in solitude, and he now attributes the feeling not only to the swelling of the self, but to a merging of the self with Nature. "Then was I first conscious of a wonderful thing in me, that responded to all the wild commotion of the outer world; and went reeling on and on with the planets in their orbits, and was lost in one delirious throb at the center of the All" (Ch. 13).

Just as the feeling of ecstatic joy that came over David in his aunt's room is in some way a memory of childhood happiness, so is Redburn's. But Redburn's feeling of wholeness comes from his feeling of reunion with Nature, not with a human family. The feeling he describes is rooted in a far earlier memory than David's, the memory of a time when, according to Freud, the infant cannot feel his own limits because he has not yet learned to "distinguish his ego from the external world as the source of the sensations flowing in upon him."

. . . originally the ego includes everything, later it separates off an external world from itself. Our present ego-feeling is . . . only a shrunken residue of a much more inclusive—indeed, an all-embracing—feeling which corresponded to a more intimate bond between the ego and the world about it. If we may assume that there are many people in whose mental life this primary ego-feeling has persisted to a greater or less degree, it would exist in them side by side with the narrower and more sharply demarcated ego-feeling of maturity, like a kind of counterpart to it. In that case, the ideational contents appropriate to it would be precisely those of limitlessness and of a bond with the universe—the . . . "oceanic" feeling.[12]

Freud associates these feelings of "limitlessness and of a bond with the universe" with the origin of a certain kind of religious sentiment which has its source not in man's need for a protecting father, but in the infantile ego-feeling just described. This feeling of a mystical bond with the universe

[12] Sigmund Freud, *Civilization and Its Discontents* (New York, 1962), pp. 14, 15.

turns up not only in Melville, but in almost every important nineteenth-century American writer. For Cooper, for Emerson, Thoreau and Whitman, for Mark Twain, the ecstatic bond with nature is a more important source of religious or quasi-religious feeling than the search for an omnipotent Father. Just as it is most characteristic of nineteenth-century American writers to seek happiness in Nature, it is most characteristic of them to seek God not in any human incarnation of a father, but in Nature itself, or in natural forces. For Melville, whose heroes *do* seek confrontation with a Father, natural forces often take the place of human or divine fathers—whales, or walls, or as in *Pierre*, rocks and mountains. For this reason the "oceanic" feeling can bring them only temporary happiness. There is a mood, Ishmael says in *Moby Dick*, in which an "absent-minded youth" may be "lulled into such an opium-like listlessness of vacant, unconscious reverie" by the "blending cadence of waves with thoughts"

that at last he loses his identity; takes the mystic ocean at his feet for the visible image of that deep, blue, bottomless soul, pervading mankind and nature; and every strange, half-seen gliding, beautiful thing that eludes him; every dimly-discovered, uprising fin of some undiscernible form, seems to him the embodiment of those elusive thoughts that only people the soul by continually flitting through it. In this enchanted mood, thy spirit ebbs away to whence it came; becomes diffused through time and space; like Cranmer's sprinkled Pantheistic ashes, forming at last a part of every shore the round globe over.

There is no life in thee, now, except that rocking life imparted by a gently rolling ship; by her, borrowed from the sea; by the sea, from the inscrutable tides of God. But while this sleep, this dream is on ye, move your foot or hand an inch; slip your hold at all; and your identity comes back in horror. (Ch. 35)

But Ishmael's dominant mood, like Ahab's, is Father-seeking. Ahab cannot rest content to lose himself in the "inscrutable tides of God." Rather, he personifies God in the inscrutable whale, and loses himself in *it*.

Emerson's famous description of what Freud calls the oceanic feeling—"I become a transparent eyeball; I am nothing; I see all; the currents of the Universal Being circulate through me; I am part or parcel of God"—was the basis of his religion, as Melville knew and in part satirized in the above passage from *Moby Dick*. This feeling could not be the basis of Melville's religion partly because it does not take into account his need for an omnipotent father. But it also does not take into account Melville's sense of tragedy—his sense that the life lived *between* the moments of ecstasy is more real than what he calls the dream of the "all."

In a letter to Hawthorne he comments upon Transcendentalism in terms which are, again, strikingly like Freud's: "This 'all' feeling, though, there is some truth in. You must often have felt it, lying on the grass on a warm summer's day. Your legs seem to send out shoots into the earth. Your hair feels like leaves upon your head. This is the *all* feeling. But what plays the mischief with the truth is that men will insist upon the universal application of a temporary feeling or opinion." In the same letter he discusses Goethe's dictum that one should *"Live in the all."*

That is to say, your separate identity is but a wretched one,—good; but get out of yourself, spread and expand yourself, and bring to yourself the tinglings of life that are felt in the flowers and the woods, that are felt in the planets Saturn and Venus, and the Fixed Stars. What nonsense! Here is a fellow with a raging toothache. "My dear boy," Goethe says to him, "you are sorely afflicted with that toothache; but you must *live in the all,* and then you will be happy!" [13]

Melville here puts his finger upon one of the central beliefs of American Transcendentalism—that life, regarded from the proper angle of vision, is basically happy; that pain, regarded from the proper angle of vision, does not exist—and recognizing it, he rejects it with scorn. For Melville was

[13] *The Letters of Herman Melville,* ed. Merrell R. Davis and William H. Gilman (New Haven, 1960), pp. 131, 130–31.

one of the few nineteenth-century American thinkers who did not confuse the search for happiness with the search for God.

In *Redburn,* Melville's preoccupation with his father ended with the proof of his death; when the hero had faced the full knowledge of his disinheritance both from his father and from the past. This knowledge was necessary to the preservation of his life. The lesson he has learned is that he must abandon the past because it has abandoned him. Redburn could not have found his way through Liverpool—that is, the world—if he had relied upon his father as his guide. And in Liverpool a young Englishman is introduced expressly to point this moral. He is another penniless gentleman's son who wants to take ship with Redburn and become an American. But he carries with him the baggage of the past—"a large mahogany [chest] which he had made to order at a furniture warehouse"—full of the rags of outworn precedents. Unable to leave his past behind, he is unfit for the future, and so dies—crushed to death between a whale and his ship. Redburn survives because he has accepted the conditions of the future by throwing the past overboard along with his father's guidebook and his father's ghost.

Although Redburn exposes his father with gusto, particularly his financial and spiritual bankruptcy, he will repeat his father's pattern of failure in his own life. When the malicious captain of his ship, still nursing a grudge against the young "son-of-a-gentleman," declares that Redburn will receive no wages at the end of his voyage—that Redburn owes *him* money—Redburn does not rebel against the injustice done him, but passively accepts it, merely "telling him that . . . I was a bankrupt, and could not pay him . . ." The last we hear of Redburn is that he has "throw[n] himself away in a whaler."

One of the expectations of American life was an endless supersedence by the future of the past. The burden put upon the sons, therefore, was to act out in their lives the proof of that expectation by soaring beyond their fathers, denying them as they create themselves. Redburn has prepared himself to supersede his father. He has carefully demonstrated, by means of this account of his first voyage, that he could not help but perceive his father's impotence and that, had he not, he could not have survived—as the young Englishman, unable to extricate himself from his past, did not. The perception alone has saved him. He will not act upon it.

The pattern of Melville's own life did not allow him to live out the American success story by leaping over his father into the endless promise of the future. Melville's father had paid for his own early success by going mad and dying, and his older brother had done the same. So Melville would not strive, but taking cover in obscurity and poverty, would live out his life against the American grain. In *Pierre,* his second autobiographical novel, Melville reverses the pattern of his hero's life, just as Dickens had done in his; Pierre seeks success where Redburn has sought failure, just as Pip accepted failure where David Copperfield has demanded success. Melville pushes his next hero deep into the American mainstream where, as Pierre Glendinning, he not only exposes his father, but acts upon that exposure. Pierre discovers that his father had all along meant him harm; had betrayed and abandoned him, the innocent and loving son. So Pierre repudiates his father. Casting him off along with his gods and all the patrimony of the past, he creates himself. But in doing so he goes mad and dies, showing that the American success story has its tragic losses, too.

At some point during his voyage Redburn says that he was a "sort of Ishmael in the ship"; and that "years after this" he found himself "a sailor in the Pacific, on board of a whaler." *Moby Dick* opens when the narrator says "Call me Ishmael." He is Wellingborough Redburn "years after"; still the deep and deeply depressed observer of life; still the passive sufferer of his Father's indifference, as the Biblical Ishmael was, and as Redburn was as well; still the survivor. But in *Moby Dick* Ishmael gives shape to his repressed will very much as Pip had done to his in *Great Expectations*. Ishmael's will creates Ahab. The disinherited, passive, wandering son creates the ambitious, furious, destructive king, who "did evil in the sight of the Lord above all that were before him."

Captain Ahab is an Isaac born into a world where there are only Ishmaels. He is a king, and he suspects that he is a king's son; but the king his Father has disappeared. He therefore demands to be sacrificed in order to prove that his father loves him, to prove that he has a father at all, to prove that the paternal gods still exist. And in his rage at his Father's treachery in running away and hiding, he will bring down his Father's whole creation, will avenge not only himself but all the world's disinherited sons: "then all collapsed, and the great shroud of the sea rolled on as it rolled five thousand years ago." Only Ishmael survives. The heroic Ahab, the man who acts upon his demonic vision, goes mad and dies; while the entirely passive Ishmael survives in safety—like the entirely passive Redburn, and like the "safe" man who told the story of Bartleby.

In *Pierre,* too, a hero will go mad and die after having extinguished, by "his own hand," all his father's house. Ahab's struggle was a cosmic allegory; Pierre's will be an allegory of Melville's life, and of America.

III PIERRE

Redburn is the poor son of a once wealthy and prominent family whose father is dead and whom "sad disappointments" have sent to sea as a common sailor. Everything that he had learned in his genteel home is useless to him on shipboard, and makes him into a kind of Ishmael among the crew; and in Liverpool he learns that guidebooks from the past, and especially his father's, are not only useless but dangerous for use in the present. Having gained this knowledge, and without otherwise enriching himself—robbed of his wages, in fact, and a self-declared bankrupt—he returns home. Along with the knowledge of his disinheritance by the past and by his father, the fact of his safe return seems to be the chief outcome of his voyage: "But yet, I, Wellingborough Redburn, chance to survive . . ." No significant actions have been taken by the hero; a voyage has happened to him, and he has passively suffered its lessons.

Pierre Glendinning is the brilliant, handsome, beloved, only son of a rich and proud widow. He is heir to an American landed estate left by his father who died after having "at intervals lowly wandered in his mind," when Pierre was twelve years old. Now nineteen, Pierre is engaged to an angelic blonde, Lucy Tartan. A mysterious dark beauty enters the neighbourhood and declares herself to be Pierre's half sister, the illegitimate daughter of Pierre's father and a French girl whom he had seduced and abandoned before his marriage. Poor and friendless, Isabel begs for Pierre's protection. If Pierre acts immediately to give his sister her rightful name, as he feels he must do, he will destroy his beloved father's reputation and his mother's faith in it. He therefore concocts a scheme which will protect father, mother, and sister, while sacrificing only himself (and incidentally Lucy). Instead of acknowledging himself Isabel's brother, he will declare himself her husband, thus protecting his parents and giving Isabel his name. He "foreknows" that his proud mother will now disinherit him—which she does, leaving his estate to a cousin whose name, Glendin-

ning Stanly, is the equivalent of Pierre Glendinning reversed. ("Stan" is Old English for "stone"; "Pierre" is
French.) Pierre now goes to New York with Isabel, where
he lives in poverty, trying to write for a living. Meanwhile
his mother falls ill, goes mad, and dies. By this time Pierre,
who is living incestuously with Isabel, has begun to doubt
the purity of his motive in "marrying" his sister. Has he
feigned marriage in order to satisfy his lust? And how does
he know that she is really his sister? He reviews the reasons:
she has told him so; she resembles an early portrait of his
father in which he is "ambiguously" smiling; and his father,
in his ravings before his death, called out "my daughter, my
daughter." Now Lucy, recovered from her long illness,
writes to say that she is coming to live in Pierre's ménage as
a kind of "nun," having realized that Pierre's motive for
breaking their engagement can only have been "divine."
Thereupon Lucy's brother, along with Pierre's cousin, Glen
Stanly, who is himself in love with Lucy, write Pierre a
threatening and insulting letter. Another insulting letter ar-
rives from Pierre's publisher, turning down his novel. Now
Pierre feels blindness, madness, and death approaching.
With his last strength, he murders his cousin Glen Stanly.
Isabel brings poison to Pierre's prison cell which they both
drink, but not before Lucy has died of shock, having
learned at last that Pierre and Isabel were brother and sister.

Melville described *Pierre* in a letter to his publisher as
being "very much more calculated for popularity than anything you have yet published of mine—being a regular romance, with a mysterious plot to it, & stirring passions at
work, and withall, representing a new & elevated aspect of
American life—" In a postscript to the same letter he
added:

I have thought that, on several accounts, (one of which is the rapid succession in which my works have lately been published) it might not prove unadvisable to publish this present book anonymously, or under an assumed name:—* *By a Vermonter* say. I beg you to consider the propriety of this suggestion, but defer the final decision to your own better experience in such matters, since I am prompted in throwing out the idea, merely in regard to your advantage as publisher.

H.M.

* or *"By Guy Winthrop."* [14]

The extraordinary mixture of self-deception and of conscious self-revelation that marks this letter is marked throughout the novel as well. Melville at times consciously conceals his meaning in *Pierre,* at times unconsciously reveals it; at times he screens what would be unacceptable to nineteenth-century readers in plainer form; at times he seems to screen from his own conscious understanding what is unacceptable to him. But what is most interesting about *Pierre*—what makes it altogether unique—is the revelation of the *process* by which hero and author peel away layer after layer of self-deception, of self-delusion, of consciousness, in order to arrive at the truth of human feeling with which the novel ends.

The plot itself is one of *Pierre*'s chief screening devices: diverting attention away from the novel's real theme, it hides more than it reveals. For example, the havoc at the end has been caused by Pierre's declared determination to protect his father, mother, and sister, at the utter sacrifice of himself alone.

From the first, determined at all hazards to hold his father's fair fame inviolate from any thing he should do in reference to protecting Isabel, and extending to her a brother's utmost devotedness and love; and equally determined not to shake his

---

[14] *Log,* I, 450.

mother's lasting peace by any useless exposure of unwelcome facts; and yet vowed in his deepest soul some way to embrace Isabel before the world, and yield to her his constant consolation and companionship; and finding no possible mode of unitedly compassing all these ends, without a most singular act of pious imposture, which he thought all heaven would justify in him, since he himself was to be the grand self-renouncing victim; therefore, this was his settled and immovable purpose now; namely: to assume before the world, that by secret rites, Pierre Glendinning was already become the husband of Isabel Banford—an assumption which would entirely warrant his dwelling in her continual company, and upon equal terms, taking her wherever the world admitted him; and at the same time foreclose all sinister inquisitions bearing upon his deceased parent's memory, or any way affecting his mother's lasting peace, as indissolubly linked with that. True, he in embryo, foreknew, that the extraordinary thing he had resolved, would, in another way, indirectly though inevitably, dart a most deep pain into his mother's heart . . . (Book x)

This is obvious subterfuge. While pretending to protect his family, Pierre is actually making preparations for its total annihilation, of all possible responses to Isabel's revelation choosing the one that "he in embryo, foreknew" would be most destructive to them all. The very prose of this passage, with its obsessive ratiocination, indicates that concealment is taking place.

Pierre's attack upon the family is in part simply an exposure of what Melville considers to be the hidden horrors of the "family romance": the convenient lies between husband and wife; the ambivalence of paternal love; the seductiveness of mother love; the sexuality of sibling love; the self love behind all the pretended self-sacrifice that goes on amongst the members of the family. In what has become characteristic of American literature, he begins the attack upon the family at the mother. Even before Isabel's revelation, Mary Glendinning is savagely exposed without the excuse that she is being protected. The hyperbole and archaism of the style screen the attack somewhat; but both the selfishness and incestuousness of her love for her son are clearly revealed, as well as its essential narcissism. At about the same time the chapters describing Mary Glendinning were being written, Melville's second son was born. When registering the birth with the town clerk, Melville mistakenly gave his own mother's name, Maria Gansevoort Melville, as the name of the child's mother.[15]

Pierre feels that he is far more seriously implicated in the incestuous relationship with his sister than with his mother, in relation to whom he was the more "innocent" of the two. He understands with absolute clarity the incestuous nature of his feelings for Isabel, as well as his motive in declaring her his wife rather than admitting that she is his sister. It is Pierre's desire for her, as much as his generous wish to protect his father's cast-out Ishmael, which makes him leave his home. This sets his mother in motion. She now disinherits Pierre, making his cousin, Glendinning Stanly, her heir—that is, heir to all of Pierre's patrimony. It is thus on account of two women—his mother and his sister—that Pierre loses his father's lands and all his inheritance. By the end of the novel, Isabel has turned into a sexual temptress not very different from Pierre's mother, as much a Jezebel as an Ishmael. But by now she has made Pierre into an Ishmael.

Women clog Pierre's life. Dependent and demanding, they drag him from his main course, which he sees as his search for "Truth"—and which, on another level, is a search for his father. "He seemed gifted with loftiness, merely that it might be dragged down to the mud." And chiefly dragging him into the mud are women: "On either hand clung to by a girl who would have laid down her life for him; Pierre, nevertheless, in his deepest, highest part, was utterly without sympathy from any thing divine, human, brute, or vegetable." His dislike of women, masked somewhat by the

[15] *Log*, I, 430.

conventionally romantic plot of the first half of the novel, is increasingly revealed. It is nowhere more openly expressed than in Melville's characterization of Lucy Tartan's mother, a minor character whom he can attack without any screen whatever. In Mrs. Tartan's repudiation of her daughter, Melville loses control: intending to expose her selfishness, he exposes his own hatred of mothers.

"Girl! here where I stand, I forever cast thee off. Never more shalt thou be vexed by my maternal entreaties. I shall instruct thy brothers to disown thee; I shall instruct Glen Stanly to banish thy worthless image from his heart, if banished thence it be not already by thine own incredible folly and depravity. For thee, Mr. Monster! [Pierre] the judgment of God will overtake thee for this. And for thee, madam, I have no words for the woman who will connivingly permit her own husband's paramour to dwell beneath her roof. For thee, frail one" (to Delly), "thou needest no amplification.—A nest of vileness! And now, surely, whom God Himself hath abandoned forever, a mother may quit, never more to revisit." (Book XXIV)

Although *Pierre* is a story about the "family romance"— one whose intention seems to be to put an end to the family forever—it is least of all concerned with the bond between husband and wife. No actual marriages are shown in the novel, and Melville is clearly most interested in the relationships between members of the family who are joined by blood ties: mother and son, father and daughter, brother and sister and, above all, father and son. Pierre himself is engaged to be married at the opening of the novel, and Melville conceals his yawning lack of interest in Pierre's relationship with Lucy Tartan, as well as his lack of interest in Lucy herself, behind the extravagantly expressed emotion Pierre claims to feel for his beloved. The prose of Pierre's and Lucy's first love speech reveals a fairly complete absence of feeling. Lucy begins:

" . . . Good mornings, good evenings, good days, weeks, months and years to thee, Pierre;—bright Pierre!—Pierre!"

Truly, thought the youth, with a still gaze of inexpressible fondness; truly the skies do ope, and this invoking angel looks
down.—"I would return thee thy manifold good mornings, Lucy,
did not that presume thou hadst lived through a night; and by
heaven, thou belong'st to the regions of an infinite day!"....
   "Bravissimo! oh, my only recruit!" (Book 1)

And the ease with which Pierre gives up all hope of marrying Lucy in order to live with his sister Isabel is apparent in
the over-wrought language which describes his anguish,
and finally in Melville's admission that there is *no* language
in which to describe it: "But here we draw a veil. Some
nameless struggles of the soul can not be painted, and some
woes will not be told. Let the ambiguous procession of
events reveal their own ambiguousness."

   The member of the family Melville is most interested in
exposing and attacking in *Pierre* is the father, but this attack
and exposure is the most veiled and indirect of all. Pierre's
father has first of all been dead for a number of years, and
so can be exposed only after the fact, and can be attacked
only indirectly. Furthermore, Pierre has curiously little
direct memory of his father; he chiefly knows him through
two portraits that were painted during his lifetime, one before and one after his marriage to Pierre's mother. It is his
musings over the contradictory aspects of his father that
these two portraits present which first reveal Pierre's feelings about him. Pierre's deeper feelings about his father are
even more indirectly presented—by means of his confrontation of a huge rock, known to him since childhood; finally,
and most fully, in a dream about a rock wall called the
Mount of Titans. Only after this dream does Pierre launch
the final attack upon his father.

   In the beginning it is Isabel, the disinherited first-born
child of Pierre's father (whose name is a feminine version of
Ishmael), who exposes Pierre's father; and she, like Pierre, is
shown to be the unwilling instrument of the exposure, as
well as the innocent victim of her father's misdeed. In the

Biblical story Abraham's first born was Ishmael; it was for the sake of his legitimate second son that he disinherited Ishmael and forced him into exile. This Pierre's father has done to his first child, Isabel. But by unfathering an Ishmael, Pierre's father has unfathered an Isaac as well. Isabel's revelation of their father's sin makes of Pierre, too, an outcast, and an outcast not only from his father but from his father's God. For to his young son, his father had seemed nothing less than a God, and his belief in his heavenly Father was founded upon his belief in his earthly father.

There had long stood a shrine in the fresh-foliaged heart of Pierre, up to which he ascended by many tableted steps of remembrance; and round which annually he had hung fresh wreaths of a sweet and holy affection. . . . In this shrine, in this niche of this pillar, stood the perfect marble form of his departed father; without blemish, unclouded, snow-white, and serene; Pierre's fond personification of perfect human goodness and virtue. Before this shrine, Pierre poured out the fulness of all his young life's most reverential thoughts and beliefs. Not to God had Pierre ever gone in his heart, unless by ascending the steps of that shrine, and so making it the vestibule of his abstractest religion. (Book IV)

Thus idealized, Pierre cannot accept his father as a flawed human creature. Although now dead to him— "Rather cast thee utterly out, than conspicuously insult thee . . . I will have no more father"—Pierre decides to protect his father's memory by sacrificing his own happiness. But this apparent protection of his father, like that of his mother, sister, and lover, is in reality another veiled attack. It is far more heavily camouflaged because, in the son's mind, it is far more dangerous to attack a father than a mother, sister, or lover, especially an omniscient father. And just as the protection is veiled attack, the reason Pierre gives himself for protecting his father—that he had not willfully harmed his son—masks Pierre's true feeling. Pierre's deepest feelings of rage come from his conviction that his father's injuries were *not* unintentional, but purposefully malicious acts of aggression against him, the innocent and loving son.

Pierre knew his father best through two portraits, one of which was worshipped by his father's spinster sister, one by his wife. Each showed contradictory aspects of him. It is these two portraits which Pierre consults after Isabel's terrible revelation. The earlier of the two, painted without his father's knowledge at the time when he was seducing Isabel's mother, reveals the side he would have kept concealed from the world if he could—the "ambiguous" and "mocking" side. But now this early portrait seems to tell Pierre that the other, later one, commissioned by his wife and representing the god-like father Pierre dimly remembers and cherishes in his heart's shrine, was not his true father:

Pierre, believe not [your mother's] painting; that is not thy father; or, at least, is not *all* of thy father. Consider in thy mind, Pierre, whether we two paintings may not make only one. Faithful wives are ever over-fond to a certain imaginary image of their husbands; and faithful widows are ever over-reverential to a certain imagined ghost of that same imagined image, Pierre. Look, again, I am thy father as he more truly was. . . . Consider this strange, ambiguous smile, Pierre; more narrowly regard this mouth. Behold, what is this too ardent and, as it were, unchastened light in these eyes, Pierre? I am thy father, boy. . . . (Book IV)

At the very end of the novel, immediately after the dream which at last reveals to Pierre his own murderous hostility toward his father, he visits a picture gallery and sees two other portraits. One, listed in the catalogue as an "unknown head," bears an astonishing resemblance to the youthful portrait of Pierre's father; the other is a portrait of Beatrice Cenci. The Cenci, Melville reminds us, is "double-hooded by . . . the black crape of the two most horrible crimes . . .

possible to civilized humanity—incest and parricide." "Now, this Cenci and 'the Stranger' were hung at a good elevation in one of the upper tiers [of portraits]; and, from the opposite walls, exactly faced each other; so that in secret they seemed pantomimically talking over and across the heads of the living spectators below" (Book XXVI). The secret traded between the two, in their god-like elevation above the crowd, seems to be their acceptance of incest and parricide; their knowledge that the two most horrible crimes known to civilized humanity are crimes no more and that God, if there is a God, has averted his face even from them. This is the final lesson of his father's inscrutable, ambiguous smile. Already guilty of incest, Pierre goes on now to commit parricide. And this parricide, which will be the sum of a murder and a suicide, is what has been planned from the beginning.

Like Redburn, Pierre is caught between two worlds, the old and the new. Pierre, whose ancestors' "far-descended Dutch meadows lie steeped in a Hindooish haze," is refugeed from another time—from a patriarchal past. When he leaves his ancestral home he cries "Henceforth, cast-out Pierre hath no paternity, and no past; and since the Future is one blank to all; therefore, twice-disinherited Pierre stands untrammeledly his ever-present self!—free to do his own self-will and present fancy to whatever end!" (Book XII). The double disinheritance is peculiarly American; is, in a sense, the crux of the national drama as Melville sees it. Melville allegorizes it on two levels in *Pierre:* on the level of the family; and on the level of the historical past. And he unifies these two levels in the theme of the disinheritance of modern man through Nature. It was the peculiar fate of the American to see his religious drama, his national drama, and his personal drama, inscribed in the natural scenery of this continent. The natural symbols which Melville uses in *Pierre* are rocks and stones. The meaning of Pierre itself is "rock"; and on a rock, in another age, a great Church was erected. Now that Church has fallen, according to Melville's allegory, and a new Peter must erect a new philosophy to take its place.

There is a rock near Pierre's home which, known only to him, he sometimes calls the Memnon Stone and sometimes the Terror Stone, according to his mood. Memnon was a young Egyptian King, Melville tells us, son of the Goddess Aurora, who was killed in a nobly undertaken battle in another's behalf. His subjects built a monument to him which, "Touched by the breath of the bereaved Aurora, every sunrise gave forth a mournful broken sound . . ." But although "Memnon's sculptured woes once melodiously resounded; now all is mute." So Pierre's Memnon Stone is mute to him. After Isabel's disclosure, Pierre goes to this stone as if to seek counsel of it. It is a "remarkable stone, or rather, smoothed mass of rock, huge as a barn . . . wholly isolated horizontally . . ." It lies sunk in the "dense deep luxuriance of the aboriginal forest . . . its crown being full eight fathoms under high-foliage mark." "It was shaped something like a lengthened egg, but flattened more; and, at the ends, pointed more; and yet not pointed, but irregularly wedge-shaped. Somewhere near the middle of its under side, there was a lateral ridge; and an obscure point of this ridge rested on a second lengthwise-sharpened rock, slightly protruding from the ground. Beside that one obscure and minute point of contact, the whole enormous and most ponderous mass touched not another object in the wide terraqueous world" (Book VII). It is very like a whale— and Pierre goes to it, as Ahab went to Moby Dick, demanding recognition and annihilation. Sliding into its "horrible interspace" he asks certain questions of it:

"If the miseries of the undisclosable things in me, shall ever unhorse me from my manhood's seat; if to vow myself all Virtue's and all Truth's, be but to make a trembling, distrusted slave of me; if Life is to prove a burden I can not bear without ignominious cringings; if indeed our actions are all foreordained, and we are Russian serfs to Fate; if invisible devils do titter at us when we most nobly strive; if Life be a cheating dream, and virtue as unmeaning and unsequeled with any blessing as the midnight mirth of wine; if by sacrificing myself for Duty's sake, my own mother re-sacrifices me; if Duty's self be but a bugbear, and all things are allowable and unpunishable to man;—then do thou, Mute Massiveness, fall on me!" (Book VII)

Some of these questions are very curious, and curiously contradictory as well. Pierre asks for annihilation "if our actions are all foreordained, and we are Russian serfs to Fate"; and he asks for annihilation, too, "if all things are allowable and unpunishable to man." The first implies that he wishes to die if he is *not* free; the second, that he wishes to die if he is altogether free, if he is *too* free. From the point of view of freedom, then, the two statements are contradictory. But it is not freedom but the *source* of freedom or of serfdom that is at issue. Pierre will serve neither an all-permissive nor an all-restrictive fate, for both, as every child intuitively knows, mean indifference, mean the absence of love. "O Father!—chiefly known to me by Thy rod—" Father Mapple prays in *Moby Dick*. The unloved, orphaned Ishmael may wander over the whole world as he pleases; it is the beloved Isaac who may be bound over for sacrifice. Pierre wants proof that his father loves him; he is willing to be sacrificed to obtain that proof. But he cannot bear to be sacrificed to an indifferent Fate—and it is that which he fears he *must* bear.

The allegory of the Memnon Stone is expanded at the end of the novel in another interpolated story involving another huge rock—this time a rock wall named by Pierre the Mount of Titans. During a "state of semi-unconsciousness, or rather trance, a remarkable dream or vision" comes to Pierre concerning the Mount of Titans, a "terrific towering palisade of dark mossy massiveness" near Pierre's ancestral home. At its base are stones, almost human in shape, which were thrown off the mountain during storms. One of these rocks took a "form defiant, a form of awfulness."

You saw Enceladus the Titan, the most potent of all the giants, writhing from out the imprisoning earth;—turbaned with up-borne moss he writhed; still, though armless, resisting with his whole striving trunk, the Pelion and the Ossa hurled back at him;—turbaned with upborne moss he writhed; still turning his unconquerable front toward that majestic mount eternally in vain assailed by him, and which, when it had stormed him off, had heaved his undoffable incubus upon him, and deridingly left him there to bay out his ineffectual howl. (Book xxv)

Rocky Enceladus and the "repulsed group of heaven-assaulters" suddenly spring to their feet, in Pierre's dream. Flinging themselves up the mountain, they batter at the precipice's "unresounding wall."

Foremost among them all, [Pierre] saw a moss-turbaned, armless giant, who despairing of any other mode of wreaking his immit-igable hate, turned his vast trunk into a battering-ram, and hurled his own arched-out ribs again and yet again against the invulnera-ble steep.

"Enceladus! it is Enceladus!"—Pierre cried out in his sleep. That moment the phantom faced him; and Pierre saw Enceladus no more; but on the Titan's armless trunk, his own duplicate face and features . . . (Book xxv)

The earth holds the Titan prisoner as he struggles to re-turn to the mountain which had "stormed him off"—the rock-face from which he had come, and to which he right-fully belongs. Armless, he is helpless to battle successfully against his parent mountain; unable to conquer it, by which he means to return to it, he hates it. Melville interprets Pierre's dream for us thus:

Old Titan's self was the son of incestuous Coelus and Terra, the son of incestuous Heaven and Earth. And Titan married his mother Terra, another and accumulatively incestuous match. And thereof Enceladus was one issue. So Enceladus was both the son and grandson of an incest; and even thus, there had been born from the organic blended heavenliness and earthliness of Pierre, another mixed, uncertain heaven-aspiring, but still not wholly earth-emancipated mood; which again, by its terrestrial taint held down to its terrestrial mother, generated there the present doubly incestuous Enceladus within him; so that the present mood of Pierre—that reckless sky-assaulting mood of his, was nevertheless on one side the grandson of the sky. For it is according to eternal fitness, that the precipitated Titan should still seek to regain his paternal birthright even by fierce escalade. Wherefore whoso storms the sky gives best proof he came from thither! But whoso crawls contented in the moat before that crystal fort, shows it was born within that slime, and there forever will abide. (Book xxv)

Enceladus, we have just been told, is Pierre. His hatred is directed against his father, the Mount of Titans, but it is a hatred born of love: if he were able to reunite himself with his father, he would then love him. But it is by means of this hatred that he proves his paternity—heaven-assaulting, he proves that he came from heaven: "whoso storms the sky gives best proof he came from thither!" If he had not come from the sky, he would be content to remain in the earth, to abide in the slime, which is his mother. It is his mother who would keep him from knowing his father, and from reuniting himself with Him; it is his mother, therefore, from whom he must free himself. Furthermore, it was through his mother that his father first betrayed him—planting his seed in her and thus confusing his paternity; planting a seed in a woman, and thus separating him from his father. For un-conceived, Enceladus would still be unseparated from his father. This is an extraordinarily radical idea of conception and of birth; and it helps explicate the deaths both of Bartleby and of Ahab.

Enceladus wishes to reattach himself to the wall which has thrown him off; Ahab wishes to reattach himself to the whale which at first encounter had only bitten off his leg;

Bartleby, after long wooing of blank walls, at last succeeds in getting within a walled tomb. In order for Enceladus to reach his father he must get free of his mother the earth, who holds him tightly in her embrace. Yet his father is the son of earth, too. The white whale, who is in some way Ahab's Father, is male—the great sperm carrier; but his great belly is also like the great womb of the world, and Ahab finds death at last tied by a cord to the whale's body like a foetus tied to a womb. He, too, must go *through* his mother in order to reach his father; must unlive the foetal life itself in order to spring back into the sperm. So the great sperm whale's sex remains ambiguous, both phallus and womb; as Bartleby's tomb within the womb of the great erect Pyramids in which he again finds his father's seed is also ambiguously sexed. Through the myth of Enceladus we understand the reason for the sexual ambiguity of the whale and of the Tombs. By dying, Melville's heroes want to unlive their foetal lives in order to rid themselves of their mothers altogether. Before the Creation, the time to which "the great shroud of the sea rolled back as it rolled five thousand years ago" at the end of *Moby Dick,* there was only God the Father.

In thus repudiating the part of his hero which is iden-tified with certain maternal ties, Melville is repudiating, too, the part that is earthbound, with all that this implies; and in repudiating the heterosexuality of his hero's conception, he is repudiating, too, the part of man which is sexual, with all that this implies. And what these things imply are, simply, almost everything human: home, children, family, sexual love, and with these things, the entire web of social life.

When Pierre realizes that he has been twice disin-herited—by his father and by the past, by his family history and by history itself, he says that he now "stands un-trammeledly his ever-present self!—free to do his own self-will and present fancy to whatever end." Now "all things are

allowable and unpunishable to man." Pierre uses this freedom to annihilate his house, to shed all his "kindred blood"
as well as his own. This is where his "self-will" has led him:
to commit a suicide that is a kind of parricide—as Ahab and
Bartleby did, too. If there is no God, then everything is permitted; and Melville's hero rises up against himself, and his
father in himself; or he rises up against a force of nature,
and his Father in Nature. In both cases, the only human
being involved is the self: both acts are narcissistic; both are
asocial. For neither act, therefore, is social redemption possible.

There was another nineteenth-century hero who decided
that if there were no God, all things are permitted. In order
to prove this, Raskolnikov committed murder. He conceived of the unFathering of the world as turning man
against man; so he committed a crime against another
human being, and eventually suffered a human punishment. A crime against another member of society permits
society to punish and to forgive; permits, therefore, the
criminal's reintegration into human society.

Raskolnikov felt his unFathering to be a simultaneous expulsion from God's presence and from the brotherhood of
men. Pierre felt his to be an expulsion from God and from
Nature. In part, this was because Americans historically saw
proof of themselves as God's chosen people in the bounty of
their continent. Nature and God were bound closely
together in the American iconography; the bounty of Nature was the sign of God's covenant with the new Israelites.
When God turned away from Americans, Nature turned
diabolic, or empty; and the nature of Nature in America—
the vast trackless plains and deserts of the West, which contained no monuments or signs of human history—looked
peculiarly deserted by God. Nevertheless, Dickens had seen
the American West without suspecting that God had withdrawn from it; and Dostoevsky saw Siberia—and in neither

of those places was either of them struck by the thought that had struck so many ordinary Americans in their travels over the American continent—that here was almost "an accursed land"; that, amid these solitudes, "nature [had] no voice . . ." But Melville said in *Pierre* that nature is the "mere supplier of that cunning alphabet, whereby selecting and combining as he pleases, each man reads his own peculiar lesson according to his own peculiar mind and mood." And it was the peculiar mind and mood of Americans to find in Nature herself evidence that man is now an orphan in the world. This mood and state of mind had been created by all the converging forces in American life which had gone into creating the "American mind." Above all, it was a consciousness which, as Melville understood, was born out of the passing of the patriarchal father, and out of the declining relevance of the past.

Dostoevsky, who had had a similar apprehension about the disappearance of God, sought reassurance within an authoritarian social order; and through it, he found his way back to God. It was a way back that led right through human society; and in the midst of human society, many nineteenth-century doubters stopped. In England, for example, the "religion of humanity" was able to take the place of the religion of Christ for a number of thinkers and writers because religious belief in England had habitually included all God's manifestations on earth—king, lords, gentry, masters, fathers. And throughout Europe there were fatherlands and motherlands, kings and queens, lords and priests, masters and fathers to help buffet the shock of doubt that was increasingly assailing traditional religious belief. So that a king could be beheaded, a father could die, God Himself could disappear, but a degree of stability remained with the remainder of a still essentially hierarchal order. Above all, a social order remained which was a reflection of a God-given hierarchy reaching back beyond the memory of man—a hierarchy whose fundamental unit was not yet the dissociated individual, but men and women and children living together in human families.

To serve this hierarchal ideal, especially as it existed within the family, Dickens bent his heroes' lives, desires, and expectations. Individuality was sacrificed to the social, especially the familial, ideal. Melville, on the other hand, sacrificed the social order, and especially the family, to the individual will. This glorification of the will, and the ideal of total self-expression to which it led him, led him also to an examination of the self that was deep and fearless, as the dethronement of the patriarchal family in America led him to an examination of the relations between members of the family, and especially between fathers and sons, which was unparalleled in his day. Melville's life did not follow the American pattern of success because he had been taught to fear success for himself; but he did not fear the condition upon which all success in America was ideologically grounded: the son's successful supersedence of his father, and his own consequent self-making.

Melville places Pierre at a time of crisis in American history as well as in his own life. Pierre's family history encapsulates all the centuries of the patriarchal European past. When Pierre is nineteen years old, he suffers a revelation which forces him to see that the past is dead—has died sometime in his father's, perhaps even in his grandfather's generation—and he now must face the future without a father and without a past. In his own lifetime, and out of his youth and inexperience, he must create a new philosophy which he can live by; unfathered, he must make a new identity for himself.

William James described the moment of the discovery of his identity, which he called his character, as the moment when he "felt himself most deeply and intensely active and alive. At such moments there is a voice inside which speaks and says: 'This is the real me!'" [16] Pierre's story is in part the story of the *un*making of an identity; the gradual disintegration of his sense of who he is which begins, significantly, when he discovers that his father was not what he had thought him to be. At that moment, Melville says, Pierre fell "dabbling in the vomit of his loathed identity." Pierre suffers what would now be called an identity crisis: his world has collapsed, and on the threshold of a new world he is no longer certain of who he is.

He knew not where he was; he did not have any ordinary life-feeling at all. He could not see; though instinctively putting his hand to his eyes, he seemed to feel that the lids were open. Then he was sensible of a combined blindness, and vertigo, and staggering; before his eyes a million green meteors danced; he felt his foot tottering upon the curb, he put out his hands, and knew no more for the time . . . and now a general and nameless torpor—some horrible foretaste of death itself—seemed stealing upon him. (Book xxv) [17]

This describes precisely the opposite state from James's description of finding his identity; here Pierre is in the process of losing his. But why does he lose his identity so quickly? What are the emotional roots of his so rapid loss of his sense of who he is? They are allied to his instant acceptance of the truth of Isabel's story, which overturns a lifetime's trust in his parents. It must be, therefore, that he was less certain of his identity than most children, that he never trusted his parents—trusted that his mother truly loved him or that his father was the God he seemed—and pretended—to be. And so he stops loving and trusting them at once, as soon as he has read Isabel's letter. "Not only was the long-cherished image of his father now transfigured

[16] Quoted in Erik H. Erikson, *Identity: Youth and Crisis* (New York, 1968), p. 19.
[17] See also Gansevoort Melville's description to his brother Herman of his last illness, above, p. 179.

before him from a green foliaged tree into a blasted trunk, but every other image in his mind attested the universality of the electral light which had darted into his soul. Not even his lovely, immaculate mother, remained entirely untouched. . . . Then he staggered back upon himself, and only found support in himself" (Book v). He has learned nothing new; he has been confirmed in an old suspicion. "For—absurd as it may seem—men are only made to comprehend things which they comprehended before (though in embryo, as it were)," Pierre says.

The infant finds his identity in his mother's loving face; the boy through his father's example and guidance; the adolescent through his culture. Thus Pierre's life is an allegory both of Melville's life and of an aspect of American history. Pierre, like Melville, had not secured his identity through his parents, as America had not secured an identity either in the European past or in the past of this continent. And never having been given a secure identity by his parents, Pierre, like Melville, cannot find one in his culture. By rooting him in an already dead patriarchal-patrician past, Pierre's parents, like Melville's, not only rooted him in sand but made him unfit to enter the dominant American technology of his day—the rush to possess and exploit and develop the continent and, in the process, to get rich quick. By failing in the rush to make money—by seeming to his son to have been driven mad by it—Melville's father made his son, too, afraid to attempt such success. But both Pierre's and Melville's identities, however tenuously held, are American identities—they are intensifications, or exacerbations, of the cultural ideal, which was to be self-made. Self-made, and unable to make anything of himself, Pierre is free to examine the truer, deeper implications of self-making, as Melville was.

History did not bear out the genteel pretensions of the Glendinnings any more than it did the genteel pretensions of the Redburns—or of the Melvilles and the Gansevoorts. The Glendinnings were living an aristocratic European idyll in the United States of America. They pretended to their son that this was still possible to do, exacting from him the respect and the feelings due the social realities of another world, a world that no longer existed, if it ever had, on this side of the Atlantic. Moreover, they pretended that they could still live by the morality of an older world, a patriarchal, traditional, historied world—and left their sons to find out that they could not. This Redburn and Pierre discovered when they discovered that their fathers could not lead them any more; that their fathers' gods were dead, and that their fathers themselves were living out a lie, were impotent. With this knowledge, Pierre can no longer live in his ancestral home. He leaves the rural past and moves to the modern city with his strange ménage of sister-wife and outcast servant; moves into a building which was once, significantly, a church, but is now like nothing so much as a present-day commune.

Without any authority which he can trust, and with the heroic determination to succeed in creating a new mode of life to suit his new insight into the death of the old, Pierre begins to break down mentally and physically; and his sense of his own identity begins to desert him. In order to leave the past he must destroy it in himself; just as in determining to make himself, he must destroy his father in himself— destroy the image of manhood that he has learned to carry in his mind and heart for nineteen years, and that has made him what he now is. For whatever the national drama and whatever the ideological stance, the family drama is always essentially the same, and the son can only grow to manhood satisfactorily by modelling himself upon a man who is his father, or who stands in place of a father to him. Pip began his history by telling of the day when he first became aware "of the identity of things," when he "found out for certain

. . . that the small bundle of shivers growing afraid of it all and beginning to cry was Pip." And instantly a fearsome father appeared to him. Magwitch "became aware" of himself when someone—"a man"—had run away from him; and Magwitch became a criminal—is a criminal already on that day, "a-thieving turnips" for his living. Magwitch became a criminal because he had lost a father—and by losing a father, he had lost the right to an identity, according to the custom of his culture. The price Pip pays for knowing and keeping his identity is a heavy one—the loss of a part of himself: of his will for power, of his attainment of sexual love. But not everyone in his culture paid so high a price for his identity as Pip; many, perhaps most, were able, within the bounds set by their society, to so acculturate their desires that within their culture they could express themselves fully—as fully as that ever is possible to do. And their reward for the limitations they suffered—like Pip's reward—was the relative security of their identities within their society.

In *White Jacket,* the novel written directly after *Redburn,* Melville said this about America's destiny and her relation to the Past:

The world has arrived at a period which renders it the part of Wisdom to pay homage to the prospective precedents of the Future in preference to those of the Past. The Past is dead, and has no resurrection; but the Future is endowed with such a life, that it lives to us even in anticipation. The Past is, in many things, the foe of mankind . . . the Future is both hope and fruition. The Past is the text-book of tyrants; the Future is the Bible of the Free. . . .

Let us leave the Past, then, to dictate laws to immovable China; let us abandon it to the Chinese Legitimists of Europe. But for us, we will have another captain to rule over us—that captain who ever marches at the head of his troop, and beckons them forward, not lingering in the rear, and impeding their march with lumbering baggage-wagons of old precedents. *This* is the Past. . . .

Escaped from the house of bondage, Israel of old did not follow after the ways of the Egyptians. To her was given an express dispensation; to her were given new things under the sun. And we Americans are the peculiar, chosen people—the Israel of our time; we bear the ark of the liberties of the world. Seventy years ago we escaped from thrall; and, besides our first birthright—embracing one continent of earth—God has given to us, for a future inheritance, the broad domains of the political pagans, that shall yet come and lie down under the shade of our ark, without bloody hands being lifted. God has predestinated, mankind expects, great things from our race; and great things we feel in our souls. The rest of the nations must soon be in our rear. We are the pioneers of the world; the advance-guard, sent on through the wilderness of untried things, to break a new path in the New World that is ours. In our youth is our strength; in our inexperience our wisdom. . . . And let us always remember, that with ourselves—almost for the first time in the history of earth—national selfishness is unbounded philanthropy; for we cannot do a good to America but we give alms to the world. (Ch. 36)

This was the American dream, the American promise. And for those Americans who were caught up in the technology of their age, it was a fulfilled dream and a fulfilled promise. If one did not succeed today, then one would succeed tomorrow: success was just around the corner—in the next job, in the next State, a little farther West.

But Melville had pulled out of the cultural mainstream, and only from time to time was he inspired to praise the majority, which was succeeding not only in uniting diverse peoples into a single nation, but in rewarding that nation with unprecedented success. Not that he dispraised the dream itself: he found it as compelling—as necessary—as the majority of Americans did. But from the unnoticed and unregarded prominence from which he observed his country and his countrymen, Melville saw what they, swept along in the rushing tide of their activity, could not see: the ambiguous sources of their gift, the ambiguous nature of their great success. He did not question the need to deal with the material riches and promise of America; he did not question the need to develop a political and economic technology of the future, or even question that America had already successfully done so; nor did he question that "with ourselves—almost for the first time in the history of earth—national selfishness is unbounded philanthropy; for we cannot do a good to America but we give alms to the world." "We are the pioneers of the world; the advance-guard, sent on through the wilderness of untried things, to break a new path in the New World that is ours." This Melville believed. What he deeply doubted was whether these things were not an ambiguous blessing to the Americans upon whom they fell; whether any men were equal to such a task; whether there was a spiritual "technology" which could satisfactorily encompass the future; whether there was an emotional stance that could make the unfathered future bearable. In the two novels he wrote after *White Jacket, Moby Dick* and *Pierre,* he created two heroic men gifted with insight into the deeper and more demonic nature of American success; Messianic men, who take upon themselves the task of finding the new way into the Future. Captain Ahab and Pierre Glendinning have the courage to face the full implications of the fact that "the Past is dead, and has no resurrection." "Let us leave the Past [Melville wrote in *White Jacket*] . . . let us abandon it to the Chinese Legitimists of Europe. But for us, we will have another captain to rule over us—" And the captain Melville next creates is Ahab, who annihilates the world. And, in a sense, *Pierre* contains Ahab's exegesis. Ahab, the hero of action, is explicated by Pierre, the hero of thought. But as Ahab, the heroic actor, can only act to destroy the world, so Pierre, the heroic writer, can only write his epitaph.

Meanwhile, nineteenth-century America ignored Melville and his dark apocalypse. Was it not proving, more and more successfully, that the world *could* be made again by men who had felt, and proved in their own lives, not only that they could survive their disinheritance, but that they could turn it to profit? And if America has discovered Melville in the twentieth century, is it because, certain at last of its survival, it can now afford to count its losses? Or is it because it feels that it must face its losses at last, in order to survive?

BIBLIOGRAPHY OF WORKS CITED

Altick, Richard D. *The English Common Reader.* Chicago, 1957.

Bagehot, Walter. *The English Constitution.* Garden City, N.Y. [1962?].

Bailyn, Bernard. *Education in the Forming of American Society.* New York, 1960.

Becker, Carl. *The Declaration of Independence: A Study in the History of Political Ideas.* New York, 1942.

Boardman, H. A. *The Bible in the Counting-House: A Course of Lectures to Merchants.* Philadelphia, 1856.

Boorstin, Daniel J., ed. *An American Primer.* Chicago, 1968.

—— *The Americans: The National Experience.* New York, 1967.

—— *The Lost World of Thomas Jefferson.* Boston, 1960.

Briggs, Asa. *The Making of Modern England.* New York, 1965.

—— *Victorian Cities.* New York, 1970.

—— *Victorian People.* New York, 1955.

Clapham, J. H. "Work and Wages." In *Early Victorian England.* Vol. 1. Ed. G. M. Young. London, 1934.

Cobbett, William. *A Year's Residence in the United States of America.* London, 1964.

The Correspondence of Thomas Carlyle and Ralph Waldo Emerson. Vol. 1. Boston, 1883.

Crèvecœur, J. Hector St. John de. *Letters from an American Farmer.* New York, 1957.

Cooper, James Fenimore. *The Prairie.* New York, 1965.

Craigie, Sir William A., and James R. Hulbert. *A Dictionary of American English.* Chicago, 1944.

Dickens, Charles. Ed. Walter Dexter. *The Letters of Charles Dickens.* 3 vols. Bloomsbury, 1938.

Emerson, Ralph Waldo, *The Selected Writings of Ralph Waldo Emerson.* New York, 1940.

Engels, Frederick. *The Condition of the Working-Class in England in 1844.* London, 1892.

Erikson, Erik H. *Identity: Youth and Crisis.* New York, 1968.

Forster, John. *The Life of Charles Dickens.* 3 vols. Philadelphia, 1897.

Franklin, Benjamin. *The Autobiography and Other Writings.* Ed. L. Jesse Lemisch. New York, 1961.

Freud, Sigmund. *Civilization and Its Discontents.* New York, 1962.

Fromm, Erich. *The Forgotten Language.* New York, 1957.

"Frontier Yarns." *Putnam's Monthly Magazine,* 8 (1856).

"The Great West." *DeBow's Review,* 15 (1853).

Habakkuk, H. J. *American and British Technology in the Nineteenth Century: The Search for Labour-Saving Inventions.* Cambridge, 1967.

Haller, William, Jr. *The Puritan Frontier: Town-Planting in New England: Colonial Development 1630–1660.* New York, 1951.

Haskins, George Lee. *Law and Authority in Early Massachusetts.* New York, 1960.

Hill, Christopher. *Puritanism and Revolution.* New York, 1964.

Hofstadter, Richard. *Anti-Intellectualism in American Life.* New York, 1962.

Houghton, Walter. *The Victorian Frame of Mind.* New Haven, 1957.

House, Humphry. *The Dickens World.* Oxford, 1960.

Hunt, Freeman. *Worth and Wealth: A Collection of Maxims, Morals, and Miscellanies for Merchants and Men of Business.* New York, 1856.

Jefferson, Thomas. *Notes on the State of Virginia.* New York, 1964.

Johnson, Edgar. *Charles Dickens: His Tragedy and Triumph.* New York, 1952.

Jones, Ernest. "Psychoanalysis and Folklore." In *Jubilee Congress of the Folklore Society: Papers and Transactions.* London, 1930.

Jordan, Robert Furneaux. *Victorian Architecture.* Harmondsworth, 1966.

Langbaum, Robert. *The Poetry of Experience.* New York, 1963.

Laslett, Peter. *The World We Have Lost.* New York, 1965.

Leyda, Jay. *The Melville Log: A Documentary Life of Herman Melville.* 2 vols. New York, 1951.

Martineau, Harriet. "Representative Men." *Once a Week,* 5 (1861).

Marx, Karl. "Alienated Labor." In *Marx's Concept of Man.* Ed. Erich Fromm. New York, 1961.

——— and Frederick Engels. "Manifesto of the Communist Party." *Selected Works.* Vol. I. Moscow, 1951.

Melville, Herman. *The Letters of Herman Melville.* Ed. Merrell R. Davis and William H. Gilman. New Haven, 1960.

Merk, Frederick. *Manifest Destiny and Mission in American History.* New York, 1963.

Meyers, Marvin. *The Jacksonian Persuasion: Politics and Belief.* Stanford, 1960.

Mill, John Stuart. *On Liberty.* In *The Essential Works of John Stuart Mill.* New York, 1961.

Miller, Perry. *Errand into the Wilderness.* New York, 1964.

Mitchell, Wesley C. *Types of Economic Theory, from Mercantilism to Institutionalism.* Ed. Joseph Dorfman. Vol. I. New York, 1967.

Morison, Samuel Eliot, ed. *Sources and Documents Illustrating the American Revolution, 1764–1788.* 2nd ed. New York, 1965.

Moynahan, Julian. "The Hero's Guilt: The Case of *Great Expectations.*" *Essays in Criticism,* 10 (January, 1960).

Nicholas, H. G. "The New Morality." In *Ideas and Beliefs of the Victorians.* Ed. Harman Grisewood. London, 1949.

Parkman, Francis. *The Oregon Trail.* New York, 1950.

Parrington, Vernon L. *Main Currents in American Thought.* 2 vols. New York, 1954.

"The Plains, as I crossed them Ten Years Ago." *Harper's New Monthly Magazine,* 38 (1869).

Plumb, J. H. *England in the Eighteenth Century (1714–1815).* Baltimore, Maryland, 1950.

Powell, Sumner Chilton. *Puritan Village: The Formation of a New England Town.* Garden City, N.Y. 1965.

Rothman, David J. *The Discovery of the Asylum: Social Order and Disorder in the New Republic.* Boston, 1971.

Ruskin, John. *The Genius of John Ruskin.* Ed. John D. Rosenberg. Boston, 1963.

Sealts, Merton M., Jr. *Melville's Reading: A Check-List of Books Owned and Borrowed.* Madison, Wis., 1966.

Seymour, Charles C. B. *Self-Made Men.* New York, 1858.

Sizer, Nelson. *The Royal Road to Wealth: How to Find and Follow It.* New York, 1882.

Smiles, Samuel. *Industrial Biography: Iron-Workers and Tool-Makers.* Boston, 1864.

—— *Self-Help: With Illustrations of Character and Conduct.* New York, 1860.

Smith, Henry Nash. *Virgin Land.* New York, 1950.

Sorokin, Pitirim. "American Millionaires and Multi-Millionaires." *Journal of Social Forces,* 3 (1925).

Still, Bayrd. *Mirror for Gotham: New York as Seen by Contemporaries from Dutch Days to the Present.* New York, 1956.

Thompson, E. P. *The Making of the English Working Class.* New York, 1964.

Thoreau, Henry David. *Walden.* New York, 1966.

Thornton, A. P. *The Habit of Authority: Paternalism in British History.* London, 1965.

Tocqueville, Alexis de. *Democracy in America.* 2 vols. New York, 1945.

Turner, Frederick Jackson. "Western State-Making in the Revolutionary Era." *American Historical Review,* 1 (1895–96).

Tuthill, Mrs. L. C. *Success in Life. The Mechanic.* New York, 1850.

Van Doren, Carl. *Benjamin Franklin.* New York, 1938.

Wall, Stephen, ed. *Charles Dickens.* Middlesex, England, 1970.

Webber, Charles W. *Old Hicks, the Guide.* London, 1856.

Weber, Max. *The Protestant Ethic and the Spirit of Capitalism.* New York, 1958.

"A Wild Western Adventure." *Chamber's Journal,* 55 (1878).

Wyllie, Irvin G. *The Self-Made Man in America: The Myth of Rags to Riches.* New York, 1954.

Young, G. M., ed. *Early Victorian England.* Vol. 1. London, 1934.

—— *Victorian England: Portrait of an Age.* New York, 1964.

INDEX